"For the Better Performance of Life's Duties"

Author: C. Ben Wright
Editor: Jane St. Anthony
Designers: Ross Rezac and Martin Skoro, MartinRoss Design

©2013 Dunwoody College of Technology
818 Dunwoody Boulevard
Minneapolis, Minnesota 55403
www.dunwoody.edu

Library of Congress Control Number:
PB 2013936982

ISBN:
HC 978-0-9858315-1-6
PB 978-0-9858315-0-9

Opposite and page 5: The south entrance to the new administration building became the main entrance to Dunwoody Institute in 1924. To the right and left of the entrance, two artisans ply their trades.

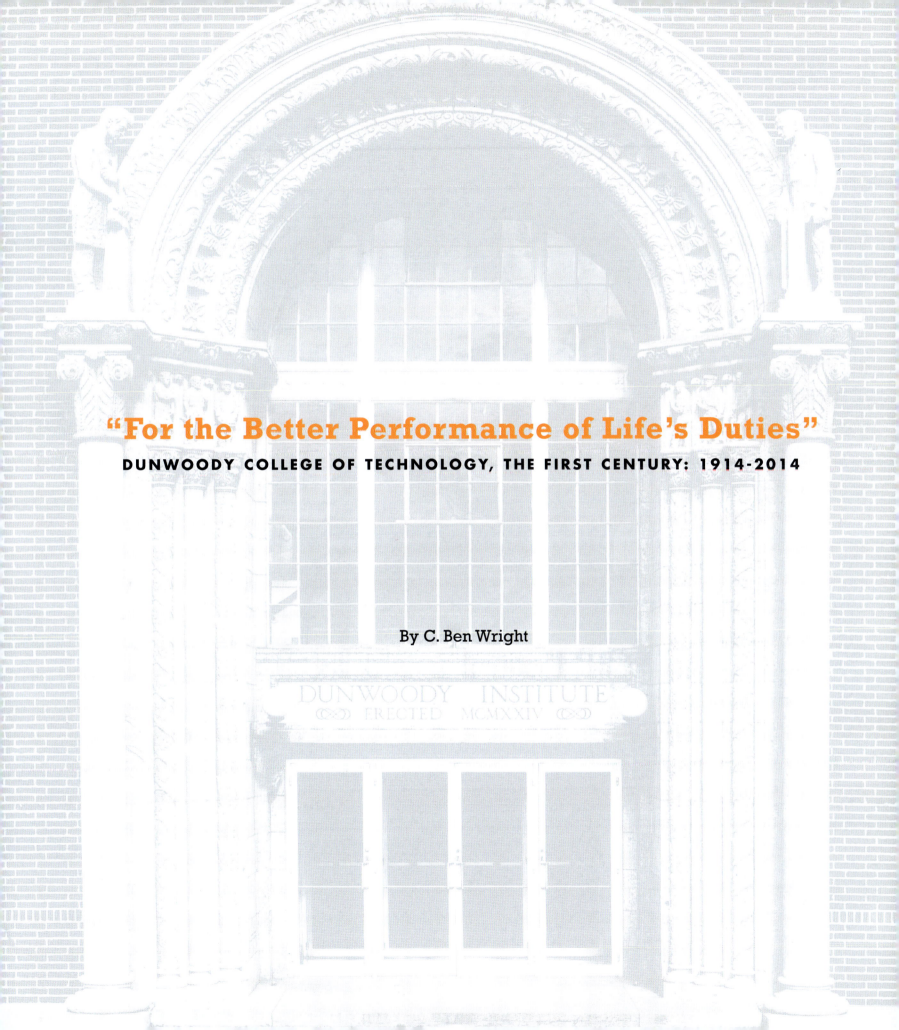

"For the Better Performance of Life's Duties"

DUNWOODY COLLEGE OF TECHNOLOGY, THE FIRST CENTURY: 1914-2014

By C. Ben Wright

This book is dedicated to all the teachers—full-time and

part-time, Day School and Evening School, technical and

general education—who have helped Dunwoody students

acquire the skills and values envisioned by

William Hood Dunwoody.

Table of Contents

ACKNOWLEDGMENTS   6

FOREWORD by David P. Crosby   8

CHAPTER I   The Founders   10

CHAPTER II   Getting Started, 1914-1924   26

CHAPTER III   The Great Depression and World War II   54

CHAPTER IV   Dunwoody in Postwar America, 1945-1968   82

CHAPTER V   Responding to Competition and Change, 1968-1989   110

CHAPTER VI   The Quality Journey, 1989-2002   138

CHAPTER VII   Highs and Lows in a Changing Economy, 2002-2012   162

CHAPTER VIII   Dunwoody at 100   188

APPENDICES   195
    Members of Dunwoody Boards of Trustees
    Leaders of Dunwoody Boards of Trustees
    Principal Dunwoody Administrators
    Alumni Achievement Award Recipients
    Alumni Entrepreneur Award Recipients
    Partnership Award Recipients

BIBLIOGRAPHY   198

INDEX   201

*To provide for all time a place
where youth without distinction on account
of race, color, or religious prejudice,
may learn the useful trades and crafts,
and thereby fit themselves
for the better performance of life's duties.*

William Hood Dunwoody

Acknowledgments

I had the pleasure and honor to work for Dunwoody College of Technology for twenty-five years. As a former student of the liberal arts, I developed a tremendous respect for the practical technical education provided by Dunwoody. My admiration for Dunwoody faculty, students, business partners, alumni, and members of the board of trustees and board of managers of the Alumni Association deepened every year that I was engaged with the college. All of these stakeholders shared my conviction that Dunwoody was a special institution with a unique mission and a distinguished history.

When I retired as president of Dunwoody in 2009, I already knew how I would spend the first few years of retirement. As Dunwoody approached its 100th anniversary in 2014, it lacked, and deserved, a published history telling the story of its first century of achievement. Having received a Ph.D. in American history from the University of Wisconsin-Madison, and having taught history as a college professor before coming to Dunwoody, I would now apply my historical training to research and write the history of Dunwoody. *For the Better Performance of Life's Duties* is the record of Dunwoody Industrial Institute and Dunwoody College of Technology since its founding in 1914.

This project would never have become a reality without the early and active support of Dunwoody President Dr. Richard Wagner. Rich values Dunwoody's legacy as much as I do, and he encouraged me to undertake this project even before he took office as president in July 2009. He permitted Dunwoody staff to assist me with the project, and he invested Dunwoody financial resources in the design and publication of the book. He also offered valuable suggestions along the way to strengthen the manuscript without micro-managing the project. I am sincerely grateful to Rich for his support.

I am indebted to Dunwoody Librarian Kristina Oberstar and Executive Assistant to the President Katie Malone who contributed countless hours to help me with important aspects of the project. I also want to thank these other employees for their assistance: Print Services Coordinator Shelly Fitterer; Marketing Manager William Morris; former Development Executive Assistant Kat Christopherson; Senior Annual Fund Officer Mary Pouch Meador; Provost Jeff Ylinen; Director of Facilities Bill Jordan; and the late Bernie Morgan, whose photographs from the 1990s were invaluable for Chapter VI.

My most important resources for the history of Dunwoody were the records of Dunwoody Institute and Dunwoody College of Technology reaching back to 1914, which are stored in the archives of the college. Second to these documents were personal interviews with more than twenty current and former leaders of the college. These interviews are cited in the bibliography. I am grateful to all of these leaders for sharing their insights and recollections with me. Five of them—Warren Phillips, Frank Starke, Gary Petersen, Ted Ferrara, and Mark Davy—also provided valuable commentary on early drafts of my manuscript, as did former Development colleague Steve Klingaman. The most ever-present and perceptive critic was my wife Donna.

To design and manage the publication of the book Dunwoody retained the services of MartinRoss Design. I am grateful to Martin Skoro and Ross Rezac, the principals of MartinRoss, for the appearance and quality of the book. Marty and Ross provided project oversight for graphic design, art direction, editing, proofing, indexing, and printing. Their editor, Jane St. Anthony, meticulously read and re-read the manuscript to ensure that it would be perfect. If it is perfect, all the credit is Jane's.

Finally I want to acknowledge my debt to the many colleagues and leaders who shaped my Dunwoody experience over twenty-five years. My personal experience inevitably affected my view of Dunwoody's history. Someone with different experiences and a different perspective would have written a different book. So, without holding my associates responsible for the interpretations in *For the Better Performance of Life's Duties*, I do want to thank them for their guidance and inspiration during my Dunwoody career.

President Emeritus Warren Phillips, former President Jim Bensen, and President Emeritus Frank Starke were great role models and mentors who influenced me and this book in countless ways. I also want to express gratitude to some of the outstanding board members who left their mark on me: trustees Charley Jackson, Don Ryks, Cliff Anderson, Chuck Kiester, Pinky McNamara, Bob Carlson, and Morrie Wagener; and alumni Les Goetzke, Lee Jessen, Floyd Schneeberg, Art Popehn, Gary Schulz, J. J. Carbonneau,

David Schlueter, Roger Storms, Steve Robinson, Mike Loegering, Harlan Hallqusit, and John Adamich. During my presidency, from 2002 to 2009, I served under five board chairpersons: Joel Elftmann, Larry Taylor, Bruce Engelsma, Andrea Newman, and Gary Petersen. All were great leaders and effective change-makers. I valued my partnership with each of them.

Special thanks to David Crosby for writing the foreword to this book. Elected to the board of trustees in 1985, chairman of the board from 1994 to 1996, David has been an influential trustee in his own right. But he also represents the Crosby family tradition of service to Dunwoody since its founding in 1914. William Dunwoody's fame and fortune were built through the Washburn Crosby Company, and his business associates at Washburn Crosby, including David's grandfather, helped establish and build The William Hood Dunwoody Industrial Institute. It seems fitting for a Crosby to introduce the story of the school's first century.

Day to day, year to year, the people who make the Dunwoody mission come alive are the college's faculty and support staff. Faculty who instruct and mentor our students, support staff who help students with academic and non-academic issues that contribute to classroom success, and administrators on the leadership team who guide the school are the unsung heroes of *For the Better Performance of Life's Duties*. Out of respect for the faculty, in particular, I have dedicated this book to Dunwoody teachers, past and present. More than anyone, they created the Dunwoody legacy by transforming William Dunwoody's vision of 1914 into applied real-world education for thousands of Dunwoody students.

C. Ben Wright

Foreword

Ben Wright asked me to write this foreword because I represent the fourth generation of Crosbys to be associated with the Dunwoody legacy. My great-grandfather John Crosby III was a partner with William Dunwoody in the Washburn Crosby Company. My grandfather Franklin Crosby and great-uncle John Crosby IV were founding members of the board of trustees of The William Hood Dunwoody Industrial Institute. A Crosby has been on the board ever since. It has been my pleasure to be that representative.

Because of the legacy and the many years I have served on the board, I knew much of the history of Dunwoody. Yet I found Ben Wright's carefully researched story of the Institute—now a college—fascinating. His story filled in many missing pieces and corrected inaccurate memories passed down from other family members. I thoroughly enjoyed Ben's well-written prose. He has placed Dunwoody's history in the context of world and national events—two world wars, a depression, industrial and communication revolutions, population changes, and value changes. The book describes the dramatic changes required by the school to provide for the needs of the economy.

The book also describes the leadership role that Dunwoody and its leaders have played in vocational education in the United States and around the world with a particular emphasis on quality.

Throughout the book, Ben maintains the focus on William Dunwoody's vision for the Institute as expressed in Dunwoody's will. Dunwoody defined his purpose as "to provide for all time a place where the youth of this city and state may, if they so desire, learn the different handicrafts and useful trades and thereby fit themselves for the better performance of life's duties."

For the Better Performance of Life's Duties does an excellent job of describing the difficulty of providing a very expensive type of education (small class sizes, hands-on instruction in labs, and heavy capital costs) within the financial constraints of a private not-for-profit institution. In his will, William Dunwoody promised education "given free to the youth of the city of Minneapolis and state of Minnesota." Over time that became impossible. The book describes very accurately the changes that needed to be made to survive and prosper. This tension will continue and will require Dunwoody to seek philanthropy to keep its programs current and affordable to its student body.

I was invited to join the board by my father, Tom Crosby, who was retiring from the board and wanted to continue the family tradition. I grew up in a home in which service to Dunwoody was a proud legacy, so I was flattered to be asked to serve on the board.

My experience on the board has been more than I had expected. Many of the issues we faced are described accurately in the book. The best example for me to use in this short introduction is *Living the Promise, Fulfilling the Dream*, a capital campaign begun in 1996. A planning group of trustees—myself included—worked with board members and staff. We met almost every month for five years. With a lot of input from Dunwoody staff, we looked strategically at almost everything Dunwoody was doing. I believe we had a real impact on Dunwoody's future. We all brought different skills to the table and all became good friends with a lot of respect for each other. I am sure other board members feel the same way about their service on the Dunwoody board.

One of the real pleasures I have had serving on Dunwoody's board, in addition to what I have mentioned, has been getting to know the many business leaders who have served with me. It might be a mistake to single out individuals, but I would like to point out some successful Dunwoody graduates who have been leaders of the board. Joel Elftmann, Morrie Wagener, Ted Ferrara, and Ray Newkirk all graduated from Dunwoody, grew businesses very successfully, and then made enormous contributions to the school.

I hope you enjoy *For the Better Performance of Life's Duties*. I certainly did.

David P. Crosby

CHAPTER I

The Founders

Prominent Minnesota family names: Dayton, Pillsbury, McKnight, Ordway, Crosby, Bell, Cargill, MacMillan, Walker. We know these names because the patriarchs of these families had children and grandchildren and other relatives who built on the legacy established by the patriarch. Conspicuously absent from this list is the name *Dunwoody*. William and Kate Dunwoody had no children. Therefore there were no Dunwoody offspring to perpetuate the name of one of Minnesota's major business leaders and community benefactors of the late nineteenth and early twentieth centuries.

Since they had no children, the Dunwoodys built their legacy through the institutions they helped to create, most of which survived in one form or another into the twenty-first century. General Mills, Wells Fargo, Abbott Northwestern Hospital, the Minneapolis Institute of Arts, Dunwoody College of Technology—these are the children of William and Kate Dunwoody. William Dunwoody was one of the founders of the Washburn Crosby Company and Northwestern National Bank of Minneapolis, which evolved into General Mills and Wells Fargo, respectively. Kate Dunwoody persuaded her husband to build Abbott Hospital, which later merged with Northwestern Hospital to form Abbott Northwestern. William Dunwoody contributed the largest cash gift in Minneapolis history to kick off the fundraising campaign that built an art museum for the Minneapolis Society of Fine Arts, and then he created a major endowment to acquire works of art for the museum. Most notably for the story that follows, Mr. and Mrs. Dunwoody together, through their last wills and testaments, bequeathed the vision and the resources that created The William Hood Dunwoody Industrial Institute, which would later be renamed Dunwoody College of Technology and celebrate its 100th anniversary in 2014. For those familiar with these great Minnesota institutions, the Dunwoodys are as important to the history of this state and our community as other pioneering leaders of the nineteenth and twentieth centuries.

If Dunwoody Institute was the child of William and Kate Dunwoody, then the thousands of students educated by their school over the next century were the grandchildren. At a Dunwoody event in 2012, the president of the school, Dr. Richard Wagner, saluted Dunwoody alumni: "You defined the institution's legacy through your professional and personal accomplishments. You became the best technicians at companies, you rose through the ranks to become managers, vice presidents and presidents, and you started companies. It is your success and discipline that has defined the Dunwoody Difference. Employers often mention that a Dunwoody graduate stands above the rest or that their company only hires Dunwoody graduates."

The Dunwoodys would have shared this pride in all of the students who benefitted from their education. They would

Opposite: William and Kate Dunwoody

have been especially impressed by those graduates who went on to build their own businesses and thereby create employment and economic benefits for the state of Minnesota. Three alumni stand as examples of the many who made a name for themselves and their alma mater during its first century:

M. A. Mortenson Sr. He received a certificate in building construction from Dunwoody Institute in 1925. After working in the construction industry for many years, Mortenson founded M. A. Mortenson Company in 1954. His company grew to become one of the largest general contractors in the United States. Some of its high-profile construction projects were the Walt Disney Concert Hall in Los Angeles and prominent sports stadiums in Minnesota, including TCF Bank Stadium and Target Field. Through the years, the company hired numerous graduates of Dunwoody Institute and Dunwoody College of Technology, many of whom became key leaders at the company.

Howard Lund A native of New York Mills, Minnesota, Howard Lund graduated from the mechanical drafting and sheet metal programs in 1936. The year after graduation Lund built an iron duck boat in his garage. Eleven years later he built an aluminum duck boat, which became the prototype for many Lund boats to follow. When Lund received an Alumni Entrepreneur Award from Dunwoody in 1999, Lund Boat Company employed 500 people, had sixty boat models, and produced 14,000 boats annually.

Maurice Wagener He graduated from Dunwoody's automotive service program in 1957. After working as a technician and service manager for a small import service shop in Wayzata, Minnesota, for a few years, Wagener bought the business in 1960. In the mid-60s he acquired two import franchises, and in 1969 he built his first automotive dealership, selling Citroen, Saab, and Alfa Romeo. By 2012 Morrie's Automotive Group sold eleven brands of cars at ten different locations in Minnesota and Wisconsin.

The school founded by William and Kate Dunwoody gave birth to the dreams and achievements not only of prominent alumni like M. A. Mortenson, Howard Lund, and Morrie Wagener, but also of the many other men and women who helped build the workforce of Minnesota, the Upper Midwest, and beyond.

William Hood Dunwoody: The Early Years

William Hood Dunwoody was born on March 4, 1841, in Chester County, Pennsylvania. His parents were James Dunwoody and Hannah Hood. The Dunwoodys were Presbyterians who had emigrated to Pennsylvania from Scotland, and the Hoods were Quakers who had come to America from England. Both families lived in Westtown township in Chester County. Like his father and grandfather before him, James Dunwoody was a farmer-entrepreneur. In 1848 he moved his family to a 122-acre farm in Newtown, Pennsylvania, a farm owned by Hannah's father, William Hood. James and Hannah had honored William seven years earlier with the name they chose for their first-born son. Eventually James bought the farm from his father-in-law, and years later William Hood Dunwoody would buy the family farm from his siblings and preserve it as a memorial to his parents.

William Dunwoody was the oldest of six sons born to James and Hannah. Although he had three bouts of serious illness during his lifetime, he would outlive all but one of his brothers. After attending a pioneer elementary school on the family farm in Newtown, he traveled ten miles to Philadelphia to begin high school in 1857. Unfortunately his high school experience ended abruptly when he came down with a fever just before graduation. Having his education cut short undoubtedly affected his later belief in the value of education for young people and his decision to create a school that would provide free education for those who might benefit from such an opportunity.

When he recovered, Dunwoody went to work in Philadelphia for two uncles in the firm of Pearce & Dunwoody, a grain and flour merchandising business. He worked for Pearce & Dunwoody until 1865. In 1866, at the age of twenty-five, he and Orrick Robertson, who would become a lifelong friend, established Dunwoody & Robertson, a grain and flour merchandising partnership. Unfortunately this new venture had to be dissolved three years later when, once again, Dunwoody's health failed him.

The question of Dunwoody's health is something of a mystery to historians. Illness ended his high school career as well as his first business venture in 1869 (and it would interrupt his Washburn Crosby career in 1898). It is not known whether Dunwoody suffered from one chronic illness or from different ailments at different times. Neither Dunwoody himself nor the historical record is specific about the medical sources of his temporarily debilitating medical problems, although there is some evidence that he had a heart condition for many years.

With business thriving, Dunwoody embarked on what would be the enduring chapter of his personal life. On December 8, 1868, he and Catherine Lane Patten were married. At twenty-four, "Kate" was four years younger than William. The marriage, which took place in Philadelphia, was blessed by both families. Kate's father and William's father, James, were good friends.

Within a year the young couple was en route to a new home. William had become ill, and his doctor advised him to seek out the clean air of the Northwest—today's Midwest— to regain his health. He and his bride relocated to St. Anthony, Minnesota, in 1869.

During his first two years in St. Anthony (which would be renamed Minneapolis in 1872), Dunwoody used his experience in the grain and flour business to purchase Minnesota flour for eastern flour interests. Having recovered his health

Dunwoody family farm, Newtown, Pennsylvania

and established new connections in Minnesota, he became a partner in two local milling companies in 1871: Tiffany, Dunwoody & Company and H. Darrow & Company. The former operated what was called the Arctic Mill, the latter the Union Mill. Both partnerships sold out three years later. In 1875 Dunwoody helped organize the Minneapolis Millers Association to buy wheat for local mills. He acted as the association's general agent until 1877, when the great challenge and opportunity of his career came knocking at the door.

The Washburn Crosby Company

In 1866 Cadwaller C. Washburn, governor of Wisconsin and entrepreneur, built his first flour mill in St. Anthony. Over the next eleven years, Governor Washburn's enterprises grew, and in 1877 he, his brother William, and John Crosby (III) formed a historic partnership: Washburn, Crosby & Company. With a second flour mill, the Washburn B Mill, in the capable hands of Crosby, Washburn now looked for someone with marketing experience who could open new markets for his flour. William Dunwoody caught his attention. An energetic yet unassuming 36-year old miller from Pennsylvania, Dunwoody shared Washburn's confidence that Minnesota flour could be sold not only on the East Coast but in Europe. Dunwoody readily accepted the governor's invitation to become the foreign sales agent for the young Washburn, Crosby & Company. In 1877 he set out for the British Isles.

Dunwoody faced a formidable challenge as Governor Washburn's representative in England. First, the British were prejudiced against Americans, considering them brash and aggressive. Second, they were suspicious of Minnesota's white flour, believing it inferior to their own dark product. During his historic trip in 1877, Dunwoody visited all the flour houses and large bakeries in London and Liverpool, and Glasgow, Scotland. Though rebuffed and frustrated, Dunwoody finally won over some of his British counterparts through his quiet yet persistent personality and extensive knowledge of the industry and Minnesota flour.

After Dunwoody made his first sale in Scotland, the British market opened rapidly. In 1877 Minnesota had sold only a few hundred barrels of flour in Europe. In 1878 that number increased to over 100,000 barrels, and by 1885 more than two million barrels were sold. In *Business Without Boundary*, a history of General Mills, Inc., James Gray wrote of William Dunwoody's 1877 breakthrough: "Dunwoody's trip . . . must be set down as the salesman's dream of glory. It changed the outlook for an entire industry, placed Minneapolis incontestably at its head, and set patterns of operation for many years to follow."

When Dunwoody returned to Minnesota, Governor Washburn quickly rewarded him for his European victory. In 1879 he re-organized Washburn, Crosby & Company, adding William Dunwoody as one of four partners, along with himself, John Crosby (III), and Charles J. Martin. Washburn proposed to add Dunwoody's name to the company's name, but the modest young man preferred to be a less public partner. For the next thirty-five years he would

William Dunwoody, approximately thirty years of age

be one of the principal leaders of Washburn Crosby and become its largest stockholder. But it never became widely recognized as Dunwoody's company.

Not long after its reorganization, Washburn Crosby faced two significant leadership succession challenges. With the deaths of Governor Washburn in 1882 and John Crosby in 1887, the partnership lost both its entrepreneurial founder and its operating manager within five years. The two remaining partners, William Dunwoody and Charles Martin, now had to deal not only with the trustees of Washburn's estate but also with a management vacuum within the business. Dunwoody addressed the management issue by traveling to Philadelphia in the spring of 1888 to recruit James Stroud Bell as Crosby's replacement. Then, in July 1889, Dunwoody and Martin created a new partnership for the company, adding John Crosby's twenty-one-year-old son, John Crosby (IV), to the board of directors. The re-incorporated company now had James S. Bell as its president and William Dunwoody as vice president.

Beginning with a financial panic in 1893, the United States entered a period of severe economic depression that

Washburn Crosby Company flour advertisement

would not abate until the end of the decade. As banks called in loans and credit became tight, the firm's president and vice president, Bell and Dunwoody, placed their personal fortunes at the disposal of the company, thereby ensuring that Washburn Crosby could continue to prosper.

But this was only the first of two occasions in the '90s when Dunwoody came to the aid of his company.

The second occurred in the late '90s when financial interests located on the East Coast and in England attempted to create a "flour trust" in the United States by buying up enough flour mills to control the milling industry. Washburn Crosby Company did not actually own its own mills. It leased them from the C. C. Washburn Flouring Mills Company, a holding company created as part of Governor Washburn's estate plan. If ownership of its mills fell to hostile external financial interests, Washburn Crosby would likely have lost its independence, and competition in Minneapolis' milling industry become a thing of the past.

As the financial threat grew, William Dunwoody was not actively engaged with the company. In 1898 he had been forced, again for health reasons, to take a one-year leave of absence from Washburn Crosby. Apparently his personal physician believed that the illness was related to anxiety and nerves, having prescribed prolonged rest and withdrawal from the tensions of his business life.

Fortunately, by March 1899, Dunwoody had returned to work. Following the annual meeting of the C. C. Washburn Flouring Mills Company in Minneapolis, Dunwoody left on a private mission to Philadelphia. There he met with financial representatives of the Washburn holding company. On April 3 he purchased 75 percent of the stock of the C. C. Washburn Flouring Mills Company.

Minneapolis milling district, c. 1900

Now William Hood Dunwoody owned the lion's share of the flour mills leased to the Washburn Crosby Company. A few months later he and the holding company sold all of their stock to Washburn Crosby. Washburn Crosby was finally in full control of its operations, and the threat of a monopolistic flour trust was broken.

The quiet, unostentatious William Dunwoody was a hero in Minneapolis. He had saved the Washburn Crosby Company. He had saved other milling companies in Minnesota. He had saved countless jobs. Minneapolis remained the milling capital of the nation. When news of Dunwoody's stock purchase became known, the employees of Washburn Crosby as well as other citizens turned out in numbers to greet and cheer the embarrassed businessman at the railroad station upon his return from Philadelphia.

With the depression over and the threat of external takeover past, Washburn Crosby entered the twentieth century with great optimism and expectations of continued economic expansion. Unfortunately, good times were interrupted in the fall of 1903 by a labor strike called by the International Union of Flour and Cereal Mill Employees against all of the city's flour mills, including Washburn Crosby. Affiliated with the American Federation of Labor and its national campaign for an eight-hour work day, the flour mill union had obtained a major concession from Washburn Crosby in 1902 when President Bell agreed to reduce work shifts from twelve to eight hours. Encouraged by this concession, union membership increased in the mills, and soon the union demanded higher wages, too. When Washburn Crosby and other companies refused to meet their demands, the union workers went out on strike.

The strike began on September 24, 1903. Although William Dunwoody was no longer actively engaged in the day-to-day operations of Washburn Crosby, he supported President Bell and his resistance to union demands.

Dunwoody had supported the movement to an eight-hour shift "because we felt that 12 hours was too long for men to keep at work," but he believed that the union's demands were unreasonable. Wages of Minneapolis mill workers, he asserted, were considerably higher than those in larger cities and surrounding areas. "[We] have to fight hard to defeat the plans of the union," he wrote the day after the walkout began. "[Flour manufacturers] cannot stand the increased cost." Three days later Dunwoody was even more adamant: "This is a bitter fight. . . . We do not intend to yield. The demands of our working people have become so unreasonable and the service so poor that we feel we must carry on the fight until the finish is satisfactory to us."

Dunwoody's attitude about his mill workers and the International Union of Flour and Cereal Mill Employees revealed how business leaders of the early twentieth century thought about labor and unionization. In the spirit of *noblesse oblige*, Dunwoody certainly cared about his workers and was willing to discuss their concerns and needs with their representatives. But neither he nor his peers were willing to let a labor union dictate terms to management. Dunwoody was convinced that the 1903 strike was more about building the flour mill union than it was about legitimate worker grievances. "Because we were generous," he maintained, "they wanted still more."

Washburn Crosby and the other milling companies broke the strike within a month by bringing in more than 600 replacement workers and by building stockades around the mills to protect the new workers from the strikers. By early November the strike was over. Having been warned that they would not be rehired if they went out on strike, most of the mill workers lost their jobs. Since many of the workers had been employed by Washburn Crosby for over twenty years, Dunwoody regretted the loss of these old-timers. However, "[They] have no one but themselves to blame," he wrote during the strike. "The orators, organizers and agitators we do not want. I feel sorry for many of [the strikers] that have been lead [sic] away by this disgrace."

Following the strike of 1903, Washburn Crosby continued to grow, without union interference, and William Dunwoody resumed his role as a more silent partner, notwithstanding his being the company's largest stockholder. In 1907, during a bank crisis similar to the one in 1893, Dunwoody again pledged his personal assets to ensure that Washburn Crosby had adequate credit. According to John Washburn, nephew of the late Governor Washburn and a director of the Washburn Crosby Company, "Mr. Dunwoody walked into the office, smiling and confident. 'Why,' he said, 'I will get you all the money you need. I have a vault in New York filled with gilt-edged bonds and every bond I have is at the disposal of the Washburn Crosby Company.'" With

such a record of personal support for his company, it is easy to understand why Dunwoody was held in high esteem by his business associates.

Other Business and Community Interests

Although William Dunwoody considered himself first and foremost a "miller," and although the Washburn Crosby Company was his principal enterprise, he built his fortune through investment and personal involvement in a multitude of related businesses. He was founder and president of St. Anthony & Dakota Elevator Company, vice president of Duluth Elevator Company, a partner in Barnum Grain Company, and president of Dunwoody Grain Company. A personal friend and business peer of railroad builder James J. Hill, Dunwoody became a director of Hill's Great Northern Railway Company, and as Hill expanded his

JOHN GERARD   FRANK W. LUND   JAMES F. BELL   H. O'B. HARDING   W. A. JONES   H. R. McLAUGHLIN

T. C. ESTEE   WILLIAM H. BOVEY   BENJAMIN S. BULL   WILLIAM G. CROCKER   G. A. THOMAS   JOHN H. MULLIKEN   WILLIAM SHERMAN

F. F. HENRY   FREDERICK G. ATKINSON·WILLIAM H. DUNWOODY   JAMES S. BELL   CHARLES C. BOVEY   SAMUEL BELL, JR.   P. B. SMITH

Washburn Crosby executive team, c.1905. William Dunwoody is third from left in the front row.

Northwestern National Bank of Minneapolis, c. 1900-1914

railroad empire west, Dunwoody's St. Anthony & Dakota Elevator Company built elevators along the line of the Great Northern in Minnesota and the Dakotas. Since Hill needed product to transport on his railroad, he urged the Washburn Crosby Company to expand into Montana. When James Bell opposed such expansion, Dunwoody established his own separate Royal Milling Company in Great Falls. Dunwoody was still president of the independent Royal Milling at the time of his death in 1914, but

eventually Washburn Crosby's successor company, General Mills, bought Royal, thereby adding it to Dunwoody's General Mills legacy. At the end of his life, Dunwoody was also a stockholder in these western companies: Great Falls Milling Company, Kalispell Flour Mill Company, and Seattle Gas & Electric Company.

Dunwoody was also very active in banking, since financing was critical to all of his entrepreneurial ventures. He

Minneapolis Institute of Arts, c. 1915

was the first depositor at Northwestern National Bank of Minneapolis in 1872, and subsequently became a director and ultimately president of the bank. Much as he had come to the aid of the Washburn Crosby Company, Dunwoody deposited $1 million at Northwestern Bank in 1907 to stabilize it during the financial panic of that year. In 1912 the directors of Northwestern National Bank and Minnesota Loan and Trust Company, of which he was also a director, demonstrated their gratitude to Dunwoody and a colleague for their 30-plus years of service by hosting a gala banquet for them at the Minneapolis Club—one of the largest and most splendid dinners held at the club up to that time.

Dunwoody not only had multiple business interests, he was also very involved in the larger community. Some of the organizations of which he was a member were Lakewood Cemetery Association, Minikahda Club, Lafayette Club, Minnesota Club of St. Paul, Minnetonka Yacht Club, Metropolitan Club of New York, Minnesota Historical Society, and Minneapolis Civic Commission. He was an active member at Westminster Presbyterian Church and a director of the Minneapolis Society of Fine Arts. Like Andrew Carnegie, whose "gospel of wealth" challenged

successful captains of industry in the late nineteenth and early twentieth centuries to give back to the community, Dunwoody was a generous though quiet philanthropist. He made contributions to his church, the YMCA and YWCA, and many organizations serving African Americans, including the Institute for Colored Youth in Pennsylvania, the Colored Orphan & Industrial Home in Kentucky, and Booker T. Washington's Tuskegee Normal & Industrial Institute in Alabama.

One of Dunwoody's most significant contributions was to the Minneapolis Society of Fine Arts. Although the Society had been founded in 1883, action to build an art museum for the city did not gain momentum until the turn of the century. Two commitments by prominent citizens marked the turning point. In 1908 Clinton Morrison privately pledged his family homestead at Third Avenue South and East Twenty-fourth Street as a site for a museum, and in 1911 William Dunwoody pledged $100,000 to launch a fundraising campaign to build a museum on the Morrison site.

Initially Dunwoody had declined to participate in the Society's fundraising campaign because 1910 had been a bad year for crops in Minnesota and thus a bad year for Washburn Crosby and other Dunwoody businesses. However, when informed of Morrison's confidential commitment of land, Dunwoody reconsidered. Morrison's son-in-law, John R. Van Derlip, had solicited Dunwoody for a gift. On January 2, 1911, Dunwoody notified him that he would contribute $100,000 to the campaign, provided that the Society raised the full $500,000 needed to build the museum. "[If] Mr. Morrison was willing to make so magnificent a gift," Dunwoody told Van Derlip, "it was the duty of everyone to fall in and help . . . ."

Dunwoody's commitment was critical to the success of the campaign. He had been number one on the Society's list of prospective donors. His participation was important not only because of his stature in the community but because he was a key leader in the milling industry, the support of which was considered essential for a successful fund drive. A gala banquet for 200 potential donors was held at the Minneapolis Club on January 10. When the Morrison and Dunwoody pledges were announced, the audience went wild. "Amid the stately white roses of the banquet tables, bedlam broke loose," wrote Jeffrey Hess in *Their Splendid Legacy*, a history of the Society of Fine Arts. "Dunwoody's offer was the largest cash donation in the city's history, and it electrified the audience." Within ninety minutes another $250,000 was pledged by seventy-two citizens, and within the next month the goal of $500,000 was reached. Ultimately the Society raised $520,180 in what was probably Minneapolis' first formal fundraising campaign. William Dunwoody was the catalyst and lead donor in this historic campaign.

Kate Dunwoody

The next year, Dunwoody was elected president of the Society's board of directors, and he was president while the new museum, the Minneapolis Institute of Arts, was being built. Unfortunately he died before the Institute was completed. The official opening of the Art Institute occurred in 1915, eleven months after Dunwoody's death. By then it was public knowledge that he had left $1 million to the Society of Fine Arts to create a trust fund to purchase works of art for the museum. Much as his cash gift in 1911 had galvanized the campaign to build the Art Institute, the 1914 bequest would serve as a catalyst to establish a first-rate art collection.

Kate L. Dunwoody

Catherine Lane Patten Dunwoody was William Dunwoody's full partner in life. They were a close couple with shared values and interests. Like her husband, she was a benefactor of the Minneapolis Institute of Arts, contributing all of her

oil paintings to the Institute in 1915. In recognition of the Dunwoodys' philanthropy, the Institute mounted a polished marble plaque in their honor inside the entrance of the new museum.

In her first year of marriage, Kate had accompanied her husband when he moved to Minnesota in 1869 to restore 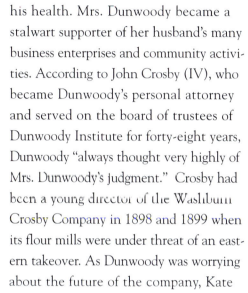 his health. Mrs. Dunwoody became a stalwart supporter of her husband's many business enterprises and community activities. According to John Crosby (IV), who became Dunwoody's personal attorney and served on the board of trustees of Dunwoody Institute for forty-eight years, Dunwoody "always thought very highly of Mrs. Dunwoody's judgment." Crosby had been a young director of the Washburn Crosby Company in 1898 and 1899 when its flour mills were under threat of an eastern takeover. As Dunwoody was worrying about the future of the company, Kate encouraged him to buy the mills from the C. C. Washburn Flouring Mills Company. Crosby's recollection was that it was she who reminded her husband that he owed it to his employees to prevent a hostile takeover of their company.

This was neither the first nor the last time that William Dunwoody took the advice of his wife. When the Dunwoodys decided to move out of their home at 52 South Tenth Street in the expanding downtown of Minneapolis, Kate persuaded her husband to donate the property to the Woman's Christian Association (WCA) of Minneapolis. She shared WCA's concern for the welfare of single young women trying to find work in large cities around the turn of the century. To provide safe housing for young women, WCA established the Woman's Boarding Home, and on June 30, 1906, William and Kate Dunwoody gave their home to WCA to be used as a dormitory. What was unusual for that time was the appearance of Mrs.

Kate Dunwoody Home

Abbott Hospital for Women

Dunwoody's name on the deed of the property along with her husband's—testimony to their partnership as community benefactors. WCA built an annex to the boarding home in 1908, and over time the Woman's Boarding Home became known as the Kate Dunwoody Home. In 1965 WCA

razed the Dunwoody mansion and annex and erected a new Kate Dunwoody Hall, which operated until it closed in 1990.

Yet another example of the Dunwoodys' shared philanthropy was Abbott Hospital. In 1902 Dr. Amos Wilson Abbott, a gynecologist, established a small hospital for women in a rented house at 10 East Seventeenth Street. This small facility had an operating room, laboratory, and beds for only fifteen patients. By 1909, when Dr. Abbott performed a corrective surgery on Kate Dunwoody, his hospital was overcrowded and not fireproof. Following her successful surgery, Kate suggested to her husband that they build a more adequate hospital for her physician. Again William Dunwoody followed his wife's advice. In 1910 he bought property at 1818 First Avenue South, where he built a private hospital for Dr. Abbott. Abbott Hospital for Women and Children opened on August 28, 1911—the same year that Dunwoody's gift to the Minneapolis Society of Fine Arts inspired the community to build the Art Institute. The new Abbott Hospital had twenty more beds than its predecessor, expanded facilities, and accommodations for twelve student nurses. Although the title was in Dunwoody's name, Dr. Abbott ran the hospital until Dunwoody's death. Abbott Hospital operated as an independent hospital until it merged with Northwestern Hospital in 1970.

The Minneapolis Institute of Arts, the Kate Dunwoody Home, and Abbott Hospital were three community institutions which Kate Dunwoody helped to found. No less important was The William Hood Dunwoody Industrial Institute, created through her husband's estate plan and strengthened through her own. Kate understood the kind of school her husband wanted to establish, and she fully supported this enterprise. That is why she attended the opening of Dunwoody Institute on December 14, 1914, and why she is considered one of the founders of the college that bears her husband's name.

The Dunwoodys' mansion, Overlook

Death of the Founders

Following a salmon fishing trip with James J. Hill and other friends in July 1913, William Dunwoody became ill and was confined to his room at the Dunwoodys' summer home at Lake Minnetonka for several weeks. During the fall his health worsened. By December, when he and Kate returned to Overlook, their Minneapolis residence at 104 Groveland Terrace, it was evident that his condition was terminal. The original source of his illness, his doctor suspected, may have been the residual effects of malaria he had contracted many years earlier. The decline was exacerbated by his prolonged heart condition. After a six-month illness, William Hood Dunwoody died on February 8, 1914, one month shy of his seventy-third birthday. The declared cause of death was ulcerative endocarditis (inflammation of the valves of the heart) and streptococcus infection.

Not surprisingly, the passing of one of Minneapolis' pioneering giants was greeted with widespread grieving and public recognition. Out of respect for Dunwoody, the offices of the Washburn Crosby Company and other businesses with which he was associated closed on the day of his funeral. The list of pallbearers reads like a who's who of the community, among them James J. Hill, Dr. Amos Abbott, John Crosby (IV), John Washburn, and George Barnum. A resolution honoring Dunwoody was adopted

William Dunwoody's memorial obelisk, Lakewood Cemetery, Minneapolis

by the board of directors of the Washburn Crosby Company. It read in part:

Straight-forward, wise, high-minded, far-sighted, William H. Dunwoody possessed a wonderfully well-balanced judgment and power which had ever been used for this company since he helped found it . . . . And such qualities as these and such a personality as his cannot be utterly lost in his death. They must survive in some degree in us, on whom his influence has worked, and they must and will be preserved in the traditions and underlying characteristics of this company. . . . His was a character rarely compounded of strength and mildness, of creative imagination and solid convictions. As ready as the youngest director of us for bold innovation, as conservative as the oldest for sound and enduring policies, he was at all times a tower of strength in both counsel and action.

Similarly the board of directors of Dunwoody's St. Anthony & Dakota Elevator Company resolved:

[That] rarely indeed have there been united in one personality such conspicuous ability, such compelling force, such scrupulous business honor; such dignity without austerity, such tact, gentleness and consideration for others; that our confidence in the permanency and continued success of this business rests largely upon the strength of the foundations which he has created and the thoroughness with which the entire organization is imbued with his principles and ideals; that we rejoice in

the universal testimonials from the men and women of his generation to his splendid character and achievements and the unique place which he filled in the community; and that we take solemn pride in having had the privilege of working so long under such superb leadership.

Kate Dunwoody received a copy of this resolution, as well as the board's expression of "our deepest sympathy in this hour of her great bereavement."

Having survived her partner of forty-five years, Kate lived only another seventeen months. Whether she realized that she had cancer of the ovaries and intestines at the time of her husband's death, or ten months later when Dunwoody Institute opened to students, is unknown. If she knew, she bore her burden quietly and with the grace and dignity that had characterized her unpretentious life. Kate Lane Patten Dunwoody died at the age of seventy on September 27, 1915. Her wake was held at Overlook, the Dunwoody's mansion, and she was buried alongside her husband at Lakewood Cemetery.

Kate Dunwoody was mourned by everyone in Minneapolis who recognized her behind-the-scenes benevolence and her critically important influence on her more public husband. Her passing was not accompanied by office closings or board resolutions, but it was certainly felt deeply by the community. What Kate and William Dunwoody left was an impressive record of civic engagement and philanthropic stewardship. Their legacy continues.

CHAPTER II

Getting Started, 1914-1924

Last Will and Testament

On Sunday morning, February 15, 1914, the city of Minneapolis awoke to news of the extraordinary philanthropy of one of its most prominent business leaders and community benefactors. William Hood Dunwoody, who had died seven days earlier, had left the community $4.6 million through an "overwhelming list of philanthropic bequests," proclaimed *The Minneapolis Sunday Journal.* The largest of the estate gifts, an estimated $2 million, would be used to establish a technical school, to be named The William Hood Dunwoody Industrial Institute.

The reading of Dunwoody's last will and testament warranted front-page headlines because Dunwoody had been a noted local leader and because an estate estimated at $7 million in 1914 dollars would have an approximate value of $158 million one hundred years later. Philanthropic gifts totaling $104 million in 2014 would be every bit as newsworthy as $4.6 million was in 1914.*

To begin with, Dunwoody's will bequeathed personal possessions such as his residence, furniture, jewelry, and horses, as well as $1.5 million, to his wife, Kate. To his brother E. Evans Dunwoody and the three daughters of his late brother John, he gave a total of $550,000. Three other relatives received $35,000, and twelve friends and associates received approximately $100,000 in cash and stock. These were the personal gifts.

Since William and Kate had no children, the bulk of the bequests went to charitable organizations. In Minneapolis the most significant gifts (aside from the founding of Dunwoody Institute) were $50,000 to the Minneapolis YMCA; $1 million in trust to the Minneapolis Society of Fine Arts to establish an endowment for the purchase of "pictures and works of art"; and the donation of Abbott Hospital for Women and Children, and $100,000 for the hospital's ongoing support, to Westminster Presbyterian Church. Other Presbyterian causes that received support were the Presbyterian Board of Relief for Disabled Ministers and Widows and Orphans of Deceased Ministers, the Board of Home Missions of the Presbyterian Church in the U.S.A, and the Board of Foreign Missions of the Presbyterian Church in the U.S.A. Each received $100,000.

Dunwoody did not forget his native Pennsylvania. He left $10,000 to the Mercantile Beneficial Association of Philadelphia and the same amount to the Merchants' Fund of Philadelphia. He donated his family farm in Newtown, Pennsylvania, plus $1 million to establish a home for convalescents on the site of the farmstead, with preference being given to patients from the Orthopedic Hospital of Philadelphia. Along with Dunwoody Institute, the "Dunwoody Home" in Pennsylvania would become a major institution created through the philanthropy of William Hood Dunwoody.

*See the websites dollartimes.com and measuringworth.com for various ways to calculate the relative value of a dollar in 1914. Although a Consumer Price Index (CPI) measurement was used to estimate the relative value of William Dunwoody's philanthropic gifts, the CPI indicator does not actually demonstrate the magnitude of his estate relative to those of other wealthy persons of his day. A different measurement, *relative share of GDP*, would place the value of his estate as high as $3.3 billion in 2009 dollars (as compared to Warren Buffet's estimated worth of $62 billion).

Opposite: Dunwoody auto mechanics training for U.S. Army during World War I

PONSIBILITY CAMPAIGNS UPON WILSON

t To Take up Task of ning Democratic Con-gress to Capital.

LEADERS HOPE R PROGRESSIVE AID

ns, However, Declare ull Moosers are Re-ning to G. O. P.

TION OUTLINED

f Administration Re-Important Element ring Radical Votes.

au

James Gray.

Feb. 14.—The recent e president, while neither rming, was enough to set politics here thinking tion which puts so much on one man and that a ned to shirk work.

of the ruling party is y and there appears to able of guiding it but The actual facts appear le he is quiet about it, velt had as much to do f congress as has Wood.

About Everything.

d about everything and his way about nearl shaped the tariff bill, turally do, since tarin central point of his

tely did he dominate currency bill and now se itself on the canal passed legislation on which had been

W. H. DUNWOODY'S WILL GIVES PUBLIC $4,601,000; $2,000,000 FOR SCHOOL

Distribution of $7,000,000 Estate Of W. H. Dunwoody

zDunwoody industrial in-stitution, Minneapolis	$2,000,000
Minneapolis Society of Fine Arts	1,000,000
zzTrustees of Westminster church, Minneapolis	175,000
Minneapolis Y. M. C. A.	50,000
Minneapolis Woman's Boarding home	1,000
Presbyterian Board of Relief for Ministers	100,000
Presbyterian Board of Home Missions	100,000
Presbyterian Board of Foreign Missions	100,000
zzzDunwoody home for convalescents, Newtown farm, Pennsylvania	1,050,000
Newtown burying ground, Pennsylvania	5,000
Merchants' Beneficial as-sociation, Philadelphia	10,000
Merchants' Fund, Phila-delphia	10,000
Mrs. W. H. Dunwoody	1,500,000
Hannah Dunwoody Bous-field, Mary Dunwoody Cartwright and Ruth Dunwoody Hardee nieces, $150,000 each	450,000
Other relatives, friends and associates	252,000
Total of estate	$6,803,000

zEstimated residue after specific bequests are paid.
zzValue of Abbott hospital esti-mated at $75,000.
zzzValue of Newtown farm esti-mated at $50,000.

RUINS SEARCHED FOR FIRE VICTIM

Wife of Man Missing in Big Downtown Blaze Prostrated —Loss Placed at $130,000.

Minneapolis Gets Industrial Institutio as Largest Item in Overwhelming List of Philanthropic Bequests

$1,000,000 GIVEN TO BUY WORKS FOR ART MUSEUM

Purchases Will Cover Thirty-Year Period—Tota of $3,226,000 to Be Spent for Benefit of Minneapolis.

BIRTHPLACE AND $1,000,000 FUND LEFT FOR HOME FOR CONVALESCENTS

Abbott Hospital With $100,000 Endowment Given West minster Church—Church Funds Get $300,000— $2,202,000 for Family and Friends.

In a testament which transcends in liberality and surpasses in importance anything in the history of philanthropy in the northwest, William H. Dunwoody who died last Sunday and who gave munificently to charity and for promotion of art and education while he lived, has directed in his will that approximately $4,601,000 be apportioned for philanthropic purposes. Of this total, approxi-mately $3,226,000 is in the form of gifts or endowments for the benefit of Min-neapolis, where he lived for forty years.

A great industrial school, wherein the youth of Minnesota may be educated free in useful crafts and trades, is provided for by the residue remaining after other benefactions have been made, and this industrial school endowment will probably reach $2,000,000.

One million dollars is given the Minneapolis Society of Fine Arts that its magnificent building, to which in his lifetime Mr. Dunwoody gave $100,000, may be provided with great works of art.

Abbott hospital, which Mr. Dunwoody built and controlled and whi is valued at $75,000, is given to Westminster church, along with an endown of $100,000.

Estate Close to $7,000,000.

An estate that will exceed $7,000,000, the acquisition forty years of identification

Articles 39 and 40 of Dunwoody's will laid out Dunwoody's plan for The William Hood Dunwoody Industrial Institute. The will directed that "the rest, residue and remainder" of his estate should be used to purchase the site, construct the buildings, and establish a permanent endowment fund to support the new school. Although *The Minneapolis Sunday Journal* had estimated that there would be $2 million remaining to establish Dunwoody Institute, the final bequest turned out to be more than $3 million.

What was the purpose of this new school? Believing that Minnesota already had more than enough post-secondary institutions dedicated to liberal arts education, Dunwoody wanted to create a school "wherein shall be taught industrial and mechanical arts, giving special importance to the different handicrafts and useful trades." As one of the founders of the Washburn Crosby Company and Minneapolis' milling industry, he specifically singled out "the art of milling and the construction of milling machinery" as priorities for his industrial institute. What was truly revolutionary about this new school was Dunwoody's directive that education at Dunwoody Institute be *"given free to the youth of the city of Minneapolis and state of Minnesota without distinction on account of race, color or religious prejudice."* In an inspirational phrase that would become the institution's formal vision statement ninety years later, Dunwoody defined his purpose as "to provide *for all time* a place where the youth of this city and state may, if they so desire, learn the different handicrafts and useful trades and thereby *fit themselves for the better performance of life's duties*."

This would be a unique school dedicated to creating economic and social opportunities for young people of all races, religions, and financial means in a community that was essentially Caucasian and Protestant, and at a time when a system of racial segregation was being re-established in our nation's capital by the so-called "progressive"

Site of Dunwoody convalescent home, Newtown, Pennsylvania, 1923

administration of President Woodrow Wilson.* Dunwoody's intent was that education at his school be free and that it provide not only practical and useful skills and trades but also prepare its students to be productive citizens who would contribute to the betterment of their communities. It is hard to imagine a school with a higher calling.

Dunwoody was very clear about how his bequest should be used. No more than one-third of his gift (i.e., no more than $1 million) was to be spent to purchase land and construct buildings for Dunwoody Institute. The balance was to be invested in a permanent endowment fund, from which the school could use 90 percent of the annual income to operate the school, reserving 10 percent of the annual income for emergency needs that might arise in any given year. Anticipating that other benefactors might want to support his school in future years, he stipulated that any subsequent contribution to Dunwoody Institute would have to be added to his permanent endowment. This condition on future gifts demonstrates how critical the school's per-

---

*In 1907 a businessman in St. Louis, Missouri, David Ranken Jr., had established a vocational school remarkably similar to Dunwoody Institute. Although the Ranken School of Mechanical Trades would become virtually the only school in the country resembling Dunwoody in philosophy, curriculum, and business support, in one respect it was very different: its founder, unlike William Dunwoody, specified that Ranken admit only Caucasians. It remained racially segregated until the 1960s.

Opposite: Minneapolis Sunday Journal headline, February 15, 1914

and four were bankers associated with his two banks, Northwestern National Bank of Minneapolis and First National Bank. Two trustees, John Crosby and Charles Bovey, were also named, along with Kate Dunwoody, as executors of Dunwoody's will.

William Dunwoody obviously trusted his friends to implement his vision and act as responsible stewards of the resources he had provided. That they took their charge seriously was demonstrated not only by the way in which they launched and managed The William Hood Dunwoody Industrial Institute but by the longevity of their service to the school. The total service of the original twelve trustees was 311 years. The average tenure on the board was twenty-six years.

Here is the founding board of trustees of Dunwoody Institute, followed by each trustee's years of service.

William H. Bovey, president of Dunwoody board of trustees, 1914-1937

F. G. Atkinson, 1914-1940
James S. Bell, 1914-1915*
Charles C. Bovey, 1914-1954
William H. Bovey, 1914-1937
Joseph Chapman, 1914-1948
Elbridge C. Cooke, 1914-1931
William G. Crocker, 1914-1922
Franklin M. Crosby, 1914-1947
John Crosby, 1914-1962
E. W. Decker, 1914-1956
John Washburn, 1914-1919
Robert W. Webb, 1914-1948

manent endowment was to William Dunwoody's plan. (This limitation on contributions to Dunwoody Institute led the board of trustees in 1940 to set up a separate corporation, The Dunwoody Alumni Fund, which could accept gifts for student scholarships and other special purposes to benefit the school.)

Board of Trustees

To convert his dream of an industrial institute into reality, William Dunwoody turned to those he trusted most, his Minneapolis business associates. In his will he named the original trustees of The William Hood Dunwoody Industrial Institute. All twelve of these men were installed as members of the first official board of trustees on November 10, 1914. Eight of these trustees were fellow business executives with Dunwoody at the Washburn Crosby Company

When the board was established on November 10, 1914, these trustees became the first officers: William Bovey, president; Elbridge Cooke, vice president; Joseph Chapman, treasurer; and William Crocker, secretary.

*On October 5, 1915, James Ford Bell replaced James S. Bell on the board; the second Bell served from 1915 to 1959.

Of these officers, two played especially important roles for the new school. William Bovey was president of the board for twenty-three years. When he resigned from the board and this leadership role in 1937, he estimated that he had given 25 percent of his personal time to the Dunwoody endeavor during these years, the equivalent of almost six years of full-time volunteer service. Joseph Chapman, to whom William Dunwoody had conveyed his personal thoughts about a potential technical school two years before his death, served as treasurer of Dunwoody Institute for its first ten years. Since the board of trustees, through its Finance Committee, controlled all of the school's finances in these formative years, Chapman was a key figure in acquiring a site for the school, allocating dollars for the construction of buildings, investing the remainder of Dunwoody's bequest in a permanent endowment fund, and directing and monitoring the school's investments thereafter.

As noted, eight of the original trustees, including William Bovey, had been Dunwoody's colleagues at the Washburn Crosby Company. In subsequent years at least one position on the Dunwoody board was reserved for an executive of the Washburn Crosby Company, later to be renamed General Mills, Inc. In addition, for one hundred years a member of the Crosby family would sit on the school's board of trustees. There were two Crosbys on the first board. John Crosby, the son of one of the two founders of the original Washburn, Crosby & Company, was Dunwoody's personal attorney. He drafted his friend's last will and testament and was one of the executors of the will. He served on the Dunwoody board of trustees for forty-eight years. His brother, Franklin Crosby, was a board member for thirty-three years. He served as chairman of the board's Building Committee, which oversaw the design and construction of buildings on the new Dunwoody campus between 1917 and 1924. During the first century of Dunwoody Institute, later Dunwoody College of Technology, six Crosbys would volunteer 167 years of collective service to the institution.

Start-Up

Following the death of William Dunwoody and the publication of his will, the trustees of his estate wasted little time getting the new school started. As close associates of Dunwoody, they had a clear idea of his vision. In 1912 Dunwoody had asked Joseph Chapman, his colleague at Northwestern National Bank, to undertake a trip to Europe on his behalf to research existing trade schools. Since Chapman was too busy to make the trip, Dunwoody arranged to have a representative from the office of the Minneapolis Board of Education make the trip on his behalf. When the official returned from Europe, he made his report to both Dunwoody and Chapman, thereby helping to solidify Dunwoody's thinking about his institute as well as opening communication between Dunwoody, Chapman, and the Minneapolis Board of Education. This communication became important six months following Dunwoody's death when the Board of Education endorsed the establishment in Minneapolis of a "vocational school for boys"—the future Dunwoody Institute.

> "I really liked that what we learned we then applied in class. We had a different project every month. An education like this is hard to come by. Dunwoody helped my life immensely."
>
> —Donn Thomas 1964

In the fall of 1914, the Minneapolis Board of Education leased to Dunwoody Institute the Old Central High School at Eleventh Street and Fourth Avenue South in downtown Minneapolis. The former high school and its annex were leased from October 26 until August 31, 1915, for the sum of one dollar. Ultimately the Old Central High School, plus space at the New Central High (Fourth Avenue South and Thirty-fourth Street), East High School (Fourth Street and University Avenue Southeast), and Madison School in St. Paul, would house Dunwoody programs during its first three years of operation, from December 1914 until August 1917.

CENTRAL HIGH SCHOOL, MINNEAPOLIS, MINN.

5106

Old Central High School, Minneapolis, Minnesota

The Dunwoody board acted quickly. A lease was negotiated and a principal hired even before Dunwoody Institute was officially incorporated. Harry W. Kavel, who had been employed by the Minneapolis school system as principal of Evening Industrial High Schools, became Dunwoody's principal in 1914 and served as the school's chief administrator until a permanent director was hired in 1915. It was Kavel's assignment to recruit faculty, oversee the development of Dunwoody curriculum, and get the Old Central High School ready for the admission of Dunwoody students.

In October 1914 the board also approved a public "Notice or Circular"—to be distributed throughout Minnesota's public schools—announcing the opening of Dunwoody Institute:

> *Boys of State of Minnesota: What Are You Going to Do For a Living? Would You Like to Become Skilled Workmen?*

The circular announced that education at the new school would be "entirely free" to residents of Minnesota between fourteen and eighteen years of age. Depending upon student demand, these trades would be offered at Dunwoody:

Harry W. Kavel, Dunwoody principal and assistant director, 1914-1922

Cabinet Making
Carpentry and Millwrighting
Machine Shop
Automobile Repair
Electrical Construction
Sheet Metal Work
Machine Drafting
Architectural Drafting
Printing
Book-Binding

In addition to "practical" courses, students would receive instruction in these "general subjects":

English
Applied Math
Drawing
Industrial History

Civics
Elementary Physics
Hygiene
Gymnastics

Over the next few weeks, enough students responded to this call and enough progress was made in retrofitting the Old Central High School that the new Dunwoody Institute was able to open its doors to the public. On December 14, which would become known as "Founder's Day," Kate Dunwoody attended the opening ceremonies for The William Hood Dunwoody Industrial Institute. Eighty students and seven instructors began instruction in Machine Shop Practice, Cabinet Making, Mill Work, and Printing. The dream of William Dunwoody was now a reality.

In January 1915 the new institute added courses in Drafting, Automobile Construction, and Electrical Construction, increasing enrollment at Dunwoody to 170 students. By September enrollment had grown to 270, and on October 4, 1915, Dunwoody enrolled an additional 800 employed workers in new Evening Trade Extension classes. By December—one year after Dunwoody Institute had opened its doors to students—total enrollment was 1,400, with 1,100 of these students enrolled in forty-eight different Evening School classes.

A New Leader

Even as the board of trustees was getting Dunwoody up and running, the institute's leaders saw the need for a more intentional and comprehensive blueprint for their new school. Therefore, in concert with the Minneapolis Board of Education, they invited the National Society for the Promotion of Industrial Education, located in New York City, to visit Minneapolis to conduct a survey of employers, educators, and civic leaders to determine the future vocational education needs of the community. The Society agreed to do a "Minneapolis Survey," and the person charged with directing the survey was the secretary of the

Dr. Charles Prosser, Dunwoody director, 1915-1945

Society, Dr. Charles A. Prosser. Work began on the survey on May 1, 1915, and it was completed in November. In January 1916 the Society held its ninth annual convention in Minneapolis to discuss the Minneapolis Survey and other issues related to vocational education.

Dr. Prosser, already a national leader in vocational education, so impressed the Dunwoody board that it set out to retain him as the chief executive of Dunwoody Institute even before he officially began work on the Minneapolis Survey. Board President William Bovey, who also served on the board of trustees of the Massachusetts Institute of Technology (MIT), had asked friends in Boston for referrals for potential leaders for Dunwoody. The friends recommended Prosser. At that time Prosser was also a candidate for the presidency at the University of Washington. According to John Crosby, Bovey compiled newspaper clippings that documented the funding and political

challenges facing presidents at public universities. He sent these to Prosser, in the hope that he would turn down the Washington job. Apparently Bovey's fear campaign worked, for on April 14, 1915, Dr. Prosser accepted Dunwoody's offer to become the first managing director of Dunwoody Institute, assuming office on September 1, while he was still completing work on the Minneapolis Survey.

Dr. Charles Prosser, a native of Indiana, had received his doctorate from Columbia University. As a public school superintendent in Indiana, he had met many young men who were interested in working with their hands and learning a vocational trade. For the seven years prior to moving to Minneapolis, he had been superintendent of schools for the Children's Aid Society in New York City, deputy commissioner for industrial education in Massachusetts, and secretary of the National Society for the Promotion of Industrial Education.

It would be Dr. Charles Prosser who would define and develop William Dunwoody's vision for Dunwoody Industrial Institute during his thirty-year tenure as director. It would be Prosser who would take over the academic leadership of this pioneering school from the board of trustees and Principal Kavel. It would be Prosser who would make Dunwoody Institute a national leader in vocational technical education.

Some of Prosser's basic beliefs were summarized by the students of Dunwoody Institute in the second edition of *The Artisan*, a monthly publication by the students and staff that ran between December 1915 and August 1924. In January 1916 *The Artisan* had this to say about Dunwoody's director:

> *Mr. Prosser believes in giving the boys a chance. He thinks that every fellow ought to have a chance to learn the thing he wants to learn and to do the things he wants to do. He believes that the Day School of the Dunwoody*

Dunwoody machine shop at the old Central High School

Institute ought to give the boys a good start for learning a trade, after which they should go into the trade as advanced apprentices at the same wage that the third year apprentice earns. . . . He believes that the Evening School should give the men who are already at work in the trades a chance to get additional knowledge and training, which will help them if they are ambitious and capable, to advance in wage or position in the shop. He hopes to see the time come when many young fellows who are employed in the shops will be able to divide their time so as to give some of it to the shop, where they make their living, and some of it to the school, where they get the training that will make them better workmen and better citizens.

Dunwoody printing shop at the old Central High School

DUNWOODY PRINT

Auto repair class at the old Central High School

When asked by the students what Dunwoody's motto ought to be, Dr. Prosser replied:

Opening the Way to Merit. Every fellow has some merit in him. It ought to be the job of the Dunwoody school to bring out all the good things in the fellows who want to learn a trade, or, who being in a trade, want to improve themselves so they may have a larger success.

Clearly the new director of Dunwoody Institute embraced the founder's vision to prepare students "for the better performance of life's duties."

Financing the School

On March 22, 1915, three weeks before Dr. Prosser was retained as director of Dunwoody Institute, the Probate Court of Hennepin County valued William Hood Dunwoody's total estate at $8,461,230.91. Subsequently, on July 15, the executors of Dunwoody's last will and testament and the board of trustees of the new school officially agreed that $3,151,473.52 had been distributed to the Institute under the terms of the will. This bequest of $3.1 million was now at the disposal of the board of trustees to acquire property, construct buildings, and set up long-term investments to sustain the new school.

When Kate Dunwoody died on September 27, her passing

set in motion the terms of her last will and testament, in which she had also designated a significant bequest for The William Hood Dunwoody Industrial Institute. Article 19 of her will (dated January 18, 1915) bequeathed all of the real property left to her by her husband, $1.5 million in securities and/or cash, and the rest of her estate to the Minneapolis Trust Company and its successors to hold in trust for Dunwoody Institute. Her intent was to create a "permanent endowment fund" for the Institute, with quarterly income payments distributed to the school. Exactly one year after Mrs. Dunwoody's death, the Probate Court of Hennepin County valued her estate at $2,036,369. Following the payment of estate expenses and other bequests, the balance remaining for the Dunwoody trust at Minneapolis Trust Company was $1,705,420. Although the board of trustees of Dunwoody Institute would not have direct control over the Kate Dunwoody Trust—a point of some contention over the next one hundred years—this second gift meant that William and Kate Dunwoody had bequeathed almost $5 million to establish and support Dunwoody Institute "for all time." In 2012 dollars, their gift was worth $110 million.

For the first decade or so of operation, the leaders of Dunwoody Institute must have felt quite secure financially. Dunwoody paid virtually nothing to lease the Old Central High School and other facilities for its first three years of operation, and the one-time start-up expenses for a new campus were relatively small. On November 24, 1915, the board of trustees authorized the expenditure of $107,000 to purchase six city blocks of land north of The Parade, a Minneapolis park on Superior Boulevard (later renamed Wayzata Boulevard and eventually Dunwoody Boulevard). These fifteen acres were supplemented by three acres donated by the Minneapolis City Council when it vacated several streets and alleys running through this area. Construction of two shop buildings on this future site of the new school in 1917 and the purchase of training equipment cost Dunwoody about $400,000, and

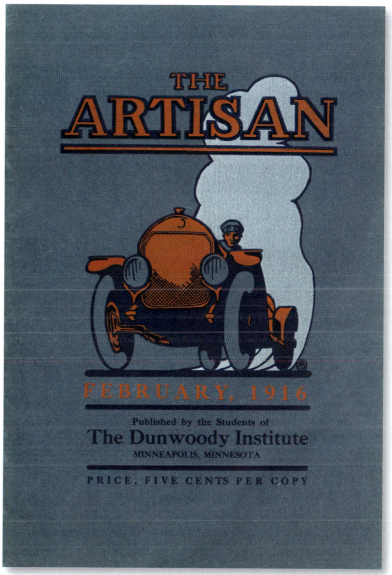

A cover of *The Artisan*, newsletter published by Dunwoody students and staff, 1915-1924

construction of an administration building in 1924 cost $220,000. In total, Dunwoody spent about $730,000 to establish a permanent home.

In spite of these start-up expenses, the William Dunwoody Endowment Fund had a principal value of $3.4 million in 1925—ten years following its creation. And the Kate Dunwoody Trust had retained its value as well, generating

$90,000 in operating income for the school in 1925.

Two reasons for Dunwoody's financial health during its first decade were the financial expertise of the board of trustees Finance Committee and the general prosperity of the United States economy from 1915 until the late 1920s. (This good fortune would end with the Great Crash of 1929 and the Great Depression that followed.) Since William Dunwoody had placed his trust and his endowment fund in the hands of his close business associates, it is not surprising that they spent considerable time and energy overseeing the investments of Dunwoody Institute. They did not turn this responsibility over to a bank or other outside investment firm; rather, they made all of the investment decisions themselves. The minutes of the Finance Committee meeting on January 20, 1925, illustrate the financial detail in which the trustees involved themselves. At this meeting the committee authorized the sale of 3,922 certificates of interest in Great Northern Ore Company for $38 per share; authorized the purchase of $100,000 of railway bonds; approved the purchase of $25,000 of Central Warehouse Company bonds; and sold a 640-acre farm in Edgeley, North Dakota, for $13,000. Along with other investors across the country, Dunwoody benefitted as the stock market and the American economy boomed.

Another reason for the financial health of Dunwoody Institute was the fiscal conservatism of the board of trustees and administration. When the board approved expenditures in 1915 for purchasing land and erecting buildings, Dr. Prosser had recommended that any funds taken from the principal of the endowment fund be regarded as a loan, to be repaid over five to six years both by limiting annual operating expenses and preserving income from the Dunwoody Endowment and the Kate Dunwoody Trust. Operating expenses for the Institute in 1915-1916—compensation for faculty and staff,* shop

*In 1916 Director Prosser was paid a salary of $7,500 and Assistant Director Kavel, $3,000.

Original board of trustees Building Committee, 1915

supplies, instructional materials for students, ongoing maintenance, etc.—were $80,000, and by 1924 they had increased to $166,000. However, such expenditures for a growing school were hardly exorbitant. And Dunwoody did manage to reinvest income each year in the William Dunwoody Endowment Fund, so that by 1925 it had restored some of the $730,000 spent building a campus.

Notwithstanding the overall financial well-being of these years, Dr. Prosser saw that the dream of a free education for all students could not go on forever. In the fall of 1916,

Dunwoody Institute introduced its first fee to students. This $2 registration fee was charged to Evening School students and subsequently rose to $3 in the 1917-1918 school year. In the October 1916 issue of *The Artisan*, Dr. Prosser explained to students the reasons for introducing a small fee, despite William Dunwoody's desire that their education be free. In the first place, the fee would help defray some of the costs of lesson sheets and other class-room supplies provided to students throughout the year. In addition, it would help pay for student subscriptions to *The Artisan*. More important than these small expenses, how-ever, was the belief that Dunwoody students needed to make a personal investment in their education if they were going to take it seriously. In the previous year many students had enrolled at Dunwoody for a few days "to look around" but then dropped out. "We value the things for which we make a sacrifice, however small," wrote Dr. Prosser. "A fee in the Dunwoody Evening School repre-sents an investment in education the same as an invest-ment or deposit in a bank, which, when once made, the student will follow to the end."

A new precedent had been established, which over the next century would have profound consequences. No longer would a Dunwoody education be entirely free. As the years advanced, modest fees would become larger until they would not be modest at all. Ultimately Dunwoody Institute would have to appeal to the courts for the author-ity to reinterpret William Dunwoody's will so that students could be asked to pay for much more of the cost of their education.*

The Dunwoody Campus

Having begun classes in the old Central High School and acquired property for a permanent campus, the board of

*Since William Dunwoody's will only stipulated that free education be provided to the residents of Minneapolis and Minnesota, non-residents were charged for the actual cost of their training. This policy of differentiating between residents and non-residents continued until the 1990s.

trustees appointed a Building Committee in November 1915, chaired by Franklin Crosby, to move forward with the design and construction of facilities for the new site. At its initial meeting on December 7, the committee directed Board President William Bovey to confer with Theodore Wirth, nationally recognized superintendent of the Minneapolis park system. The purpose of the meeting was to elicit advice about landscaping and the location of buildings on the Dunwoody campus, which was directly across the street from The Parade, a prominent city park. It also authorized Bovey to engage a local firm, Hewitt & Brown, as architects for the campus plan.

Soon after, Director Prosser, Assistant Director Kavel, and the principal architect, Edwin H. Hewitt, embarked on an investi-gative trip to the East Coast to observe eight established trade schools. Among the schools vis-ited were Wentworth Institute, MIT, and Boston School of Technology in Boston, Pratt Institute in New York, Carnegie Institute in Pittsburgh, and Purdue University in Indiana. Prosser, Kavel, and Hewitt interviewed their educational counterparts, whose suggestions were reported to the board of trustees when the Dunwoody team returned to Minneapolis in January. Subsequently this input was incorporated into a master plan developed by Hewitt.

> "I was working full-time, going to school full-time, but was having fun. It was a good fit. I met great friends and remain in contact with many. Dunwoody helped me pursue my education at a higher level."
>
> —David Eastling 1971

The 1916 master plan for the Dunwoody campus was ambitious, envisioning the construction of five large shop buildings running north and south, an administration building running east and west along Superior Boulevard, and stand-alone auditorium and gymnasium buildings adjacent to the administration building. A schematic of the Hewitt plan illustrates the optimism and ambition of Dunwoody's founders. Due to emerging financial constraints

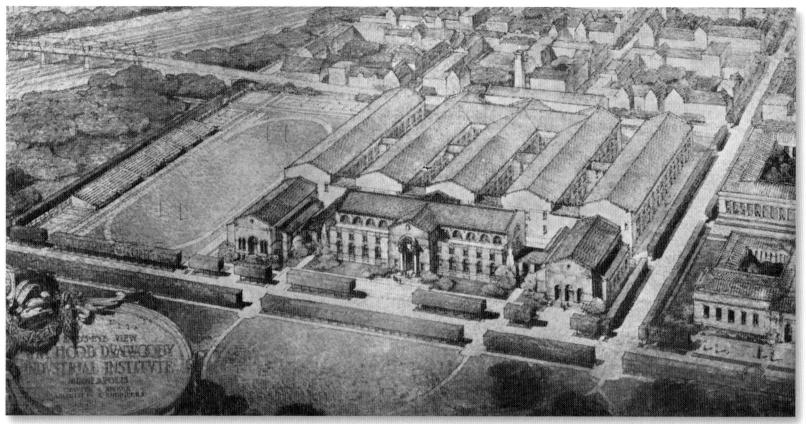

Master plan for Dunwoody Industrial Institute campus, 1916

in ensuing years, only two of the shop buildings and a modified administration building, incorporating a gym and auditorium, were ever built.

The first building priority of Hewitt, Prosser, and the board was two shop buildings, each 280 feet long and 75 feet wide, with 25,000 square feet of space on each of two main floors. On August 23, 1916, the Building Committee approved a contract with general contractor Pike & Cook to build the two buildings, and with S. J. Groves & Sons to perform excavation and grading of the site. Like Hewitt & Brown, both were Minneapolis companies. The only non-local company engaged for the project was MacArthur Concrete Pile Company of New York and Chicago, known nationally for its expertise in concrete piling.

The Dunwoody pilings would prove to be a challenge for the school throughout its history. The property on which the new campus was being built had been an ancient channel of the Mississippi River and, more recently, a city landfill. Like The Parade Park across the street and Bryn Mawr Meadows to the west, the land here was very unstable. Although wooden pilings were originally considered adequate to support the new buildings, the decision was made to play it safe and use concrete pilings. To ensure that Dunwoody's buildings stood on solid foundations, MacArthur Company installed 600 pilings for each building, varying in depth from twenty to forty-six feet. These pilings would hold up fairly well in the years to come. The administration building erected in 1924 would be a different story.

One feature of Hewitt's building design, in particular,

related directly to Dr. Prosser's educational philosophy. Flexibility would be a key to the Dunwoody layout. Since all of the technical programs would be modeled after current industry practice, and since all trades were different, each department space needed to remain relatively undefined so that it could be adapted for change as time went on. And because classroom instruction and hands-on practice in laboratories were inseparable from a pedagogical point of view, all of the shops in the Dunwoody buildings were located immediately adjacent to their technical classrooms. In this way, a Dunwoody teacher could talk about a particular industry practice or principle and then walk directly into the adjacent shop to illustrate that practice or principle on appropriate equipment. Theory and practice would be inseparable at Dunwoody.

Construction began on the Dunwoody campus in October 1916, and by August 1917 the new buildings were ready for occupation. After two and a half years at the Old Central High School, the students and staff moved to their permanent campus at the start of the 1917-1918 school year. The Automotive and Machine shops occupied the main floor of the east building, with Sheet Metal, Building Construction, and Printing on the second floor. Electrical and Radio shops were on the second floor of the west building, with Baking, the library, gym, and administrative offices on the first floor. The student cafeteria, lockers, and student recreational areas were in the basement. The new buildings were officially dedicated on October 31, 1917.

For the first eight decades of Dunwoody's history, Dunwoody students and alumni would especially remember one feature of the new buildings, the time clocks. Modeled after American industry, Dunwoody Institute initiated a system of "clocking in" and "clocking out" to hold students accountable for their hours "worked" and their punctuality, much as an employer might clock their work day. In the years to come, employers of Dunwoody graduates would point to the time clock as one indicator of a "Dunwoody

Pilings for the foundation of Dunwoody's new shop buildings, 1916

New shop buildings at Dunwoody Institute, 1917

Difference"—tangible evidence of a future employee's potential reliability. Indeed many employers would come to regard a student's attendance as a better predictor of performance on the job than the student's academic grades.

As Dunwoody enrollment grew over the next few years, so did the need for more space. Accordingly in 1923 the board's Building Committee determined that it was time to implement the next phase of the Hewitt campus master

Shop arrangement in new building, 1917. Note classrooms to the left of the shop.

plan. By now, for financial reasons, Dunwoody had to cut back on the original plan. Instead of constructing three buildings along Superior Boulevard, the decision was made to build one smaller administration building that would include a gymnasium that would also serve as an auditorium. Construction began on the new building during the summer of 1923, and it was completed by the fall of 1924. The building was dedicated as a memorial to William and Kate Dunwoody at an opening ceremony in February 1925. With the three Dunwoody buildings interconnected, the Dunwoody campus really amounted to one large building with a grand new entrance facing Superior Boulevard and The Parade. It would be forty years before Dunwoody Institute would add to its campus again, and by then the Hewitt plan would be virtually forgotten.

As with the two shop wings, the new administration building had foundation problems. Pilings had to be driven even deeper than at the northern end of the campus. Within a few years, the new building was beginning to sink on its foundation, requiring additional engineering measures in the 1930s. Complicating the foundation problems for the whole site was the close proximity of the water table to the ground's surface. In October 1924, Dr. Prosser informed the board that heavy rains were causing damage in the basement since the buildings lacked the sewer capacity to carry away water. In January, the same month as the dedication of the new administration building, the board authorized an expenditure of $1,200 to purchase a pump to remove water from the basement whenever necessary. Such problems would continue throughout the school's history.

Dunwoody in World War I

As the new campus of the young institute took shape and

New administration building, 1924. This building facing south was dedicated to founders William and Kate Dunwoody.

students prepared to move to the permanent location, the school was beginning to be drawn into world events that directly affected the United States. Beginning in August 1914, a few months before the first Dunwoody students enrolled at the Old Central High School, the major nations of Europe entered into the bloodiest war in human history, the so-called "Great War." Not until 1939, when an even greater war broke out, would this war be called World War I. Between 1914 and 1917 the administration of President Woodrow Wilson had attempted to keep the United States out of this "foreign" war. But in April 1917, following Germany's resumption of a policy of unrestricted submarine warfare—which had already cost American lives on the high seas—the president asked for and received a declaration of war by Congress against Germany. The United States and its citizens were now part of a great nationalistic crusade, what Wilson called "a war to end

war," one that would make the world "safe for democracy." With Great Britain and France physically and financially exhausted by three years of war, the United States rapidly mobilized the economy and all government agencies in order to get troops to Europe before Germany and its allies won the war. The Wilson administration instituted a draft to ensure adequate manpower for the war, and it organized a propaganda campaign to foster and capitalize on the patriotic zeal that immediately swept the nation. Like the American Civil War before it and the Second World War to follow, this would be total war, involving soldiers and civilians alike.

Dr. Prosser immediately made it clear that Dunwoody Institute would do its part to support the war effort. Soon after the U.S. declaration of war, the school invited about 3,000 current students and alumni to attend a mass meeting to facilitate their enlistment in the armed forces. Since most of Dunwoody's technical programs provided training in skills that would be of practical use to the military, it was fitting that the school support President Wilson's mobilization program. At the initial meeting in the spring of 1917, 280 Dunwoody men were enrolled in twenty-one trades of interest to the U.S. Army; 141 of these were auto drivers. Although the faculty and administration encouraged students to remain in school as long as they could, for their training might be of greater service to the country later on, they also encouraged students to enlist in branches of the service if their technical skills could be immediately useful.

In May Dr. Prosser wrote with pride in *The Artisan*:

> *Patriotism is not dead in the Northwest Territory nor in the good old State of Minnesota. If the response which has come from the students of Dunwoody is any indication of loyalty in the Nation, no lover of this country need fear the final outcome of the struggle where every man must do his part in order that the Republic may be saved and democracy may endure.*

Very soon Dr. Prosser himself was called upon to serve his nation. The Smith-Hughes Vocational Education Act, which Prosser had helped to author, went into effect on June 1, 1917. This legislation promoted vocational education throughout the United States, supporting cooperation between the Federal government and the states to encourage vocational education for agriculture and industry, and among the states, to train teachers in vocational subjects. Congress appropriated $500,000 to implement Smith-Hughes in 1917, and the plan was to increase this annual appropriation to $3 million by 1926.* The Smith-Hughes Act was a huge milestone in the history of vocational education in the United States. It established the principle of Federal support for vocational education, thereby giving a status and priority to this area of public education which it

Dunwoody's administrative leaders during World War I

had not had before. And it was important for Dunwoody Institute because its leader, Dr. Prosser, was selected to be the first National Director for Vocational Education, a position he assumed almost immediately.

*The wartime demand for manpower trained in the vocational trades was so great that by November 1917, the Federal government had allocated $850,000 to the states under Smith-Hughes, an appropriation that would grow to $1.8 million in 1918 with the expectation that the appropriation would increase to $7.3 million by 1926.

Bakers training for U.S. Navy during World War I (Dr. Prosser and Acting Director Kavel, front center)

The board of trustees was reluctant to see its director leave. But it recognized his importance to the mobilization effort, realized his absence would be temporary, and understood that his new role would enhance the school's stature nationwide. Prosser left behind a very able leadership team to carry on for him. For the duration of the war, Assistant Director Harry Kavel, who had been Dunwoody's first administrator prior to Prosser's appointment in 1915, served as acting director. The principals of Day School, Evening School, and Extension Work were Ralph T. Craigo, M. Reed Bass, and L. A. Emerson, respectively.

In addition to supporting the enlistment of students at the onset of the war, Dunwoody sped up the completion of its new shop buildings in the summer of 1917 so that it could adapt the school to military training for the army and navy. Although Day School and Evening School for civil-

ian students continued throughout the war, Dunwoody virtually turned itself into a military training post. For the army, Dunwoody began by creating an auto truck class and then developed new courses in radio and telegraphy in order to train 155 men for a battalion for the U.S. Signal Corps Reserve. For the navy, it began by printing advertising materials for the Minneapolis Naval Recruiting Station, and then it launched a baking course to staff a company of bakers.

Although William Dunwoody's will had called for instruction in the art of milling and the construction of milling equipment, it was World War I that provided the impetus to establish a baking curriculum at Dunwoody Institute. In September 1917 Dunwoody enrolled its first baking students in response to the need for bakers in the military. When the new buildings opened that fall, equipment

Dunwoody's Aviation department during World War I

Dunwoody naval battalion during World War I

costing $25,000 was installed in the new baking shop in the west wing. To get bakers into the service as quickly as possible, Dunwoody developed three training options: a three-month course, a six-month course, and a nine-month course. Soon Dunwoody-trained bakers joined two army baking companies headed for France. One baking company of 101 men could supply one division of 30,000 soldiers in the field—an indication of the impact of practical Dunwoody training on the war effort.

Dr. Prosser's role as Director for Vocational Education in Washington gave him a unique opportunity to bring Dunwoody to the attention of military planners. Sooner than other trade and technical schools on the East Coast,

Dunwoody put its campus, its faculty, and its programs at the service of the U.S. War Department. The "Naval School" created at Dunwoody in 1917 was farther from the Atlantic seaboard than any comparable training site. Due largely to Prosser's national prominence and the board's willingness to follow his lead, the navy sent 400 men to Dunwoody for training in early August. Then, in January 1918, at the request of the War Department, the school began training aviation mechanics for both the navy and the army. A month later, the army selected Dunwoody to train 2,000 aviation mechanics. To accommodate the size and cost of this project, Dunwoody turned over the actual running of the new aviation training program to the army and leased a separate building in St. Paul, the Overland Building, for the program. Dunwoody, however, coordinated the instructors, equipment, and local support for the project.

On May 13, 1918, six months prior to the armistice that ended World War I, Dunwoody Institute held its third annual commencement ceremony in the auditorium of the Old Central High School. At this event, Acting Director Kavel, Board President Bovey, and Dr. Prosser all extolled Dunwoody's service to the war effort. Since President Wilson's declaration of war the year before, more than 5,000 men had received training at Dunwoody, most of it war-related. "This is the war of mechanics and technicians," proclaimed Dr. Prosser. "I care not how brave men may be, how their hearts may be fired with courage, how well equipped they may be to use machines. If there is not along with the officers and along with the privates and along with the sailors, those who are able to keep that machine and those devices in order, the Germans would win this war." With one statement, Prosser summed up Dunwoody's contribution to the war effort.

Return to "Normalcy," 1919-1924

During the presidential campaign of 1920, President-to-be Warren Harding coined the word "normalcy" to express the American public's desire to return to "normal" after several years of "progressive" crusades both at home and abroad. With the end of the Great War in Europe and President Wilson's rancorous fight with the U.S. Senate over the Versailles Peace Treaty and his cherished League of Nations, American voters turned to the affable, if unprepared, Warren Harding to lead the nation in 1921. Thus began the Roaring 20s and a decade of unprecedented American economic prosperity.

Dunwoody Institute was ready for a return to normalcy as well. Early 1919 brought an end to all direct work for the armed services. However, since World War I had a devastating impact on millions of soldiers worldwide, the school now addressed the integration of disabled veterans into civilian life. The Federal Board for Vocational Education, created two years earlier under the Smith-Hughes Act, played a key role. All handicapped soldiers and sailors were now eligible for federal funding for rehabilitation training, whether in public schools, private schools, or industry. This training could be short-term or take up to four years. Students received funding for tuition, books, and at least $65 a month for living expenses. By May 1919 Dunwoody had enrolled seventy veterans in rehabilitation training, most in the Automotive, Machine, and Electrical departments. Minnesota veterans attended Dunwoody free of charge, as did other Minnesota students. Depending upon the actual costs of their programs, non-residents paid $10 to $25 per month.

Another reflection of Dunwoody's return to peacetime pursuits was a new focus on the training of vocational teachers for the peacetime economy. When the State of Minnesota accepted federal aid in 1919 under the Smith-Hughes Act, it set up a State Board for Vocational Education to administer public vocational education in Minnesota. The board assigned most responsibility

> "Dunwoody was a great background for me. A day doesn't pass in manufacturing without me being reminded of my training at Dunwoody, the work ethic, the skills I learned and the camaraderie of my Dunwoody family of friends."
>
> —Jim Tilbury 1974

Rehabilitation students in machine shop following World War I

Dunwoody's Tractor School following World War I

for training vocational teachers to the University of Minnesota, but it also included Dunwoody Institute as a major hands-on site for the training. From the beginning, Dunwoody instructors were permitted to enroll without charge in University of Minnesota education courses, while university students were permitted to enroll in technical courses at the Institute. Although Dunwoody was not a public school, its role in promoting vocational education statewide, which began under Dr. Prosser's leadership, would continue for decades.

Yet another new direction in early 1919 was Dunwoody's invitation to young men in rural Minnesota to take intensive short courses in farm mechanics, which included welding, machine shop, electrical wiring, automotive repair, and others. By February of that year the school had enrolled fifty students in a new Tractor School, which was run by Dunwoody's automotive department, thereby recognizing the emergence of mechanization on the American farm of the 1920s.

Dunwoody knew that things were back to normal when Dr. Prosser resumed his position as director of the Institute in November 1919. As the first director of the Federal Board for Vocational Education, Prosser had given life to the Smith-Hughes Act and put Dunwoody on the national map of vocational education. Although absent, he had continued to exercise his influence on the school throughout the war and during the year following the armistice. With Prosser's return, Acting Director Harry Kavel returned to his position as assistant director.

Upon returning to Minneapolis, Dr. Prosser observed the changes that had occurred at Dunwoody since it opened five years earlier. The war had clearly demonstrated the value of mechanical and technical trades, one result being that the school now enrolled about 3,000 students, with a waiting list of 368. Not only had Dunwoody grown, with its own campus and a larger student body, but the composition of the student body was also different. Students were now older than they had been before the war. Forty-eight percent of Day School students were twenty-two years of age or older in December 1919. A majority were still twenty-one or younger, but the number of older students was apparent. "The typical day school student now is older, larger, stronger, more mature and better prepared in general education," Prosser noted.

Prosser now saw two types of students at Dunwoody. First there were young adolescent students who enrolled in a technical course of study before going to work in a trade. These students learned the skills and work ethic necessary to become productive entry-level employees upon graduating

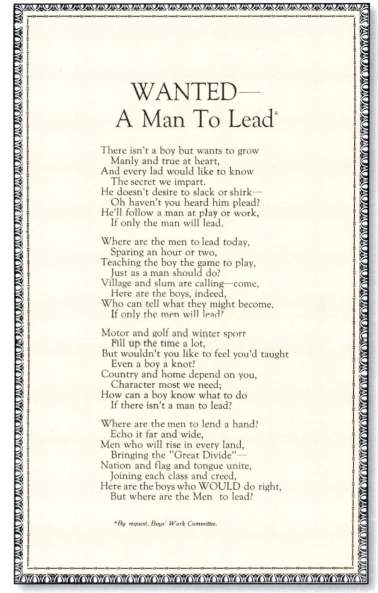

Motivational exhortation in *The Artisan*, 1921

from Day School. Then there were the more experienced students, whom Prosser called "in and outers." These students were either Day School graduates returning to Dunwoody for continuing education or working adults who enrolled in one or more Evening School courses in order to become more skilled. Increasingly most students were becoming "in and outers" so that they could remain productive or become more productive workers. Over time,

Building Construction shop following World War I

Prosser believed, Dunwoody was creating a new class of worker, a "non-commissioned officer of industry."

What was the economic value of this new class of worker? In May 1920 the editors of *The Artisan*, Dunwoody's student and faculty magazine, attempted to quantify the value of a Dunwoody education. During the 1919-1920 school year, Dunwoody had enrolled 4,347 students (1,229 in Day School, 2,718 in Evening School, and 400 in Extension and other part-time classes). Assuming that one year of

Dunwoody training increased the average earning power of each of these students by $150 and that all of these students worked for 30 years, then the total economic benefit for this group of students would amount to $19,561,500 by the year 1950.* This formula probably inflated the value of a Dunwoody education to part-time students, and it said nothing about the value of Dunwoody students to their

*Since the editors of the May 1920 *Artisan* made some mathematical errors, their estimate of economic value has been recalculated using their same assumptions.

employers or to the economy at large, but it represented an early effort to demonstrate that Dunwoody was making an important economic contribution to the state of Minnesota and the nation.

Over the next four years, Dunwoody Institute continued to build on the achievements of its formative years and establish itself as a going concern. By the time the school turned ten years old in 1924-1925, students, faculty, and staff had occupied their new administration building, and the school had grown to 4,669 in total enrollment (1,400 in Day School, 3,133 in Evening School, and 136 in Extension classes). The core Dunwoody programs and departments had been established, and they included Automotive, Baking, Building Construction, Electrical, Machine, Mechanical Drafting, Painting, Printing, Power, Sheet Metal, Highway Construction/Surveying, and "Related Trades." These areas of concentration would evolve and change over time, but the industrial institute envisioned by William Hood Dunwoody and started by his hand-picked board of trustees was now an established entity.

One important programmatic milestone and one administrative change that took place at the school in the early 1920s deserve special mention.

Dunwoody's new Baking program had been so successful during World War I that the American Association of the Baking Industry, representing commercial bakers nationwide, decided to locate its newly formed American Institute of Baking (A. I. B.) on the Dunwoody campus in 1920. A. I. B. established its administrative office and research and testing laboratories adjacent to Dunwoody's training department, thereby creating a symbiotic partnership between the baking industry and Dunwoody's baking program. Dunwoody's Baking School now became a national institution which would attract bakers and bakers-to-be to Minneapolis for the next eighty years.

EAT MORE BREAD

Dunwoody believes that Students
LEARN best by DOING.

Dunwoody Baking Students Make

GOOD BREAD

This Bread Must be Sold.

Dunwoody STUDENTS and EMPLOYEES
Can Buy it for SEVEN CENTS a Pound.

Get the Habit!

TAKE A LOAF HOME EVERY DAY

Advertisement for Dunwoody bakery products, 1921

Two years after A.I.B. became a fixture at Dunwoody, the school lost one of its founding leaders. On January 1, 1922, the board of trustees accepted the resignation of Assistant Director Harry W. Kavel, who ostensibly left Dunwoody to go into the life insurance business. Kavel had been the first administrator of the school when it began operations at the old Central High School in 1914, and he had been

Dunwoody's basketball team, 1923

acting director during Dr. Prosser's wartime leave of absence. What makes Kavel's resignation somewhat curious is the adoption in November 1921 of a confidential board of trustees report which had reviewed Kavel's "connection" to the Institute and then the rather low-key farewell tribute to Kavel in the December issue of *The Artisan*. Unfortunately there are no sources that shed more light on this important personnel change.

With Kavel's departure, Dr. Prosser reorganized his administrative team. Ralph T. Craigo now became Dunwoody's assistant director of Day School, and M. Reed Bass became assistant director of Evening, Extension, and Part-time Schools. This was the team leading Dunwoody Institute as it entered its second decade.

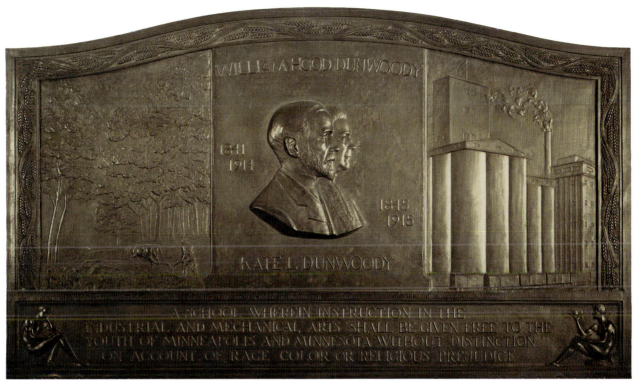

A bronze plaque, installed in the administration building in 1925, memorializes William and Kate Dunwoody.
The plaque includes a quotation from William Dunwoody's last will and testament.

CHAPTER III

The Great Depression and World War II

The first three decades of Dunwoody's history can appropriately be called "the Prosser years," since Dr. Charles Prosser served as managing director of Dunwoody Institute from 1915 to 1945. He led Dunwoody through years of prosperity and economic depression and through two world wars, established the educational model for the school, and built Dunwoody's reputation as the preeminent technical school of its type. Widely regarded as the "father of vocational education" in the United States, Prosser, along with William and Kate Dunwoody, deserves recognition as a principal founder of Dunwoody College of Technology.

Prosser's Educational "Laboratory"

Beginning in 1915 Dr. Prosser and his academic colleagues set up the curriculum and the educational principles that defined and guided Dunwoody Institute during the years of his administration and beyond. In effect Dunwoody became a functioning "laboratory" for the educational philosophy of Prosser and other leaders of vocational/technical education during the first half of the twentieth century.

Ten years after assuming the leadership of Dunwoody Institute, Prosser and Charles R. Allen, a colleague at the Federal Board for Vocational Education, coauthored *Vocational Education in a Democracy*, a seminal work on the emerging discipline of vocational education. In this book, Prosser and Allen laid out many of the principles that were being put into action at Dunwoody. "The progress of science and invention," Prosser and Allen wrote, "has not only resulted in an increased demand for the technician and inventor, but has also created great numbers of new jobs and profoundly modified the processes in many old jobs." These changes had led to an increased need for and interest in vocational education. Education in general and vocational education in particular, the authors believed, would "secure stability and progress in a democracy."

The fundamental principle of vocational education, according to Prosser and Allen, was "habit psychology." "It is only through the establishment of habit by repetitive training that capacity to think or do in the field of production is developed," they argued. There were three general types of habits that needed to be developed: process habits, thinking habits, and habits appropriate to an employed person's specific work environment. By cultivating the desired habits, vocational education would ensure that students performed their jobs correctly when they entered or reentered the work force. In this way they would improve themselves, help their employers, and contribute to the public good.

From this habit psychology, Prosser and Allen postulated general theories of vocational education, which they summarized as a list of characteristics of an efficient educational plan. All of these were adopted by Dunwoody Institute. Many of them are cited here.

- The training environment is the working environment itself or a replica of the working environment.
- The training jobs are carried on in the same way as in the occupation itself.

Opposite: Dunwoody radio repair class in the 1920s

Radio broadcast of Dunwoody's student orchestra in the 1920s

- The trainee is trained specifically in the manipulative habits and thinking habits required in the occupation itself.
- The training is given to those who need it, want it, and are able to profit by it.
- Adequate repetitive training in experiences from the occupation fixes right habits of doing and thinking to the degree necessary for employment.
- The instructor is himself master of the skills and knowledge he teaches.
- Training is carried to the point where it gives the trainee a productive ability with which he can secure employment or hold employment.
- Training meets the market demands for labor whatever these may be in any given occupation.
- Training is given on actual jobs and not in exercises or pseudo jobs.
- The content of the training which is taught is obtained from masters of the occupation, not theorists.
- The training needs of any group are met at the time they most require help and in the way that gives the most help.

Prosser and Allen formulated these principles by 1925. Dunwoody Institute continued to apply them for the next twenty years. They were the essence of what became known as the Dunwoody Way or the Dunwoody Difference. Illustrations follow.

Painting students apply their craft in Dunwoody's new administration building.

Replica of the work environment: Shops in Dunwoody's technical departments performed actual production work related to their trades. For example, the Automotive department performed mechanical and electrical repairs on students' and employees' cars; the Electrical department repaired and rebuilt batteries, small motors, and fans; the Printing department did all of the school's printing; and the Baking department baked bread and pastries and sold them to students and employees. Since safety was a key priority for employers, Dunwoody included safety instruction in all of its programs and, in 1926, launched "Safety Week" for students and instructors.

Training jobs: Since a person's performance on the job was either acceptable or not acceptable, Dunwoody

instructors graded student work in shop as either **Pd** (passed) or **Fd** (failed). In shop, students were graded for speed (30 percent), accuracy (50 percent), and industry (20 percent).

Student attitude: From the beginning, indoctrinating students in a positive work ethic was a hallmark of the Dunwoody education. At a 1926 student assembly, Dr. Prosser surprised students when he told them, "If you would be successful, you must fool the boss!" He explained this statement by urging them to do "the unexpected": be on time, be clean-cut, well-dressed, and orderly. "Don't do what [your bosses] expect of you," he said. "Do more!"

Instructor qualifications: Teachers at Dunwoody were masters of their trades, not educators per se. They were

All Dunwoody students were required to punch in and punch out in Timeclock Hall.

practical doers, not theorists. Although Dunwoody Institute would eventually become Dunwoody College, in his day Dr. Prosser clearly differentiated between "trade schools" like Dunwoody and "colleges." In his opinion, Dunwoody was founded to give trade training to young people for entry-level employment or additional skill training to employed workers, whereas colleges were designed to give persons a more general education or prepare them for professions like engineering. Unlike Dunwoody trainees, college graduates were usually not prepared for any particular job; their education was more theoretical than practical. It followed, therefore, that Dunwoody instructors had to be masters of the occupations and trades that would employ Dunwoody graduates.

Graduate placement: The purpose of Dunwoody training, Dr. Prosser and others frequently stated, was to help a student get a job, hold the job, and ultimately earn a promotion. A student's "productive ability" would be embodied in four attributes desired by employers: skill, knowledge, reasoning, and attitude. In April 1945 *The Dunwoody News* (which had followed *The Artisan* as the Dunwoody student newspaper) labeled these the "Big Four," or SKRA.

S= mastery of the **skills** of a trade

K= job and trade **knowledge**

R= **reasoning**, the ability to solve problems

A= a student's **attitude** toward his job, his employer, and his fellow workers

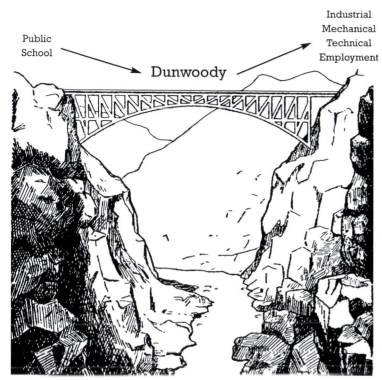

Public
School

Industrial
Mechanical
Technical
Employment

Dunwoody

Illustration of Dunwoody's "bridge to employment"

increase in businesses in Minneapolis in recent years had been fueled by the abundance of electrical power in the city. The rapid growth of Minneapolis, in turn, had created demand for further expansion of the electrical power industry. Not surprisingly, Dunwoody Institute developed training programs to meet the growing demand for electrical technicians.

Responsiveness to any group: Curricular offerings were one response to market demand; another was Dunwoody's readiness to develop customized programs for business, government, and other organizations. Training programs for the U.S. Army and Navy during World War I were a major example, as were Evening School programs developed for local and national businesses during the 1920s, 1930s, and 1940s. In 1925 *The Dunwoody News* listed a variety of cooperative relationships that the school had established with businesses, trade organizations, and other schools, including Mergenthaler Linotype Company, National Retail Bakers Association, National Paper Hangers Association, the University of Minnesota's College of Education, Stout University, and the Iowa and Wisconsin state boards of education.

Another example of Dunwoody's academic flexibility was the development of a special four-month "General Shops" program, which was offered between 1925 and 1945. The program was designed to help younger students select a trade. Following a four-month introduction to the automotive, electrical, machine, and sheet metal trades, students transferred from this "vestibule" program into one of the main technical programs, receiving credit for the trade-specific training in the General Shops program. Since Dunwoody students had become older, General Shops was

> "I feel gratitude to Dunwoody for all that I have gained because Dunwoody was not afraid to take a chance with me, a poor and uneducated Asian back in the days of World War II, when there were great prejudices against minority groups."
>
> —Francis Y. Dang 1938

Market demand: Although William Dunwoody's will called for instruction in the industrial and mechanical trades, Dr. Prosser did not believe that any trade should be favored at Dunwoody. Writing in *The Dunwoody News* in 1925, the director said, "Up to the limit of the resources of the school, instruction can be given for any trade, any occupation, any employment." Dunwoody Institute "gives any man, any time, anything it offers." What followed from this flexibility was a readiness to offer programs or courses demanded by business and industry. This attitude was manifest as early as 1914 and 1915 when the new school introduced programs to serve the automobile, printing, and electrical industries. At that time the automobile industry was rapidly increasing due to consumer and business demand for more speed in transportation. The auto industry was the catalyst for growth of the metal, glass, rubber, paint, and gas and oil industries. Printing was the sixth largest industry in the United States and the fourth largest in Minnesota, and it was increasingly important to all areas of business. As for the electrical industry, the

finally eliminated as a program option toward the end of World War II.

One more feature of the Dunwoody Way that originated during the Prosser years was the General Subjects requirement for Day School students. General Subjects were the non-trade courses like mathematics, English, and drawing. For years to come, Dunwoody alumni recalled General Subjects with ambivalence. Since most students were technically oriented and primarily interested in learning the skills of a trade, they were not usually enthusiastic about General Subjects. However, in retrospect, many alumni spoke of the value of these less immediately practical courses. They might have agreed with Assistant Director Ralph Craigo in January 1945 when he made the case for English as an important "tool" for both students and alumni. "Without some English," he wrote in *The Dunwoody News*, "almost all the work of the country would be discontinued." He also noted that poor English could be a "very serious obstacle" for competent technicians seeking promotions in the workplace.

Reprinted with permission from Minnesota Historical Society.

Unemployed and homeless men gather in Gateway Park in downtown Minneapolis during the Great Depression.

Dunwoody during the Great Depression

Except for a brief recession following World War I, the United States experienced unprecedented economic prosperity during the Roaring Twenties. As historian George Moss expressed it, the years from 1923 to 1929 were "one of the longest epochs of good times in American history." The economy grew at a rate of 7 percent per year during these years, gross domestic product rose 40 percent, and manufacturing output increased 30 percent. National per capita income increased 30 percent, and since there was limited inflation, Americans' living standards improved dramatically. The stock market increased 176 percent during the '20s, and the number of Americans owning stock went from 2 million to 17 million. The optimism of Herbert Hoover, Republican candidate for president, seemed warranted in 1928: "We seem only to have touched the fringe of our potentialities."

The Great Crash of October 1929 changed everything. The Wall Street boom which had stimulated economic growth in the late '20s came to a sudden and shocking halt on "Black Thursday," October 24, 1929. The average value of the *New York Times* list of industrial stocks had risen from 106 in 1924 to 452 in 1929, and the Dow Jones industrial average had gone from 99 in 1925 to 381 in 1929. When the stock market crashed, all of these gains were wiped out. By the end of the year, the *New York Times* average had dropped 50 percent to 224. By the summer of 1932 the *Times* average was down to 58 points, and the Dow Jones average had fallen to 41. By then almost 80 percent of the total value of American stocks, around $74 billion, had been erased by the Great Crash and its aftermath.

The impact of the Crash on the American economy was more serious than the loss of stock values for investors. The Great Crash precipitated the most severe economic depression in the nation's history, the Great Depression, which lasted over a decade. Statistics indicate the depth of the economic collapse between 1929 and 1933. During these years approximately 100,000 businesses failed and nearly 6,000 banks closed, wiping out $25 billion in personal savings. In 1929 new capital issues, a sign of investment, totaled $10 billion; in 1932 they totaled $1 billion. Corporate profits fell from $8.4 billion to $3.4 billion. The Unites States economy now produced half of what it had produced before the Crash. National income went from $88 billion to $42 billion. Average manufacturing wages declined 60 percent and average salaries by 40 percent.

The most devastating impact was on employment. It is estimated that by the bottom of the Great Depression, in 1932 and 1933, anywhere from **one-fourth to one-third** of the American labor force was out of work. Taken together, unemployment and underemployment were close to **50 percent**. Unemployment in manufacturing and the building trades (two areas served by Dunwoody Institute) reached 40 percent and 80 percent, respectively. For young people (Dunwoody's student demographic), the numbers were especially bad: 50 percent for 15-19 year olds and 36 percent for 20-24 year olds. By the late 1930s, unemployment in the United States remained over 20 percent. The Great Depression and its horrendous unemployment did not end until the U.S. government and defense-related industries stimulated the economy through major spending leading up to the nation's involvement in the Second World War.

> "Dunwoody prepared me not only in my specialized tech area, but also just generally. Dunwoody provided the base—I needed that foundation. Learning wasn't easy for me; my Dunwoody instructors were always there to help."
>
> —Gerald Krzmarzick 1956

The establishment of Dunwoody Institute between 1914 and the mid-1920s had coincided with good economic times. The onset of the Great Depression posed a new set of challenges for the young institution. Chief among these were the financial challenges.

During the early years of Dunwoody Institute, operating funds for the school came primarily from the annual investment income generated by the William H. Dunwoody Endowment, managed by the board of trustees' Finance Committee, and the Kate Dunwoody Trust, managed by First Minneapolis Trust Company. Since both sets of investments rose and fell along with the rest of the American economy, it was inevitable that they would be seriously affected by the Great Crash and the Depression that followed. At the peak of the stock market boom in 1928-29, these funds produced $216,000 in operating income for Dunwoody Institute. By 1932-33 this income had fallen to $178,000; by 1938-39 it had dropped to $132,000—a decrease of 39 percent in ten years. With less revenue available to run the school, the board of trustees was forced to cut Dr. Prosser's annual operating budget by 27 percent, from $183,000 in 1928-29 to $134,500 in 1938-39. Whereas Dunwoody had seen operating surpluses in the 1920s, it had deficits in 1932 and 1933 of $3,597 and $6,238, respectively.

> "Going to Dunwoody was a great life experience and a real quality start."
>
> —David Smith 1970

Dr. Prosser and his leadership team responded to the budget cuts in predictable ways. In 1932 they instituted a 10 percent pay reduction for non-instructional staff, subsequently adopting 5 percent cuts for all employees. Some teacher vacancies were left unfilled. Financing of a retirement plan for Dunwoody employees was put off until 1943. Campus maintenance projects were deferred. For example, as the foundation of the administration building continued to sink, Dunwoody elected to spend $1,000 in 1934 to install jacks under the building rather than $10,000 to install additional pilings. When the inexpensive option did not work, the board's Building Committee was forced to allocate $40,000 in 1938 to address the worsening problem. (In 1945 Dunwoody spent another $22,000 to stabilize the foundation.) The annual budget for the purchase of new

shop equipment and repair of existing equipment also suffered during the Depression. In 1931 Dr. Prosser complained to the board about the "grave problem" of obsolescence of Dunwoody's training equipment.

Cutting or limiting expenses was one response to the economic crisis of the '30s. Another was to look for other sources of revenue, notably student fees and charitable contributions. Dunwoody had introduced the first token fee for students back in 1916. By the mid-1920s, Day School students who were Minnesota residents were charged $5 every six months for their instruction; they were also required to provide their own shop clothes, one or two books, and some hand tools. By the 1933-34 school year, a resident's fee for ten months had increased to $17, which represented only about 6 percent of the actual cost of his Dunwoody education. Non-residents and Baking students, on the other hand, were charged a fee more commensurate with Dunwoody's per-student expense, $300 for ten months. These charges produced $25,808 in revenue for the Institute that year. Four years later, to compensate for the loss of operating income from its endowed funds, Dunwoody increased the annual fee for full-time Minnesota students to $30, thereby generating $82,788 in operating revenue. By progressively increasing student fees, Dunwoody began the process of increasing a student's participation in the funding of his own education. The cost of a Dunwoody education was still very inexpensive for a Minnesota resident attending the Institute, but it was no longer free.

Consignments and donations of equipment and supplies were another response to Dunwoody's financial challenges. Since the school had less money to buy equipment, business partners and suppliers began to donate and lend equipment to the Institute. Thus began a process and a trend that would gain momentum over the ensuing decades. During Dunwoody's 1936-37 fiscal year, for example, the school received almost $30,000 worth of consignments and

Printing class in the 1930s

donations for the Automotive, Welding, Air Conditioning, Electrical, and Baking departments. Employers of Dunwoody trainees recognized that it was in their self-interest to equip the Institute's technical shops with up-to-date technology and supplies.

The William Dunwoody Endowment Fund and the Kate Dunwoody Trust remained the most important assets of Dunwoody Institute during the 1930s, as they had been since 1915 and would continue to be in the future.

Following the Great Crash, the board of trustees re-evaluated the school's investment portfolio and investment policies, and it focused as well on the investment performance of First Minneapolis Trust Company, which controlled the Kate Dunwoody Trust.

Included in the endowment portfolio were significant investments in real estate. As of the 1928-29 fiscal year (July 1, 1928-June 30, 1929), prior to the Crash, the board of trustees' Finance Committee had invested 28 percent of the Institute's current assets, $815,130, in real estate mortgage loans, farmland contracts, and other properties. Farm-related investments alone constituted 11 percent of the portfolio. By the 1932-33 fiscal year, farm investments had increased to 14 percent and all real estate to 29 percent.* As the Great Depression deepened, banks and other investors—and Dunwoody actually functioned like a bank during these years—had to deal with the growing problem of borrowers who were unable to meet their loan obligations. At a meeting of the board of trustees in October 1933, trustees expressed concern about the status of farm mortgage loans and contracts for deed. Already dealing with the issue of loan foreclosures, the board authorized the Finance Committee to agree to discounts on mortgages being refinanced through government loan programs. Refinancing was considered a preferable alternative to foreclosure. In January 1934 it approved the refinancing of two farm loans and reduced the interest charge on a third loan so that the borrower could pay his taxes on the property, thus keeping the loan alive. Since the financial pressures on farmers did not abate, the board authorized the Finance Committee to sell three farms in Swift County in April 1935 "for anything that can be gotten for them."

"There's still a need for technical education today. Dunwoody instills discipline and stresses accuracy. Everyone in my class entered the industry and did very well in their careers."

—Dave Anderson 1971

One change made by the board beginning in the mid-1930s was to reduce Dunwoody's investment in real estate, particularly farm mortgages. Between 1933 and 1939, farm-related investments were reduced from $391,000 to $122,000, a decrease of 69 percent. Overall, real estate investments went from 29 percent of the Institute's invested assets in 1933 to 18 percent in 1939. The $479,000 invested in real estate at the end of the '30s represented a 41 percent decrease

in this segment of the endowment portfolio since the late '20s.

An even greater portion of the endowment was invested in bonds. In 1929, 67 percent of Dunwoody's invested assets, $1,958,000, was invested in a variety of bonds. Although the dollar value of these investments fell to $1,799,000 by 1933, bonds still accounted for 67 percent of the Institute's portfolio. Fifty-four percent of these dollars were invested in railroad bonds, and 41 percent were invested in state, county, municipal, and school district bonds. Much as the board of trustees had invested in real estate in the Upper Midwest, it had also purchased bonds throughout the region.**

As the board was re-evaluating its investments in real estate, it also reconsidered the amount of money it had tied up in bonds. In January 1938 the board of trustees adopted investment guidelines recommended by Dunwoody Treasurer Henry S. Kingman and the Wells-Dickey Company, a firm hired by the Finance Committee to manage the school's investments. The new guidelines authorized the Finance Committee to reduce its investment in bonds, especially railroad bonds, and to increase its investment in stocks. What Kingman wanted was "more income and somewhat increased risks."

With this direction, the Finance Committee continued to diversify the endowment portfolio. By June 1939 bonds were down to 56 percent of invested assets, or $1.4 million, and railroad bonds were less than 39 percent, or $565,000. Since 1933 Dunwoody's investment in bonds had declined 18.5 percent and railroad bonds 42 percent. On the other hand, investments in preferred and common stocks increased 461 percent. In 1933 only 4 percent of

---

*One of the more interesting real estate investments was a $45,000 mortgage for Woodhill Country Club, which was located on property originally owned by William Dunwoody.

**In Minnesota, Dunwoody owned 2 state bonds, 27 county bonds (for 13 counties), 15 municipal bonds (for 7 cities), and 16 school district bonds (for 7 school districts); in North Dakota, it owned 6 state bonds, 4 county bonds, 3 municipal bonds, and 5 school district bonds; in Wisconsin, it owned 11 county bonds, 3 municipal bonds, and 3 school district bonds; in Iowa, it owned 5 municipal bonds and 15 school district bonds; and in South Dakota, it owned 4 state bonds.

Air-conditioning class in the 1930s

current investments, $113,000, had been invested in stocks; by 1939, stocks made up 24 percent of the portfolio, or $634,000.

A major responsibility of Dunwoody's board was to be good stewards of the assets invested in the William Dunwoody Endowment. Despite the daunting economic challenges of the 1930s, the board did an excellent job of managing and preserving the resources entrusted to it by the school's founders. Conservative investments and conscientious

management of the investments limited Dunwoody's market losses during the Great Depression. In 1939 the invested assets of the endowment were $2.6 million,* down only

*It is difficult to determine the relative value of the William Dunwoody Endowment over the years since neither the Finance Committee nor the Institute's financial auditors conducted annual market reviews of the endowment. For purposes of the annual audit, the "principal amount" of the endowment was compared to $3,167,149, the historical valuation on July 30, 1915. For example, the "principal amount" recorded in the 1924-25 audit was $3,479,138, whereas the balance sheet for that year shows "current assets" in investments of $2,931,280. For the 1930s, invested assets are the best guide to the market value of the William Dunwoody Endowment.

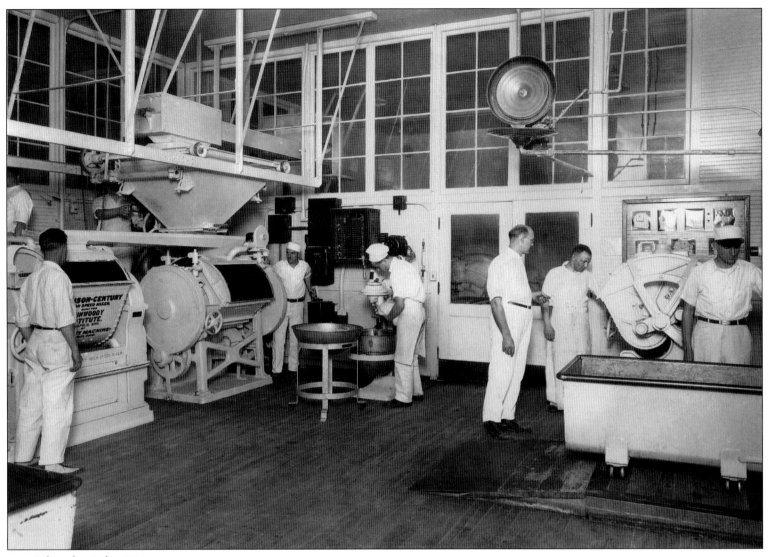

Baking class in the 1930s

10 percent since the Great Crash, whereas the Dow Jones average was still down 61 percent. These losses caused hardships for the school, but they could have been worse. Early in the Depression, loss of financial resources forced the closing of almost 5,000 public schools across the country in one year alone.

Beyond the direct control of the board of trustees were the assets of the Kate Dunwoody Trust. As stipulated by Kate's last will and testament, these funds were administered by First Minneapolis Trust Company for the benefit of Dunwoody Institute. Since this arrangement provided regular, predictable income for the school, the board of trustees rarely questioned the management or performance of First Trust. However, in 1930 Dunwoody did challenge First Trust's purchase of bonds for the Kate Dunwoody Trust from the company's own holdings. Maintaining that this practice had cost the trust $118,000, the Institute initiated legal action. The two sides resolved this conflict in July 1931, when First Trust agreed to make a number of specific investment changes in return for Dunwoody's releasing First Trust from any liability for previous losses.

The positive effect of this agreement was that Dunwoody would henceforth receive a net increase of $6,500 in annual income from the trust. That the Kate Dunwoody Trust lost only 7 percent in value between 1929 and 1939 demonstrates that First Minneapolis Trust Company was, on balance, a responsible steward of Dunwoody's resources.

Education for a Lifetime

Remarkably, in spite of the high levels of unemployment during the 1930s, many Dunwoody graduates of the Depression era recalled their Dunwoody education with great appreciation and nostalgia. Here are some comments made by Dunwoody alumni many years after their graduations.

Dunwoody gave me the lift I needed during the Depression to appreciate what I could accomplish.

Dunwoody gave me the start I might never have had otherwise. It found me a good job, and after the war I had full employment.

Dunwoody gave me the start I needed when times were tough.

It got me off the farm and prepared me for a lifetime trade.

The education I received at Dunwoody gave me the skills I have used all my life and made me successful.

Dunwoody opened the door to the future. It taught me how to get a job, how to hold it, and [how] to get a better one. It taught me that quality would always sell and always be in demand. It really taught me how to work.

Dunwoody made my life.

Such effusive testimonials show the gratitude Dunwoody students felt for the unique opportunity provided to them by Dunwoody Institute during hard times.

Reflecting upon Dunwoody's enrollment patterns during the previous two decades, Dr. Prosser observed in 1943 that Day School had filled to capacity during the 1930s, notwithstanding the high unemployment rates. Since jobs were so hard to find during the Depression, many young men decided to learn a trade that might lead to employment later. Evening School, on the other hand, struggled to maintain its enrollment levels of the 1920s because fewer workers were employed and could afford extension training. Still, in April 1938, Prosser reported to the board of trustees that Dunwoody had just reached not only its highest enrollment of civilians in Day School history (about 1,600) but also one of its largest Evening Schools ever (about 2,600). By 1939 Dunwoody had a waiting list of 783 applicants for Day School, and it had to add a late shift from 10:45 a.m. to 6:15 p.m. to accommodate all of the students. In terms of total student hours in Day School, Evening School, and part-time enrollments, Dunwoody had peaked at 1,538,869 hours in 1918, during World War I. Total student hours did not go above 1,000,000 again until 1938, when they reached 1,226,926.

> "I enrolled in the mechanical design program and was pleased with the high caliber instructors . . . all the information the teachers jam into one day—you really get the best bang for the buck."
>
> —Cody Smith 2012

With one exception, the profile of the Day School student body did not change much during the 1930s. In 1937, for example, 52 percent of Dunwoody students were sixteen to twenty years of age; 11 percent were twenty-one to thirty; and 4 percent were thirty-one or older. Or, expressed slightly differently, 84 percent of the students were young men between the ages of sixteen and twenty-five. Thirty-eight percent of the students came from the Minneapolis/St. Paul urban area, 49 percent from rural Minnesota, and 13 percent from outside of Minnesota. These percentages were similar to those in the 1920s. Only in the category of

Dr. Prosser addresses Dunwoody students in the auditorium/gym in 1937.

previous education had the student demographic changed. In 1929, 32 percent of admitted students had an 8th grade education or less; 26 percent had completed their 9th and 10th grades of high school; 34 percent had completed 11th and 12th grades; and 8 percent had attended college. By 1937 the level of education had increased. Though the percentage of students with college backgrounds did not change, the number of entering students who had completed 11th and 12th grades increased from 34 to 63 percent. Dunwoody was still enrolling young students, but in 1937 more of them had more years of high school education before enrolling at Dunwoody.

Although Dunwoody modified and added new courses and programs as needs emerged, the core of Dunwoody's program offerings, especially in Day School, remained fairly consistent throughout the years. In the 1930s the principal programs were clustered in these departments: Automotive, Baking, Building Construction, Electrical, Highway Construction and Surveying, Machine Shop

and Mechanical Drafting, Printing, Sheet Metal and Air Conditioning, and General Shops. In February 1938, when daily enrollment reached its highest level since World War I, the departments with the largest student enrollments were General Shops, 300; Air Conditioning and Electrical, 205 each; Machine Shop, 144; Building Construction, 129. In September 1939 these were the eight largest departments at Dunwoody, listed in order: Electrical, Air Conditioning, Machine Shop, Automotive, Building Construction, Printing, Mechanical Drafting, and Baking.

Aside from the loss of operating revenue, the employment, or "placement," of Dunwoody graduates at a time when employers were drastically cutting their work forces might have been the school's greatest challenge. In late 1929 *The Dunwoody News* boasted that the demand for Dunwoody graduates exceeded the supply, and this demand was nationwide. Although this rosy situation changed with the onset of the Depression, Dunwoody continued to place its graduates during the 1930s. During the 1936-37 school year, the Institute awarded 673 certificates and diplomas. During the same year it received 716 employer requests for Dunwoody-trained technicians. The Dunwoody name was often sufficient to get someone a job. With many students finding employment on their own, Dunwoody recorded the placement of only 420 students that year. However, in June 1937, the school was unable to fill eighty-six employer requests for Dunwoody graduates because it did not have that number of students looking for work.

Two important leadership changes took place at Dunwoody in 1937. Early in the year Assistant Director M. Reed Bass,

a Dunwoody administrator since 1915, who had co-authored a book on evening industrial schools with Dr. Prosser, left Dunwoody to become the director of the Ranken School of Mechanical Trades in St. Louis, Missouri. Then in November, William H. Bovey, a key founding trustee of the Institute, resigned as president of the board of trustees, a position he had held since 1914. The board passed a suitable resolution recognizing Bovey for his strong leadership and dedicated service, presented him with a silver loving cup, and bestowed on him the honorary title of President Emeritus. At the same meeting, the board named Russell Bennett as its new president. Like Bovey, Bennett would

Front office in administration building

Russell H. Bennett, president of Dunwoody's board of trustees, 1937-1948 and 1953-1957; chairman of the board, 1957-1961

have a long tenure as president of the board, from 1937 to 1948 and from 1953 to 1957. After the board reorganized its leadership positions in 1957, he served as the first chairman of the board until 1961.

A third leadership change of note occurred a year later, in October 1938, when the board elected a new treasurer of Dunwoody Institute. Henry S. Kingman had been treasurer and chairman of the board's Finance Committee since 1929. Management of Dunwoody's finances was extremely time-consuming for the Finance Committee and especially for the treasurer. The board decided in 1938 to retain Kingman's brother, Joseph R. Kingman Jr., as treasurer, with an annual salary of $5,000, while retaining Henry Kingman in his volunteer role as chairman of the Finance Committee. President Bennett welcomed Joe Kingman as someone who could give his "entire time and attention" to Dunwoody's financial affairs. The Finance Committee

was so pleased with Kingman's appointment as a full-time financial administrator that it decided the next year not to renew Dunwoody's investment management contract with the Wells-Dickey Company.

Dunwoody during World War II

On December 14, 1939, Dunwoody celebrated its 25th anniversary. During its twenty-five years of service it had trained close to 75,000 students in a wide variety of courses and programs. As Dr. Prosser had observed the year before, the Institute had "won an undisputed position as the outstanding trade and industrial school of the country." But even as Dunwoody marked the achievements of its first twenty-five years, a new international crisis threatened the nation. On September 1 the military forces of Nazi Germany invaded Poland, precipitating declarations of war against Germany by Great Britain and France. Meanwhile in Asia, Japanese military aggression against China had brought war to that area of the world two years earlier. Although the United States would not become actively involved in the fighting until 1941, World War II had begun, and like the Great War of 1914-1918, it, too, would inevitably touch Dunwoody Institute.

As early as April 1939, when Adolf Hitler was intensifying his territorial demands on Poland, Dunwoody had begun to prepare for war. After Dr. Prosser informed the board of trustees of the possibility of developing an aviation mechanics course for the U.S. government, the board authorized the administration to explore potential defense training programs. In 1940 and 1941, Dunwoody negotiated contracts with the War Department and defense-oriented companies to begin training mechanics for the coming war. At a special meeting called to update the board about Dunwoody planning for defense training in June 1941—two weeks before the German invasion of Russia and six months prior to the Japanese attack on Pearl Harbor—Dr. Prosser reported that 135 students were

Opposite: *Minneapolis Sunday Tribune* headline and cover story, November 1, 1942

War Production Training during World War II included telephone training at Dunwoody.

enrolled in Machine Shop training subsidized by Northern Pump Company, Honeywell, and General Mills. With the nation's defense industry facing a shortage of 1.4 million machine shop workers, Dunwoody received a government grant to train machinists and welders in Evening School beginning that September. By the end of September, Dunwoody had received 2,250 applications for the 150 Machine Shop openings and 50 Welding openings in these free Evening School classes. In addition to the tuition subsidies, Dunwoody received $60,000 in new equipment as part of the defense buildup. Throughout the fall of 1941, the school's Machine Shop ran at capacity, with 140 students enrolled in Day School and the extra sections scheduled both before and after regular hours.

December 7, 1941—"a date which will live in infamy," in the words of President Franklin D. Roosevelt—finally brought the United States into the Second World War. Japan's military attack on Pearl Harbor, followed a few days later by Germany's declaration of war against the United States, immediately ended the nation's pseudo-neutrality. The war was now truly a world war, and like the world war twenty years earlier, it would be another total war that engaged all of the resources of the United States, including those of

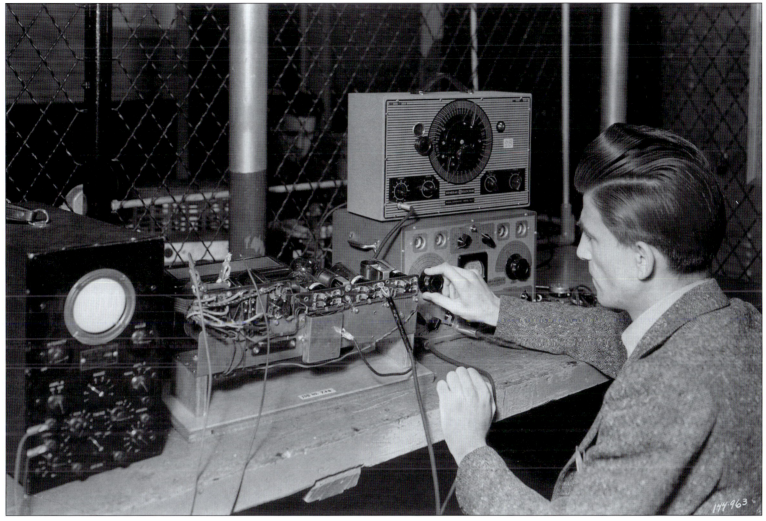

Radio training for U.S. Civil Service Commission during World War II

one private technical school in Minneapolis, Minnesota. Within three months of the United States' entry into World War II, Dunwoody Institute was operating twenty-four hours a day, five days a week, as well as on Saturdays and Sundays, providing a variety of training for the defense industry. Between July 1941 and February 1942, half of the 4,000 students trained in Day School and Evening School had enrolled in classes leading to defense-related occupations. As the military buildup intensified after Pearl Harbor, this percentage increased. Contracts with Northern Pump Company, Twin Cities Ordnance Plant, and Rock Island Arsenal financed the training of machinists and welders,

who were now in such demand that Dunwoody had to force Machine Shop students not enrolled in government-funded classes either to transfer to other departments or to check out of school. In the spring of 1942, *The Dunwoody News* noted one unfortunate side effect of the defense buildup: some trades, such as automotive, electrical, and printing, which were classified by the War Department as "non-essential pursuits," were gradually being "pushed out into the cold." Their enrollment would suffer during the war. When Dunwoody's Day School for the 1942-43 school year began in August, enrollment had declined considerably from the previous year. By early October more than 30

World War II "Rosie the Riveter" poster

1943. During the previous war, the Institute had trained 6,483 men for military service; during the first two years of World War II, it trained 8,712 for military service and defense occupations. During the 1941-42 school year, Dunwoody registered 1,984 students in defense training. This number grew to 6,728 during the 1942-43 school year, with Machine Shop and Welding enrolling the largest number of students—4,241 in a variety of Machine Shop courses and 1,530 in Welding courses. Dr. Prosser informed the board of trustees in January 1943 that Dunwoody had placed 3,190 students in jobs over the past two years, which did not include all of the students who had enlisted in the armed forces. Federal Cartridge Company and Northern Pump Company were two of the major employers of Dunwoody trainees at this time.

The mobilization of the American economy for World War II had one very significant historic effect on Dunwoody Institute. As American men enlisted or were drafted into the armed forces, it became necessary for the United States to make use of women to transform the domestic economy into a war economy. Suddenly women were welcomed into jobs and roles that had traditionally been reserved for men. Dunwoody was no exception. In 1928 the "Founder's Day" issue of *The Dunwoody News* had defined the Institute as a "he school." "Undoubtedly," the newspaper's editors wrote, "[William Dunwoody] believed that as far as possible, woman's place was in the home and that it was a duty of the man to prepare himself to make himself efficient so as to support that home as it should be maintained." Dunwoody Institute may have been open to all men since 1914, irrespective of race, color, or religion, but it took the economic realities of World War II to open the school to women, at least temporarily.

Bowing to these realities, the board of trustees voted in October 1942 to permit the training of women for the duration of the war. Soon thereafter, on December 1, 1942, Dunwoody admitted eighteen women for training on

percent of the students who had started school during the summer had left Dunwoody either to enlist in the armed forces or to take jobs with employers now desperate for workers. To meet the emergency needs of the war, Dunwoody introduced intensive short courses in "pre-Army" and "pre-Navy" training, including the operation and maintenance of tanks, guns, planes, trucks, tractors, and gas engines. It also began training radio mechanics for the U.S. Army Signal Corps, and over the next six months Dunwoody became the Signal Corps' official telephone training center for the Upper Midwest.

Even as the enrollment of so-called "civilians" declined during the first year of the war, the training of men and women for the war effort increased dramatically. In January 1943 *The Dunwoody News* compared Dunwoody's record of defense training in all of World War I to that of 1941-

bench work and machine tool operation—the first in Dunwoody's history. These women would be in high demand in defense plants producing war equipment. Women employed in the U.S. defense industry during the war were personified by the patriotic figure known as "Rosie the Riveter." Dunwoody's own Rosies made an immediate impression on their institution. After only one week of training, their classroom performance compared favorably to that of the male students in terms of grades on shop jobs and the number of jobs completed.

By February 1943 seventy women were enrolled in a variety of Dunwoody courses, and the numbers were increasing. Edward Asproth, the instructor for the women's pre-employment program, commented in *The Dunwoody News* that the quality of the women's work was "well above" that of the average male class and that their test scores were higher. He also observed that the women were "more studious" than the men. However, due to their greater "nervousness and hesitancy," they completed less work than the men. Between 1941 and 1945, Dunwoody Institute trained about

Women welders being trained at Dunwoody during World War II

15,000 men and women, most of them for the war effort. Among the school's training partners were the U.S. Office of Education, U.S. Army Ordnance Department, U.S. Army Signal Corps, Northern Pump Company, Federal Cartridge Company, International Harvester Company, General Mills, Donaldson Company, Honeywell Company, McQuay Company, and beginning in late 1943, the U.S. Veterans Administration. By the end of World War II, 214 veterans were enrolled at Dunwoody, about 40 percent able-bodied and 60 percent requiring some physical rehabilitation.

> "I wouldn't be where I am today without Dunwoody. I came to the Twin Cities in 1945 with only $38 and an eighth-grade diploma. I was 18 and didn't pass the navy physical, so I enrolled in the Electrical program at Dunwoody."
>
> —Dale Hartman 1946

Not surprisingly, employers of Dunwoody-educated personnel were impressed with the quality of Dunwoody's training programs. These are a few of the employer commendations printed in *The Dunwoody News* in November 1942.

> *The William Hood Dunwoody Industrial Institute has contributed personnel to our organization in the past few years and we wish to commend you highly for the good work you have done and are doing . . . .*

> *This is a letter of appreciation for the training of sixteen of our most highly skilled machinists and draftsmen . . . . Each one of these boys has been a key employee in our shops and engineering departments.*

> *Dunwoody has been our source for electric shop apprentices for so many years that we would not know where to turn if your activities were curtailed. . . . It has been our experience that Dunwoody's happy combination of theoretical and practical training puts its graduates well above the average in ability to progress rapidly in industrial work. Our factory is engaged exclusively in war production, and we shall continue to recommend the Dunwoody Institute to anyone in our employ interested in further study in their particular trade.*

The U.S. War Department was no less impressed. Toward the end of World War II, the chief of the Civilian Personnel Division in the Ordnance Office wrote to Dr. Prosser: "The record you and your staff have achieved in teaching fundamentals to ordnance maintenance personnel over the past two years has been a contributing factor to the overall maintenance training program [at Rock Island, Illinois]." Dunwoody's "able training" of ordnance employees, he continued, had contributed to their "doing such an essential job of maintaining ordnance equipment." It must have been gratifying to Prosser, the board of trustees, and the entire Dunwoody team to know how important its training role was during the war.

Much as the Second World War lifted the United States out of the Great Depression, it also improved Dunwoody's financial position. Although the school's operating budget remained unchanged from 1939 to 1945, government funding of defense training programs was a boon to Dunwoody. War Production Training reimbursements from the U.S. Office of Education totaled $117,224 in 1941-42, $298,748 in 1942-43, and $270,117 in 1943-44. As the war neared its end in 1945, this funding source declined while funding from the Veterans Administration increased. Income from student fees decreased by 72 percent between 1939 and 1945, and income from the William and Kate Dunwoody invested funds still remained 27 percent below what it had been before the Great Crash of 1929. Nevertheless, throughout the war, Dunwoody was able to contribute surpluses back to its investment account at the end of each fiscal year. The war enabled Dunwoody to operate in the black.

As Dunwoody prepared for the anticipated postwar influx of veterans funded through either the Disabled Veterans Rehabilitation Act or the G.I. Bill of Rights,

Students eating in Dunwoody cafeteria in early 1940s

the board of trustees made an important policy decision that would have future implications for the school. On August 20, 1943, the board passed a resolution requiring the U.S. Government and the State of Minnesota to reimburse Dunwoody for 100 percent of the cost of training veterans, whether disabled or able-bodied. Recalling the intent of William Hood Dunwoody to provide free education to underprivileged youth, the resolution noted that the decline of annual operating income from the Dunwoody endowments meant that free education was no longer available to some of Dunwoody's regular applicants. Over the next two months, the board instituted a monthly fee of $35 for veterans, thus inaugurating a policy of charging higher fees for veterans, on the assumption

that government agencies could afford to reimburse Dunwoody for the actual cost of a student's education. Although such a policy made sense from a financial point of view, many veterans came to believe that the policy was discriminatory. After loyally serving their nation during the war and afterward, they resented having to pay more to attend Dunwoody than those who had not served in the armed forces. This would become a point of contention for some Dunwoody alumni for years to come.

Another source of future revenue for Dunwoody would be philanthropic contributions. Dunwoody did not receive many contributions during the 1930s and 1940s, but it

Director Charles Prosser (right) with his successor, Treasurer Joseph R. Kingman Jr.

did create the organizational framework for future gifts. According to William Dunwoody's will, any contributions to Dunwoody Institute had to be added to his permanent endowment fund. Therefore, when the Institute received a gift of property from trustee James Ford Bell in 1937, the proceeds of $31,625 from its sale were added to the William Dunwoody Endowment. Later, in 1944 and 1945, the school received $193,850 in gifts from twelve donors, both individuals and businesses, and these funds were also added to the endowment. These gifts were highly valued by the board of trustees and administration. But what if the Institute wanted to solicit contributions for shop equipment, student scholarships, or other special projects?

One answer lay in the establishment of an organization authorized to accept gifts for purposes other than the William Dunwoody Endowment. And who better to ask for support than those who had benefitted most from a Dunwoody education—Dunwoody alumni? Accordingly, in October 1939, the board of trustees approved in principle the creation of a new corporation, the Dunwoody Industrial Institute Alumni Fund. The Alumni Fund was

incorporated on June 11, 1940. It would be governed by a board of managers composed of seven to nine members: one Dunwoody alumnus, two members of the staff of Dunwoody Institute, the treasurer of the Institute (i.e., Joseph Kingman), and three to five members of the Institute's board of trustees. The original members of the board of managers were Robert Lowry, Fred Landon, Joseph Kingman, Russell Bennett, Henry Kingman, and Robert Webb. Landon was elected president of the new organization; Bennett, vice president; and Joe Kingman, secretary/treasurer.

Creation of the Dunwoody Alumni Fund marked the beginning of active fundraising for Dunwoody Institute. Over the next three years the board of managers raised $6,000 from 632 alumni and friends of the school. After five years it had raised over $10,000. These early results were not auspicious, but a mechanism had been established to solicit charitable gifts from alumni, businesses, and other potential supporters. Thirty years later Dunwoody would raise millions of dollars in private contributions. Moreover, the nascent Alumni Fund and its board of managers were the precursors to a much more active Dunwoody Alumni Association that would begin to emerge in the 1960s.

End of an Era

On May 15, 1945, exactly one week after Germany's surrender ended World War II in Europe, Dr. Charles A. Prosser announced to the Dunwoody board that he intended to retire as the Institute's director on September 20, his seventy-fourth birthday. While regretting "the inexorable march of the years," the board reluctantly accepted Prosser's decision. At the same meeting, it also performed its duty and named a successor for Prosser. It elected Treasurer Joseph R. Kingman Jr. as Dunwoody Institute's next director, effective in September.

At the same meeting, Board President Russell Bennett read a resolution of appreciation that conveyed the tremendous esteem in which Prosser was held by the board of trustees, some of which is quoted here.

> Dr. Prosser has built a nationally renowned educational institution, one that has become a model and guide for vocational schools everywhere. It has indeed been referred to as the 'national shrine for vocational educators.'

> Industry in the Northwest has benefitted by the availability of trained workers; the profession of engineering has been greatly helped by the accession of this great number of its indispensable assistants— the mechanics, machinists, welders, electricians, and artisans of the many other trades—whose combined efforts have given us the nationally high standard of living that we enjoy.

> Dr. Prosser has thus earned the lasting gratitude of industry, of the engineering profession, and of civic and educational groups in the Northwest, and in the nation. Great as have been his accomplishments in organized vocational education, it is perhaps safe to say that his greatest achievement has been the preparation for life and for socially useful living of the individual men and boys that have passed through our portals. Each of our students has felt in Dr. Prosser the impact of a forceful yet kindly nature; his precepts and examples have strengthened the fibre [sic] of all who have come under him. Through him and his staff and his organization, these many thousands have learned useful trades and gone forth to labor in the building of a better world.

These lofty sentiments were not limited to the Dunwoody community. Prosser had received honorary degrees from Hanover College, Alfred University, DePauw University, and Stout University. In 1933 he was the recipient of a tribute by the National Association of State Directors for Vocational Education at the annual convention of the American Vocational Association, where twenty-five of his professional colleagues wrote papers included in A

Testimonial in Recognition of his Service to Vocational Education. His reputation as the father of vocational education was so widely accepted across the nation that later, after his retirement, at least one high school and one college were named after him.*

As he contemplated his pending retirement, Dr. Prosser composed a memo, entitled "Dunwoody's Past, Present and Future," in which he reflected on Dunwoody's thirty-one years of achievement and factors contributing to the school's success. Presented to the board on April 13, 1945, this memo also included Prosser's recommendations for Dunwoody's continuing success.

> "Dunwoody gave me the education I needed to get a good job that I loved."
>
> —Alan Wussow 1969

Prosser cited achievements since 1914. Among them were:

Dunwoody's national reputation and leadership. The Institute was widely regarded as "the largest, best equipped and most efficient" technical school.

The increased number and types of students and areas served. Dunwoody had enrolled over 125,000 students, increasing the average age of a student and expanding the geographic area served from Minneapolis to other states and countries.

The increased number and variety of courses offered. Day School now operated fourteen departments providing entry-level training for 400 different jobs, and Evening School met the needs of a large number of employed workers.

Enhanced services for students and employers. Placement served an increased number and geographic range of employers; special training programs had been developed to meet the unique needs of industry and government.

*Prosser Career Academy in Chicago and Prosser School of Technology in New Albany, Indiana

Expanded school facilities, including shop equipment. At least one-third of Dunwoody's equipment had been donated.

Improved quality of instruction. Cooperative programs with the University of Minnesota and Colorado State College had improved the continuing education of Dunwoody teachers and supervisors

Financial responsibility. All of these accomplishments had been achieved in spite of rising operating costs and declining income from endowment funds.

Accounting for Dunwoody's achievements were Prosser's "factors in our success." These included:

- Serving more than 4,000 "underprivileged citizens" annually
- Practical education for employment and "life education" to foster good citizenship
- Flexible admissions policies
- Training by doing rather than talking
- Following the habit psychology
- Being an experimental laboratory
- "Growing and vital cooperation" with employers
- Cooperation with other educational organizations
- Ongoing analysis of occupations to determine what should be taught and how
- Employing effective teaching methods and materials
- Requiring all students to improve their performance as they progress

Dr. Prosser concluded his memo for the board with specific recommendations for Dunwoody's continuing success. These included continuation of many of the "success factors" listed above. Some of the other recommendations were:

- Consistent with William Hood Dunwoody's intent, Dunwoody Institute should always maintain the lowest possible fees and serve as many students as possible within the school's financial means.

- Hiring of instructors should be based on trade competency, not academic degrees.
- Training for the trades should be supplemented by the preparation of students for life (what William Dunwoody had called "the better performance of life's duties").
- Dunwoody should maintain a continuous program of instructor training, requiring both teachers and department heads to return to their trades at regular intervals.
- Dunwoody should continue its "middle of the road policy" between business and organized labor, never taking sides in labor disputes.
- Dunwoody should consider developing a third year of training for advanced students (no more than twenty students per trade). Such a course would be Dunwoody's contribution to the growing movement to expand vocational education nationally.

How fitting that Dr. Prosser, at the time of his retirement, was still looking ahead, not only to the future of Dunwoody Institute but to the future of vocational education. He returned to this theme in August 1945, when he delivered an address at Purdue University on "Then and Now: Twenty-eight Years and the Smith-Hughes Act." As one of the authors of the seminal 1917 legislation, Prosser had lost none of his evangelical zeal for the vocational education movement. Between 1917 and 1940 more than 20 million students had been trained by schools receiving Smith-Hughes funding. During World War II, Smith-Hughes schools trained another 10 million students. "In a very real way," Prosser told his Purdue audience, "our vocational schools became the deciding factor in the overthrow, we hope forever, of fascism." However, the achievements of the past twenty-eight years notwithstanding, Prosser reminded the audience that "the battle for a national system of democratic education has not yet been completely won." While acknowledging that public high schools should continue to prepare 20 percent of their students for college and that vocational schools should prepare another 20 percent for skilled occupations, public secondary schools still needed to find a way to prepare

The Great Depression and World War II

the remaining 60 percent for gainful employment. This would be the challenge facing the postwar generation.

One month after the Purdue speech, Joseph Kingman replaced Dr. Prosser as director of Dunwoody Institute, also retaining the office of treasurer. On September 26 the board of trustees and the Minneapolis Civic and Commerce Association honored Prosser at a dinner at the Nicollet Hotel. At the dinner he was recognized by Minneapolis Mayor Hubert H. Humphrey and by representatives of the U.S. Department of Vocational Education, Minnesota Department of Education, U.S. Secretary of the Navy, and American Federation of Labor of Minnesota. The Civic and Commerce Association named Prosser a lifetime honorary member and the board of trustees unveiled portraits of Prosser and the late Board President William Bovey, which would hang in the halls of Dunwoody Institute to commemorate the legacy of these two great leaders.

"At Dunwoody I learned to be detail oriented. I lived by a few simple truths: better build it right, because it'll stand there for 40+ years, and it's not going to fix itself."

—Ben Ellsworth 1956

CHAPTER IV

Dunwoody In Postwar America, 1945-1968

With the formal surrender of Imperial Japan in Tokyo Bay on September 2, 1945, the most destructive war in the history of the world came to an end. Although World War II had lifted the United States out of the Great Depression, neither economists nor ordinary Americans were confident that the nation would not sink back into hard times once the temporary stimulus of war spending ended. Much to everyone's surprise, a postwar depression did not occur. In spite of some short-term readjustments, the United States was about to embark on an unprecedented economic boom from the 1940s to the 1960s.

Along with economic prosperity came new and, if possible, even more frightening international challenges. The Cold War with the Soviet Union, which began in earnest two years after the end of World War II, led the United States into new wars in Korea and Indochina as well as crises with the Soviet Union over Berlin, Cuba, and other global hot spots. The specter of nuclear war between the two adversaries threatened the peace of Europe, Asia, the Middle East, and even North America. The rearmament of the U.S. military during the Korean War and the growth of a permanent defense establishment as part of the Cold War contributed to American prosperity in the 1950s and 1960s, much as the defense buildup during the Second World War contributed to the economic recovery of the early 1940s.

During the postwar years of economic growth and Cold War tensions, Dunwoody Institute continued to play a leadership role in the world of vocational and technical education. Dunwoody took full advantage of the 1944 G.I. Bill of Rights to train hundreds of World War II veterans for the workforce. Inspired by former Director Charles Prosser, Dunwoody administrators became active in promoting and supporting the creation of public vocational schools throughout the state of Minnesota. Beginning in the 1950s, with major grants from the Ford Foundation and the U.S. Agency for International Development, Dunwoody helped to establish technical schools and technical programs overseas; the International Division became a major new element of Dunwoody's program mix. And the bread-and-butter programs of Dunwoody's Day School and Evening School continued to provide skilled technicians for grateful employers.

Dunwoody Leadership, 1945-1957

Dr. Charles Prosser's retirement as director in September 1945 signaled the beginning of Dunwoody's transition to the postwar era. On September 21 Joseph R. Kingman Jr., the school's treasurer since 1938, became director of the Institute, retaining his role as treasurer as well.

Kingman was not a unanimous choice to succeed the acclaimed Dr. Prosser. According to Board President Russell Bennett, Kingman's lack of experience in school administration as well as his lack of vocational education credentials "raised pedagogical eyebrows." However, Bennett and the board held many closed-door meetings to discuss the succession issue, and ultimately Bennett persuaded his colleagues that Kingman was their man. Reflecting upon Kingman's performance twenty years later, Bennett gave him high grades for reorganizing the administration and improving staff morale. "If I were to select the one quality which he possesses to a

Opposite: Dunwoody Carpentry students build a house in the gym, 1948.

Board President Russell Bennett (left) and Joseph R. Kingman Jr., Dunwoody treasurer, 1938-1970; director, 1945-1957; president, 1957-1965

men" as Dunwoody teachers; the creation of "job lists" and "job sheets"; adoption of the time clock system for taking attendance; establishment of the Highway Construction and Surveying program; and recruitment of Dunwoody students from around the state of Minnesota rather than just the Twin Cities. Along with Sahlin, Craigo was one of the key educators who helped bring Dr. Prosser's philosophical ideas to life at Dunwoody.

Although Joe Kingman held the title of director, it was apparent to Dunwoody staff that Craigo, Sahlin, and Butler were the de facto successors to Prosser as the educational leaders of Dunwoody Institute in the postwar years. Kingman managed the finances of the school and worked directly with the board of trustees, as Prosser had, but first Craigo and then Butler, his successor as head of Day School, actually ran the operations side of the school, overseeing the faculty, support staff, and students. Younger than Sahlin, Butler replaced Prosser as assistant treasurer of the board in 1945 and was elected assistant secretary of the board in 1946. After 1948 he gradually emerged as the face of Dunwoody in the educational world, with Kingman remaining more in the background. Over time, Butler would gain status in Minnesota—if not nationally—comparable to that of Dr. Prosser.

greater degree than any other . . . ," Bennett wrote in 1964, "it would be the quality of personal modesty. Joe not only shared credit for Dunwoody's progress with his associates, but in many cases I feel that he abnegated his rightful share."

Upon taking up his new position, Kingman immediately appointed three assistant directors: Ralph T. Craigo, assistant director for Day School; Walter F. Sahlin, assistant director for Evening School; and John A. Butler, assistant director of Business Management. These four men were the administrative leadership team of Dunwoody Institute until 1948, when Craigo, who had been on the Dunwoody staff since 1914, retired. At that time, Kingman moved Butler to the position of assistant director for Day School and left Butler's former position unfilled.

According to Walter Sahlin, who had been Craigo's colleague since the school's founding, Craigo initiated or helped implement many innovations during his thirty-four year tenure, including division of the program day into half-shop and half-classroom instruction; development of "related instruction" to parallel shop work; the hiring of "practical trades-

At the board level, the transition was gradual yet significant. When the board of trustees held its first annual meeting at the end of the war, six of the fifteen trustees had served since the founding of Dunwoody Institute thirty-one years earlier, and one (James Ford Bell) had been on the board for thirty years. Over the next fourteen years, all of these long-serving founding trustees would either die or retire from the board. Franklin Crosby, long-time chairman of the Building Committee, died in 1947. Joseph Chapman, board treasurer from 1914 to 1924, retired in 1948, as did Robert Webb. John Crosby, William Dunwoody's attorney, retired in 1951 and then held the title of trustee emeritus until his death in 1962. Charles Bovey retired in 1954, Edward Decker died in

1956, and James Ford Bell retired in 1959. In addition to these founders, Cavour Langdon, who had joined the board in 1922 and served as treasurer from 1924 to 1929, retired in 1945, and Harold Hunt, a trustee since 1923, retired in 1959.

As the old guard moved on, the board of trustees continued to add new trustees to its ranks. A few of the Dunwoody leaders of the future who joined the board between 1947 and 1957 were George C. Crosby, son of Franklin Crosby; Dr. Laurence Gould, president of Carleton College; John S. Pillsbury Jr., scion of Minnesota's second great milling giant, the Pillsbury Flour Mills Company; Paul Wishart, president of Minneapolis Honeywell; Clifford H. Anderson, president of Crown Iron Works; and Robert C. Wood, president of Minneapolis Electric Steel Castings Company.

John A. Butler, assistant director, 1945-1957; director, 1957-1974

One source of long-term continuity at Dunwoody was Russell Bennett, who had been president of the board since 1937. Believing that he had served long enough in this position, Bennett resigned in 1948 and was replaced by Henry S. Crosby, the son of trustee John Crosby. Unfortunately Crosby's tenure lasted only four years; he was killed in a plane crash in March 1953. Following the tragedy, the board turned to its seasoned leader, Russell Bennett, and persuaded him to reassume his role as president in April 1953. Bennett remained president until 1957, when he was elected to the new position of board chairman, which he held until 1961.

Bennett's move to the position of chairman was part of a leadership restructuring that occurred in October 1957. Bylaw changes adopted by the board that year created the office of board chairman, who would now be the leader of the board of trustees, much as the president had been since 1914. Henceforth the title of president would belong to the chief administrator of the school, in this case Joseph Kingman. Accordingly the board now elected Kingman president and treasurer and promoted John Butler to the position of director. George Crosby and Paul Wishart

became vice presidents of the board, and Walter Sahlin became associate director.

From 1957 on, leadership roles at Dunwoody began to change. The president was no longer the principal *volunteer* leader of the board of trustees. That role now belonged to the chairman. The president now became the highest ranking *employed* administrator of the Institute. Throughout the 1960s, the president shared administrative authority with Director John Butler, who, like Dr. Prosser before him, essentially ran the educational and operations side of the school. Not until Butler retired in 1974 did the president, then Dr. John Walsh, consolidate all of the administrative roles under his position. Beginning with Dr. Walsh, the president would begin to function as Dunwoody's one chief executive officer, with the position of director relegated to a more subordinate status.

> "I cannot imagine what I would have been without my Dunwoody training. I have used all that I learned and beyond throughout my life."
>
> —Joseph Hillenbrand 1949

The G.I. Bill of Rights

Even before the end of the Second World War, Dr. Prosser and his colleagues had begun to focus on the training needs that would face Dunwoody Institute in the postwar era. In an article entitled "What Lies Ahead?" printed in *The Dunwoody News* in December 1943, Dr. Prosser identified two challenges awaiting Dunwoody: how to serve World War II veterans and how to respond to a growing demand

for the expansion of vocational education nationwide. One of these would be met through the G.I. Bill of Rights, the other through Dunwoody's active support of the creation of public vocational schools throughout the state of Minnesota.

In June 1945, following the surrender of Germany but prior to the defeat of Japan, almost 15 million American men and women served in the armed forces. Over the next twelve

Refrigeration instructor Floyd H. Schneeberg. Eventually Schneeberg became assistant director of Day School. After leaving Dunwoody for industry in the 1960s, he became president of the Dunwoody Development Fund and co-founder of the Century Club and Arizona alumni reunion. In 1986 he received Dunwoody's Alumni Achievement Award.

months, this number dropped to 1.5 million; approximately 13 million military personnel were demobilized within one year. How would these millions of Americans be absorbed into the peacetime economy? How would the United States avoid a return to the high levels of unemployment that had existed before the war?

In 1944 Congress answered these questions. On June 22, President Roosevelt signed into law the Servicemen's Readjustment Act, otherwise known as the G.I. Bill of Rights. Spearheaded by the American Legion, the G.I. Bill was intended to prevent demobilized veterans from encountering Depression-era unemployment. Veterans received several benefits under this revolutionary legislation: subsidized training and education; a loan guarantee for the purchase of a home, farm, or business; unemployment pay of $20 per week for fifty-two weeks; and assistance with finding a job. The educational benefits were especially important for veterans who enrolled at Dunwoody Institute and other post-secondary institutions. A veteran was entitled to one year of full-time training plus time equal to his or her duration of service in the armed forces, to a maximum of forty-eight months. Up to $500 per year would be paid to a veteran's educational institution for tuition, books, and other training materials. The veteran received a subsistence allowance of $50 per month, which was increased to $65 in 1946 and $75 in 1948.

Between the establishment of the G.I. Bill in 1945 and its expiration in 1956, more than 5 million veterans learned trades or crafts through on-the-job training or by attending trade and vocational schools across the nation. A smaller number, around 2.2 million, attended four-year colleges and universities under the G.I. Bill. Altogether it cost the United States $14.5 billion to assimilate its veterans into postwar society through the G.I. Bill. The program was so successful and so popular that Congress subsequently followed the first G.I. Bill with separate G.I. Bills for the Korean and Vietnam wars.

Even as war training at Dunwoody peaked in 1942-44, the Institute began to enroll veterans returning from active service in 1944 and 1945. Beginning in the fall of 1945, the enrollment of veterans exploded, at first with disabled veterans and then increasingly with students under the new G.I. Bill. Between 1945 and 1951, six school years, Dunwoody enrolled more than 16,000 students in Day School programs. Veterans—12,783 of the students—comprised 79 percent of the student body, an average of 2,130 annually. Although the enrollment of veterans declined over the subsequent decade, veterans still made up 44 percent of Day School enrollment between 1951 and 1961. As the number of students decreased, overall enrollment fell from its peak of 3,023 in 1947-48 to an annual average of 1,544 from 1951 to 1961.

Reflecting upon the influx of veterans after the war, Refrigeration instructor Floyd Schneeberg recalled that Dunwoody was forced to operate two work shifts for instructors, from 8 a.m. to 3 p.m. and from 11 a.m. to 6 p.m., with three schedules for students. Students enrolled in Section A had shop from 8:15 a.m. to 11:15 a.m. and classroom instruction from noon to 3 p.m. Section B had class from 8:15 a.m. to 11:15 a.m. and shop from noon to 3 p.m. And Section C had class from noon to 3 p.m. and shop from 3 p.m. to 6 p.m. Dunwoody was a very busy place during these years.

Schneeberg was one of many Dunwoody alumni interviewed by Randall W. Hansen for his unpublished manuscript, *The Servicemen's Readjustment Act of 1944 and its Beneficiaries* (2003). The purpose of Hansen's study was to document the impact of the G.I. Bill of Rights on the World War II generation of American veterans, sometimes called "The Greatest

Dunwoody's motor winding shop in the Electrical department, 1947

Generation." Central to his work was the story of Dunwoody Institute and the Dunwoody students who benefitted from the G.I. Bill. Testimonials from a few of them give a sense of their gratitude for the historic legislation that made it possible for them to attend Dunwoody.

LeRoy Wolf (Electrical, 1947-49): "What would my life have been without the G.I. Bill and the rock-solid foundation of the Dunwoody experience? I have often said, 'My military experience was worth a million dollars, but I wouldn't do it again for another million. Yet it gave me the opportunity to use the G.I. Bill to go to Dunwoody and make it all worthwhile.'"

Raymond Renner (Refrigeration, 1946-47): "Life is fine. Looking back now, there was a time of not knowing what to expect in our life. Frankly the G.I. Bill and Dunwoody made a heck of a difference for us."

Students in the Highway Surveying program use Dunwoody's campus as a training laboratory, 1948.

Richard Dinneen (Highway Surveying, 1947-48, 1949-50): "The G.I. Bill home loan program enabled me to acquire my first home, and the G.I. educational program provided me three years of post-high school education. Without my college and Dunwoody education, I seriously doubt that I would have ever become a registered professional engineer."

Wilfred Pehling (Electrical, 1945-47): "Dunwoody and the G.I. Bill—what a very special benefit for a young man like me who wanted to reconstruct his life. I was such a poor student in high school, but Dunwoody had a place for many others like me to start."

Chester Tollefson (Mechanical Drafting, 1945-46): "Dunwoody was a godsend. After going through the mechanics of arranging to go to Dunwoody and buying a home, I had never thought much about the G.I. Bill. Looking back now, I conclude that it was a Great And Wonderful Thing."

Dunwoody auto body class, 1949

Ivan Beal (Radio and Electronics, 1945-47): "Hail to the G.I. Bill and Dunwoody!"

Randall Hansen's interviews with representatives of the postwar generation provide colorful recollections of Dunwoody alumni. A more "scientific" study of alumni opinion was conducted by Milton Larson and Simon O'Loughlin in 1956 as a research project for their master's degree program at the University of Minnesota. By polling 309 Dunwoody graduates from 1950 to 1955, Larson and

O'Loughlin discovered some interesting information about alumni in those years.

Despite the decline in veteran enrollment in the early 1950s, almost 60 percent of Larson and O'Loughlin's alumni cited the G.I. Bill as their major source of funding for their Dunwoody education. (Outside employment was the second most important funding source.) Not surprisingly, 56 percent rated Shop as their most valued subject studied at Dunwoody. Next in importance were Job Knowledge (28 percent), Trade Knowledge (11 percent), and Applied Subjects (5 percent). Fifty-three percent of the graduates were employed in trades for which they had trained, 17 percent in related occupations. Fifty-six percent were working within thirty miles of Minneapolis and St. Paul, 15 percent in greater Minnesota, and 29 percent outside of the state. Thirty-eight percent were union members, and 35 percent had been or were serving apprenticeships. Dunwoody's placement efforts had helped 44 percent find their first job, while 34 percent had found jobs on their own. Still, almost 60 percent believed they had received adequate placement assistance from the school.

Placement, wages, and promotions were the obvious signs of Dunwoody's success. The average weekly wage for 1950-55 graduates in their first job was $61.11, and it was $91.53 in their current job. Their annual compensation had increased from approximately $3,178 to $4,760. On average, from 1950 to 1955, 22 percent of the graduates had received three or more job promotions, 18 percent had received two promotions, and 25 percent had received at least one promotion. No wonder that alumni expressed appreciation for their Dunwoody training. Larson and O'Loughlin concluded: "Dunwoody Industrial Institute is very effectively meeting the needs of young adults for trade training."

Growth of Public Vocational Education in Minnesota

Even as he entered into retirement in 1945, Dr. Prosser had his eye on the future of vocational education beyond Dunwoody. In his April memo to the board of trustees, "Dunwoody's Past, Present and Future," he had observed that it took one hundred mechanics to support every college-educated professional engineer in industry. Whereas many engineering colleges existed across the United States, few institutions educated the technicians who were so badly needed. Responding to a nationwide movement to promote public vocational education, Congress was then considering a national vocational education bill to provide $97.5 million to the states to fund vocational education. The state of New

40th anniversary cover of *The Dunwoody News*, December 10, 1954

York had already allocated $14 million to build fourteen vocational schools, and the Minnesota Legislature was considering the establishment of eight schools around the state.

Dr. Prosser did not mention in his memo to the board that he was a catalyst behind passage of the Area Vocational Technical School Law 121 in 1945. Chief sponsor of the landmark legislation was Walter Rogosheske, who represented the 45th District in the Minnesota House. Before introducing his bill, Rogosheske visited Dunwoody Institute

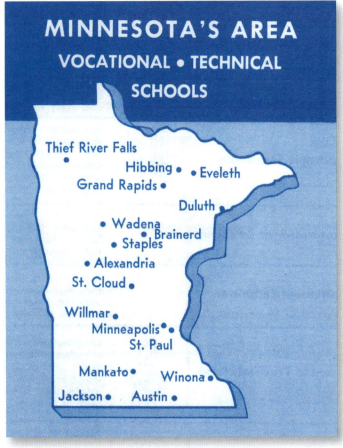

MINNESOTA'S AREA VOCATIONAL • TECHNICAL SCHOOLS

Thief River Falls

Hibbing • • Eveleth

Grand Rapids •

Duluth •

• Wadena
• Brainerd
• Staples

• Alexandria

St. Cloud •

Willmar •

Minneapolis • •
St. Paul

Mankato • Winona •

Jackson • Austin •

Locations of Minnesota's public vocational schools, 1947-1966

and questioned Dr. Prosser closely about his philosophy of vocational education. As the author of the Smith-Hughes Act and "father of vocational education," Prosser was, of course, all too willing to advise Rogosheske. Dunwoody's director never considered or worried about the possibility that the establishment of public vocational schools would ultimately create future competition for the Institute.

During the next ten years, Minnesota established area vocational technical schools in eight locations: Mankato (1947), St. Cloud (1948), Winona (1948), Thief River Falls (1949), Duluth (1950), Austin (1951), St. Paul (1952), and Minneapolis (1955). Even before he became director in 1957, Assistant Director John Butler emerged as Prosser's successor in championing public vocational education in

Minnesota. Butler's lobbying forum was the Minnesota Vocational Association, a statewide association of professional educators, who elected him president in 1947. In his role as MVA president, Butler helped obtain funding from the legislature to support public vocational education at both the high school and post-high school levels, thereby "placing support of vocational instruction after July 1, 1947 at a very favorable point," he wrote in an MVA publication. Later that year Butler was active in planning the first annual conference of MVA in Minneapolis, which was attended by more than 1,000 persons and attracted Minnesota Governor Luther Youngdahl and former Dunwoody Director Dr. Prosser as featured speakers. With the presidents of the University of Minnesota, Gustavus Adolphus College, and Mankato State Teachers College, Butler was appointed by the Minnesota commissioner of education to a committee to study post-secondary education in Minnesota. Here was evidence that he was recognized as an up-and-coming leader in vocational education.

By the time that Butler succeeded Joe Kingman as Dunwoody director in 1957, he and his colleagues were ready to throw their support behind the second wave of public vocational school expansion. Between 1959 and 1966, Minnesota built fourteen additional vocational schools, making a total of twenty-two public schools established since 1947. As of the 1963-64 school year, enrollment in the new public schools totaled 51,585, including full-time, part-time, and day and evening students. In the same year, the state schools offered 170 different technical programs, as compared to the three programs available at Mankato in 1947.

When MVA printed a special brochure in 1965 to commemorate the twentieth anniversary of the Area Vocational Technical School Law of 1945, the endorsement by John Butler and Dunwoody Institute figured prominently. Butler wrote:

To their everlasting credit, the leaders and members of the Minnesota Legislature and those responsible at the state

and local levels for the system of public schools quickly recognized the growth potential of our industries and wisely acted to educate and train a workforce with the essential capabilities. The Area Vocational Technical Schools are eminently suited to provide the vital occupational training for present and future needs. The officials and staff of Dunwoody Institute are proud to have been privileged to work closely over many years with the organizations and individuals who have promoted and secured greater opportunities for industrial and technical education. We share the pride in celebrating this 20th anniversary of the passage of the Minnesota Area Vocational Technical School Law.

Dunwoody's support and leadership of the vocational education movement manifested itself in other ways. For example, by the early 1950s the school was funding memberships in MVA for 100 percent of its faculty. In 1961 Governor Elmer Andersen appointed John Butler to the State Board of Education, highlighting his prominent status as the "dean" of vocational education. And as the public technical schools

Printing instructor Lloyd Stevens (second from left) with Dunwoody international students, 1952.
Eventually Stevens became chairman of the Printing department.

spread around the state, Dunwoody Institute was the educational model emulated by most of them. Dunwoody Presidents Emeritus Warren Phillips and Frank Starke (who had been curriculum coordinator and then director/president at Alexandria Area Vocational Technical School before coming to Dunwoody in 1995) later recalled that the new technical schools borrowed curriculum and teaching materials freely from Dunwoody. Many faculty and staff left Dunwoody to set up the new programs in the state schools, and they did not hesitate to take their Dunwoody instructional resources with them. William Hood Dunwoody and Dr. Charles Prosser likely would have been pleased to

note how the Dunwoody Way was replicated many times over during the postwar era of educational expansion in Minnesota.

International Training, 1950s–1960s

In 1951 the American Vocational Association (AVA) held its annual conference in Minneapolis, attended by 3,500 vocational teachers and administrators. Dunwoody leaders were active in planning the convention and also hosted a tour of Dunwoody Institute for 700 AVA members during the conference. "I have visited many vocational schools," one educator from Thailand said to Director Joe Kingman

Dunwoody's international training team departs for Indonesia, fall of 1953.

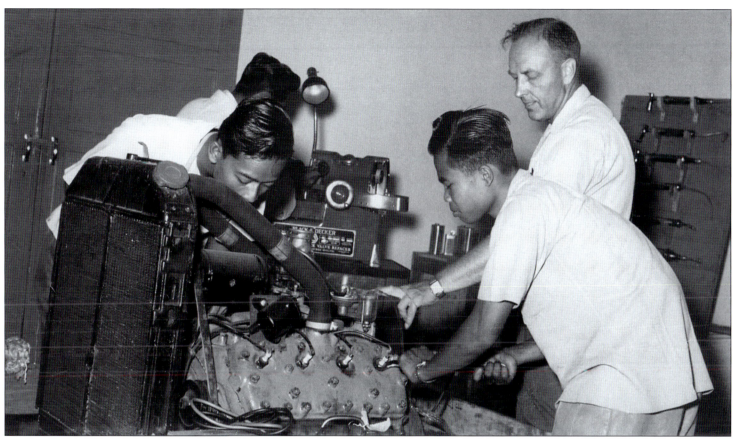

Auto instructor Allan Johnson (far right) works with Indonesian students in Bandung.

after the tour. "This is the finest of all!" Dunwoody's reputation was about to become international.

Like almost everything else, Dunwoody's foray into international education had begun with Dr. Prosser. In 1930 and 1931 he had conducted surveys of vocational training needs for both the Philippine Islands and the Hawaiian Islands, and he had returned to Honolulu in 1943-44 to advise a school there on postwar mechanical and vocational planning. After Dr. Prosser's retirement, Dunwoody's first venture overseas occurred in 1950, when nine technical teachers from the Republic of Korea traveled to Dunwoody for six months of study in the Electrical, Machine, Automotive, Welding, and Sheet Metal departments. Sponsored by the U.S. Economic Cooperative Administration, this project essentially kicked off three decades of active international work.

The first major international project took place in Indonesia from 1953 to 1960. Initiated by a $15,000 grant from the Ford Foundation, the project began in April 1953, when Assistant Director John Butler and Dr. Milton G. Towner, director of the Staff College of the Federal Civil Defense Administration, traveled to Indonesia to meet with officials of the Ministry of Education to assess the country's vocational training needs. The result was the inaugural phase of a seven-year Ford Foundation project to establish an Indonesian Technical Teacher Training Institute in Bandung. In September 1953 Dunwoody sent a team of six teacher-trainers, led by Dr. Towner as adviser/director, to Bandung to set up the Indonesian school. Concurrently seven Indonesians came to Minneapolis to receive teacher training in machine shop, woodworking, electricity, automotive, diesel, machinery maintenance, and printing.

Since international work was about to become an important focus for Dunwoody, the school created a new International Services Division in November 1953. Dr. K. Nagaraja Rao, a native of India who had been a consultant to the Indonesian government during Butler's Asian trip, was brought to Dunwoody to coordinate the Ford Foundation project.

Three years later, Butler recruited another key leader for the Indonesian project, future Dunwoody President Warren E. Phillips. In 1956 Butler sent Phillips to Bandung as an instructor. The next year he asked him to conduct a study for the Ford Foundation, which resulted in an expansion of the Indonesian program. By the time that the Indonesian

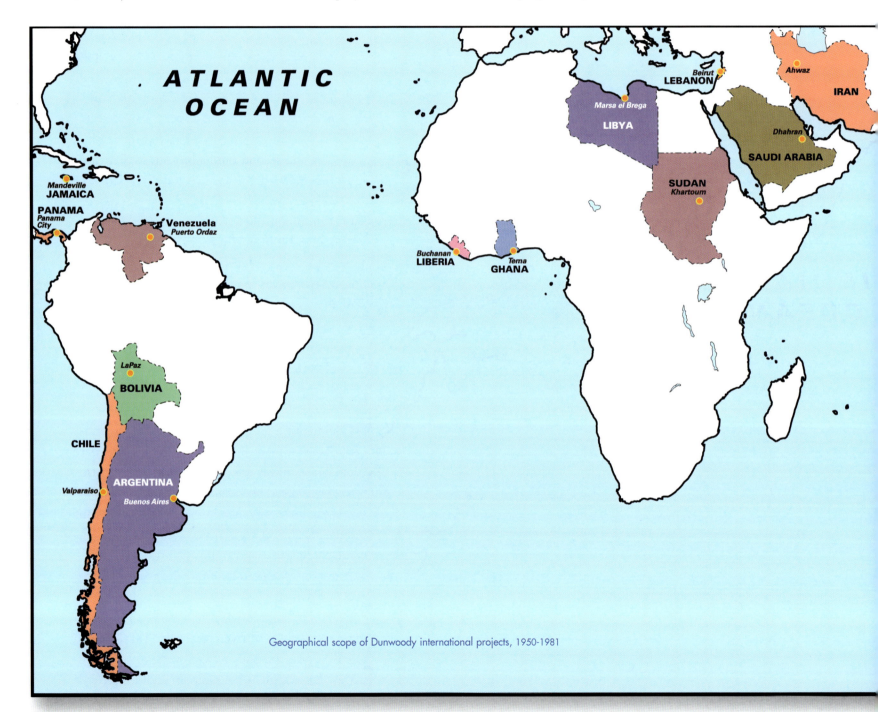

Geographical scope of Dunwoody international projects, 1950-1981

project ended in 1960, Dunwoody had administered $1,136,680 in Ford Foundation grants. Over the seven years of the project, forty-one Indonesians studied at Dunwoody Institute, and four officials of the Indonesian government visited Dunwoody to observe American technical education in action. When the project closed down, Phillips, by now

associate adviser, returned to Minneapolis and became a counselor in Dr. Rao's International Division.

One year after launching the Ford project in Indonesia, Assistant Director Butler made a follow-up trip to Asia. During the summer of 1954 he visited the Technical Teacher Training Institute in Bandung and then traveled to Insein, Burma, to study the viability of creating a similar teacher training program there. The upshot was the initiation of a second Ford Foundation project, a Dunwoody-organized Government Technical Institute (GTI) in Insein. This project was followed two years later by a third Ford project and second Burma project, support for a Rangoon Technical High School (RTHS). By 1958 five Dunwoody advisers were working at GTI in Insein, and five GTI trainees were being trained in Minneapolis. Four Dunwoody advisers were stationed at RTHS while five RTHS trainees were studying at Dunwoody. The budget for GTI in that year was $228,315 and for RTHS, $100,825. In addition to these projects, Dunwoody had received a grant of $43,100 to advise the government of Burma on other aspects of vocational and technical education.

Commenting on Dunwoody's growing international work in his first annual report to the board of trustees in his role as director in 1958, Butler wrote: "Dunwoody Institute seems to be a sort of 'Mecca' for foreign educators interested in seeing a practical program of industrial, trade, and technical education and training in operation in America." He then informed the board that the Ford Foundation had made a grant of $15,400 to the Lodhipur Institute in Shahjahanpur, India, which would send seven teachers to Dunwoody for the training necessary to set up a trade and industrial department at Lodhipur. In addition to

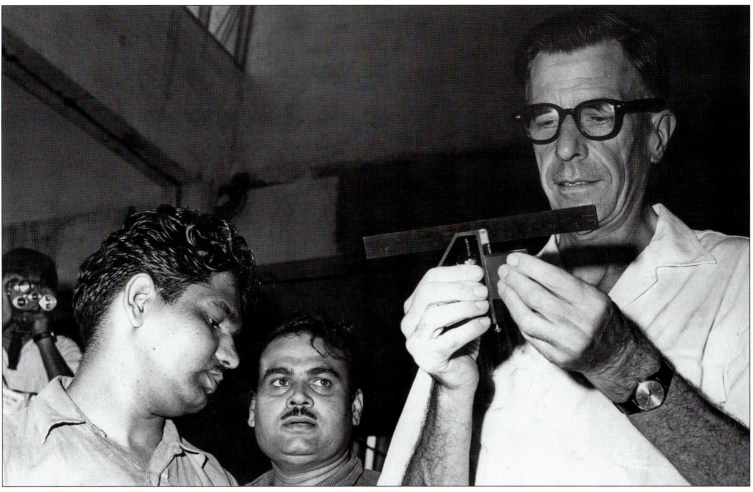

John Kenneth Galbraith, U.S. Ambassador to India, visits Central Training Institute in Bombay in 1962.

teacher training, Dunwoody's job would be to advise the Indians on the purchase of $20,000 of equipment for the new department.

Since 1953 Dunwoody had administered four projects in Indonesia, Burma, and India, with grants from the Ford Foundation totaling $2.9 million. Dunwoody's role had been dual: to establish technical training schools in these countries and to bring their nationals to Dunwoody to receive more teacher training. Almost twenty Dunwoody advisers had gone overseas during these five years, and more than 350 foreign trainees had attended Dunwoody in the past ten years.

The pace and volume of international work did not slow during the next ten years. As the original Ford Foundation projects wound down, Dunwoody launched six new projects in the 1960s, with funding from Ford, the U.S. Agency for International Development (USAID), and some private companies. These were the projects:

- Central Training Institute, Bombay, India, 1962-1968 (USAID)
- Khartoum Senior Trade School, Khartoum, Sudan, 1963-1967 (USAID)
- Instituto Superior del Profesorado Tecnico, Buenos Aires, Argentina, 1964-1968 (Ford Foundation)

- Escuela Tecnico Profesional, Valparaiso, Chile, 1964-1968 (Ford Foundation)
- Amiliyah Vocational School, Beirut, Lebanon, 1965-1968 (Ford Foundation)
- Alumina Partners of Jamaica, Spurtree, Jamaica, 1967-1969 (Kaiser, Reynolds, and Anaconda aluminum companies)

Between 1962 and 1968, the budgets for these six projects totaled $3.3 million. Reporting to the board of trustees about the 1967-68 school year, Director Butler observed that the year had been busy and productive for Dunwoody's International Services Division, with ninety students from sixteen countries enrolled at Dunwoody. Expenditures for international work totaled $469,000, and the Institute was under contract for $368,000 of continuing work during the next year. Dunwoody would remain active in international work through the 1970s into the early 1980s.

Postwar Financial Challenges

Despite the infusion of tuition revenue in the late 1940s—thanks to the G.I. Bill of Rights and the extraordinary external funding for international projects during the 1950s and '60s—many of Dunwoody's familiar financial challenges persisted after World War II.

The end of the war brought a temporary improvement in Dunwoody's financial picture. Fee revenue provided by the Veterans Administration increased from $22,849 to $265,336 from 1945 to 1946, and fees from non-veteran students also increased. In October 1946 Director/Treasurer Joe Kingman reported to the board of trustees that the Institute's total assets—now $5.7 million—were greater than they had been at any time in the school's history. Kingman's brother, Henry S. Kingman, Finance Committee chairman, noted that the Dunwoody Endowment had grown to $3.5 million, an increase of almost $500,000 over the original bequest. Income available from Dunwoody's investments helped to offset some of the increases in postwar operating expenses.

In 1949-50 the endowment generated $200,509 in operating income for the school—the largest amount since 1930. And in 1950-51 it produced $224,101—the largest amount since 1926.

Nonetheless the ever-increasing costs of running a technical school like Dunwoody was an ongoing issue. Director Kingman summarized the challenge for Dunwoody students and employees in May 1948 in *The Dunwoody News*. The cost of vocational education, Kingman wrote, was more than that of any average high school or college. First, the size of an average Dunwoody class of seventeen was smaller than that of most high schools and colleges. Second, a technical school like Dunwoody incurred greater expenses for equipment and consumables. Remaining current with the changing needs of business and industry was an ongoing challenge.

As the enrollment of World War II veterans began to decrease in the early 1950s, Dunwoody's response to the decline in operating revenue was to cut operating expenses by reducing staff.

"The best thing I received from Dunwoody was the work ethic!"

—Dan Lind 1967

Unfortunately budget cutting was not a viable long-term solution if Dunwoody were to remain the leader in vocational/technical education. Although board members commended the Kingman administration for reducing overhead in 1951-52, they also recognized the school's need to address the long-term revenue issue. In February 1951 Board Vice President John Crosby, who had drafted William Dunwoody's last will and testament, commented to his fellow trustees on the necessity of the Institute's remaining "up to date and in step with industry and [other] progressive and forward-looking educational institutions." Board President Henry Crosby made a similar point a year later when he challenged the board to assess Dunwoody's position in the field of vocational education, focusing especially on the need for possible changes. Then in January 1953, the board passed a resolution asking Kingman and his staff to study the issue of resident tuition in relation to the school's operating costs and to explore the legal constraints imposed on tuition levels by William Dunwoody's original directive that instruction at Dunwoody be free.

Increasing fees for Dunwoody students had already begun in 1951. The monthly fee for a resident student in the late '40s had been $5 and for non-residents $44. In addition, residents and non-residents had both paid a one-time registration fee of $15. When calculated over the eleven training periods of the school year, residents paid annual fees totaling $70 and non-residents $499. At the beginning of the 1951-52 school year, the monthly fee for residents was doubled to $10, while non-residents continued to be charged $44. Residents now paid $125 for a year's worth of instruction. Six years later, prior to the 1957-58 school year, Dunwoody increased a student's registration fee to $20, and the monthly fee for residents to $25 and for non-residents to $48. Residents were now paying $295 for their eleven training periods and non-residents were paying $548. Non-resident tuition had

hardly increased over the past ten years while resident tuition had increased 321 percent. Since most of Dunwoody's students were residents of Minnesota, non-residents were not viewed as a great source of potential operating revenue.

Notwithstanding these fee increases, the board of trustees and the Kingman administration still felt constrained by the Dunwoody will. In the fall of 1958, Cant, Taylor, Haverstock, Beardsley & Gray, Dunwoody's law firm, began to formulate the Institute's legal case for reinterpreting the will. There were two key provisions of the will that the school wanted to modify: the requirement that instruction be "free," or minimal, for Minnesota residents; and the requirement that all philanthropic gifts to the Institute be added to the endowment. Both provisions made it difficult for the school to cover increasing operating expenses with tuition revenue or charitable contributions.

President/Treasurer Kingman provided Cant, Taylor, et al., with evidence that the "nominal" $25 monthly fee charged

THE DUNWOODY NEWS

Published by The William Hood Dunwoody Industrial Institute, an endowed institution, not conducted for profit, for training in Industrial and Mechanical Arts

Vol. XXVIII — Minneapolis, Minn., November 4, 1949 — No. 5

Community Chest Gets $1004.78 in Contributions

A total of $1004.78 was collected at Dunwoody for the Community Chest this year, as a result of a two day drive on Tuesday and Wednesday, October 25 and 26.

On the whole, giving by the Dunwoody employees was up this year, with student giving falling from last year's mark. Totals by department (employees and students) are as follows:

Accounting ....$ 26.00
Air Conditioning 89.52
Auto 191.05

Fruit Cake Orders

Don't forget to order your fruit cakes early! A. J. Vander Voort, head of the Baking department, stated that last year many people were not able to get fruit cakes because they ordered them at the last minute when the Baking department was already swamped with orders. So order yours now. Remember, fruit cakes can be stored for an indefinite time if kept in a receptacle like a bread box.

ES Courses Prove Popular, Extra Sections Set Up

Interest in several of the Evening School courses offered at Dunwoody is running very high this year. Walter F. Sahlin, assistant director, has found it necessary to organize extra sections of certain classes.

Courses proving so interesting that one, and sometimes two extra sections have had to be added are the following in the Auto department: A4, A5-6 and A24. These cover respectively Carburetors; Carburetion, Ignition, Starting and Lighting; and Engine Tune-up and Analysis.

Fruit cakes for the Christmas holiday season became an annual tradition of Dunwoody's Baking department.

Machine Tool student Lester Goetzke in 1957. Goetzke eventually founded his own business, Midtown Manufacturing. In 1989 he received Dunwoody's Alumni Achievement Award.

to Dunwoody students did not provide enough revenue to keep up with the growth of operating expenses. In 1957-58 it cost $58.47 per hour to educate one Dunwoody student, as compared to $16.81 per hour twenty years earlier. The cost of Day School instructor salaries had increased from $104,615 in 1930 to $382,556 in 1958, and non-instructional costs like campus maintenance, utilities, and non-teacher

salaries from $161,057 to $601,013. The earnings of $300,000 from the Dunwoody Endowment, Kingman argued, were not adequate to provide free education to as many resident students in 1958 as the $147,000 in earnings had in 1936.

On January 15, 1959, Cant, Taylor, et al., submitted Dunwoody's petition to Hennepin County District Court.

In 1964 Dunwoody administrators cut a 50th anniversary cake baked and decorated by Dunwoody Baking students. Left to right: President Joe Kingman Jr.; Assistant Director of Evening School, John C. Hansen; Director John Butler; and Assistant Director of International Services, Dr. K. N. Rao.

essentially authorized the Institute to raise fees and accept gifts without limitations or restrictions.

Although Dunwoody's board and administration did not use this legal ruling to justify a dramatic rise in student fees, they enacted modest monthly increases for residents and non-residents prior to the 1959-60 school year. By the 1967-68 school year, residents were being charged $525 and non-residents $745 for eleven months of training, increases of 81 percent and 36 percent, respectively, since the 1959 court ruling. From the late '40s to the late '60s, the school had raised annual fees for Minnesota residents by 650 percent and for non-residents by 49 percent. This trend would continue until William Dunwoody's dream of free instruction became a distant memory.

Dunwoody Institute had created the Dunwoody Industrial Institute Alumni Fund in the early 1940s as a means of raising philanthropic contributions for purposes other than additions to the Dunwoody Endowment Fund. Between 1940 and 1958, Dunwoody raised $274,773 through the Alumni Fund for student scholarships and various small projects, averaging $38,500 annually from 1953 to 1958. Now that the Institute could accept gifts for any purpose, Dunwoody had greater flexibility in the solicitation of contributions. Soon the board of trustees, along with the board of managers of the Alumni Fund, would become actively engaged in fundraising as a way of relieving pressure on the school's operating budget.

One month later, the court ruled in favor of Dunwoody's petition. The court defined "free instruction" for Minnesota residents as a pro-rata share of instructors' salaries; the Institute was permitted to determine what this pro rata share would be.* In addition, it could charge residents for non-instructional expenses such as equipment, supplies, maintenance, and utilities. Non-residents and Evening School students could be charged for the full cost of their instruction. The court also authorized Dunwoody to accept financial contributions for purposes other than the endowment. As Board Chairman Russell Bennett informed the board of trustees at its April meeting, the district court had

During the 1960-61 fiscal year, Dunwoody not only raised $50,000 through the Alumni Fund but another $215,000 from other sources: a bequest of $50,000 for the endowment; a grant of $100,000 from the Ford Foundation to support the International Services Division; and gifts and consignments of equipment and supplies totaling $65,000. The $265,000 in contributions was the largest amount received by the Institute since 1914-15, when it received the original bequests from Mr. and Mrs. Dunwoody.

*In 1977 the district court removed Dunwoody's obligation to continue providing pro rata data regarding instructors' salaries. From then on the board of trustees and administration were no longer required to justify tuition increases.

This was encouraging progress. However, what the board of trustees really wanted was to increase the number and amount of unrestricted operating gifts to the school. To this end, it created a trustee fundraising committee with Robert C. Wood as its chairman. Wood remained chairman of this board committee for several years. In April 1962 he outlined the two purposes of his committee: to obtain larger contributions from companies with whom his fellow board members were associated and to obtain gifts from companies not already supporting Dunwoody. From this time on, fundraising would be a new priority of the board of trustees. Another example of the Institute's greater focus on fundraising was the 1963 decision by the Alumni Fund's board of

managers to change the name of their organization to the Dunwoody Development Fund—thereby removing the exclusive focus on alumni and placing the emphasis on longer-term financial *development* rather than shorter-term fundraising.

The most significant gift that Dunwoody received during the 1960s, aside from Ford Foundation and USAID grants for international projects, was the partial donation of the Warren-Cadillac building by the estate of Henry E. Warren. In 1954 Director Joe Kingman had recommended that the board's Building Committee study the feasibility of erecting a new building on the Dunwoody campus to house the Automotive and Welding programs, as well as warehouse

Warren-Cadillac building at the corner of Wayzata Boulevard and Lyndale Avenue South

facilities. Even though the board had allocated $5,000 in 1956 to develop preliminary engineering plans for a new building, estimates of $1 million temporarily killed the idea—until it was revived in a new form. In 1964 Henry Warren made Dunwoody an offer too attractive to pass up.

"I've never forgotten the Big 4: Skill, Knowledge, Reasoning and Attitude (SKRA)."

—Russell Sod 1946

Warren held a unique franchise for his Cadillac business at the corner of Lyndale Avenue and Wayzata Boulevard, directly east of Dunwoody Institute on Aldrich Avenue. Warren-Cadillac, Inc. was the distributor for all Cadillacs sold in the Upper Midwest. With his franchise due to expire on October 31, 1965, Warren—who was in failing health— was concerned that neither he nor his estate would receive top dollar from Cadillac when it replaced his regional distributorship with a more conventional retail dealership. On June 30, 1964, Warren sent a letter of intent to Dunwoody in which he outlined his proposal. He intended to give $360,000 worth of shares of Warren-Cadillac to Dunwoody Institute; in return, Dunwoody would purchase $400,000 of Warren-Cadillac stock. Warren planned to liquidate his business in 1965, at which time he would give to Dunwoody Institute the Warren-Cadillac building and adjacent real estate, and Dunwoody would give back the shares of stock it received in 1964.

Upon the recommendation of President Kingman and his administrative staff, the board of trustees unanimously approved accepting the terms of Warren's offer. In October the board recognized Warren by electing him an honorary trustee of the Institute. Warren died on February 19, 1965. The somewhat complicated details of his gift were left to the trustees of his estate. Subsequently Dunwoody borrowed $337,412 from the Dunwoody Endowment with which to pay the Warren estate. In return the Institute received a bequest of $694,438. Dunwoody took possession of the Warren-Cadillac property on December 1, 1965. The net charitable contribution from the Warren estate to Dunwoody was $357,026.

During the next year and a half, Dunwoody spent almost $275,000 to retrofit the Warren-Cadillac building, now named the H. E. and Helen R. Warren Building, for instructional shops and classrooms. Finally, during the summer of 1967, Dunwoody's Automotive and Welding departments moved into the remodeled Warren Building. This was the first significant expansion of the Dunwoody campus since 1924.

Meanwhile, as instructors and students were moving across Aldrich Avenue to begin training in their new facilities, trustee Bob Wood and his fundraising committee had been raising money to restore the funds borrowed from the Dunwoody Endowment to acquire the Warren property. By 1968 the board of trustees and the board of managers of the Dunwoody Development Fund had successfully repaid $154,000 of the original loan, having obtained gifts from General Mills, Honeywell, and other corporations.

As in prior decades, the principal financial responsibility of the board of trustees was its stewardship of the William Dunwoody Endowment Fund, managed by Treasurer Joe Kingman and the Finance Committee, and the Kate Dunwoody Trust, managed by First National Bank. Between 1946 and 1968, the market value of these two investment funds had increased 139 percent, from $4.6 million to $11 million, and the annual income generated by the two funds had increased by 162 percent, from $163,091 to $426,976. The problem was that the operating expenses for Dunwoody Institute had increased by 211 percent, from $409,562 to $1,273,932. Instructional expenses accounted for part of the increase, but the larger increase came from general overhead, including building maintenance, equipment and supplies, utilities, and compensation for managers and clerical staff. These expenses had grown by 259 percent since the end of World War II. And since student fees, investment income, and other sources of revenue had only grown

Paul B. Wishart, chairman of Dunwoody's board of trustees, 1961-1968

"counterculture" of long-haired "hippies" and left-wing revolutionaries who repudiated almost everything sacred to the World War II generation that had built the prosperous culture of the 1950s and '60s.

Dunwoody Institute had embraced change during the postwar years by welcoming GIs home from the war, actively promoting the creation of public technical institutes in Minnesota, and helping to establish several Dunwoody-type schools overseas. However, by the late 1960s there was some evidence that Dunwoody was no longer leading change as much as it was upholding the educational status quo.

John Butler was the personification of the Dunwoody status quo. A devoted disciple of Dr. Charles Prosser, he took pride in maintaining the philosophy and pedagogy of Prosser's creation. His annual director's report to the board of trustees in 1968 was strikingly similar to his first director's report ten years earlier, both in format and in substance. Total student enrollment at Dunwoody in 1957-58 had been 4,250; in 1967-68 it was 4,421. The largest Day School Departments in 1958 were, in order, Electrical (including Radio and Electronics), Automotive, Air Conditioning (including Sheet Metal), Machine Shop, and Mechanical Drafting. These were still the largest departments in 1968. In 1958 Dunwoody had conducted special training programs for three railroads, the Minnesota Highway Department, and IBM's plant in Rochester, Minnesota; in 1968 it provided special training for seven labor unions, Northern States Power Company, Electric Machinery Company, and Pako Corporation. In 1958, 85 percent of Dunwoody's Day School students had been high school graduates while 12 percent had had one or more years of college education; ten years later, 98 percent were high school graduates and 13 percent had college backgrounds. There had been 111 full-time employees in 1958, including 64 Day School instructors; by 1968 there were 117 full-time employees, of whom 71 were Day School teachers. In short, the school had not changed much during Butler's decade as director.

by 187 percent, Dunwoody continued to struggle with the challenge of making ends meet while remaining the leader in its special educational niche.

"The Times They Are a-Changin'"

Although change had certainly characterized the history of the United States and Dunwoody Institute since the end of World War II, the political, social, and cultural changes that swept across the nation during the 1960s were unprecedented. Dunwoody Institute was not overwhelmed by the kind of campus turmoil at the University of Wisconsin-Madison, the University of California at Berkeley, and other post-secondary institutions, yet it was affected. With his song "The Times They Are a-Changin,'" folk singer and Minnesota native Bob Dylan captured the essence of a decade during which civil rights protests escalated into urban riots, and peaceful antiwar demonstrations into violent confrontations in the streets of Chicago. The "cool" playboy antics of Frank Sinatra's "Rat Pack" gave way to the

> "Mastering each architectural segment required total dedication. Every month was a new segment and you had to successfully complete it before progressing to the next level. Students punched a time clock and instructors were strict about being on time."
>
> —Ann Fincham 1979

By all accounts, Butler had perpetuated Dr. Prosser's no-nonsense approach to education, for faculty as well as students. Teachers and other staff—as well as students—were required to punch in and out on a time clock. Dunwoody instructors were underpaid compared to faculty in the new public technical schools, and Butler refused to pay them overtime for working late sections. Gradually some employees and students began to challenge Butler's authoritarian "my way or the highway" administration. In 1966 and 1968, faculty defeated two unionization drives, but the votes were close—36-28 and 34-22. Since leaders of these drives worked in the General Subjects department, Butler got rid of his problem by changing staffing in the department from full-time and permanent to part-time and temporary. When Dunwoody students defied Dunwoody's conservative dress and personal grooming codes, Butler simply expelled them. Eventually one long-haired student filed and won a law suit against Dunwoody, forcing the school to modify its approach to personal grooming. Not even John Butler could hold back the tidal wave of the 1960s.

Leadership changes during the '60s were not particularly dramatic, but they did presage a less certain future for Director Butler and Dunwoody. In October 1961 Russell Bennett—who had led the board of trustees from 1937 to 1948 and again from 1953 to 1961—resigned as board chairman. He relinquished this role to Paul Wishart, chairman of the board of Minneapolis Honeywell Regulator Company.

Six months later, Associate Director Walter Sahlin, a Dunwoody student in 1914-16 and a staff member since 1917, retired after forty-five years of service to the school. President Kingman and Director Butler's leadership team now included Floyd Schneeberg, assistant director for Day School; John C. Hansen, assistant director for Evening School; and Dr. K. N. Rao, assistant director for International Services.

Board Chairman Wishart announced a more significant change in January 1965: President Kingman would retire from his position as president in June. No mention was made of a successor, although Wishart informed the board that Kingman would continue to serve as treasurer—a role he had held since 1938—for another five years.

Given the common perception that John Butler had become the face of Dunwoody Institute during the Kingman era, it is intriguing that the board did not automatically promote the director to president. At its annual meeting in October 1965, it elected Butler to the board for the first time but left the office of president vacant. In fact, it amended its articles of incorporation in January 1966, making the office of president optional, stipulating that the board chairman would act as Dunwoody's chief executive officer in the absence of a president. For three years, from 1965 until 1968, Dunwoody functioned without a president.

Whether the board ever asked or wanted Butler to become president is not known. His associate Warren Phillips recalled that Butler never aspired to the office. Butler's mentor, Dr. Prosser, had been director. All of the leaders of the new area vocational technical institutes were directors. Since Butler had essentially run Dunwoody Institute for President Kingman, being director of Dunwoody was the most prestigious and influential position he could imagine. Why would he want to bother himself with financial matters, fundraising, and board affairs the way Kingman had? As long as the position of president remained vacant, he wouldn't have to share administrative authority with anyone. Even former President Kingman wouldn't be close at hand, since he would occupy a new office in downtown Minneapolis during his final years as treasurer.

With the announcement of Kingman's retirement as president, the board of trustees realized that Dunwoody would be facing inevitable changes in the near future. Therefore, in January 1965, the board asked the Dunwoody administration to "reexamine" the objectives and role of Dunwoody Institute. Since Kingman's retirement was imminent, John Butler took the lead on this study, which was presented to the board in April 1965. Entitled "A Study of the Objectives and Role of the Dunwoody Industrial Institute," this impressive report was coauthored by Director Butler, Assistant Directors Hansen and Rao, and Warren Phillips, now coordinator of Day School.

As an analysis of the current position of Dunwoody Institute, trends in the labor force, and the status of vocational/technical education, the Butler Study was quite comprehensive. Noteworthy yet not surprising was its conservative recommendation "that Dunwoody Institute continue and strengthen its present plan of operation and its programs of practical and technical industrial education . . . ." This was not a recommendation for revolutionary change; it was a recommendation to continue doing what Dunwoody had done successfully for fifty-one years.

Two years later Dunwoody's leaders must have been ready for a more change-oriented vision. This time it commissioned a New York-based management consulting firm to study the school's current situation as well as future challenges and opportunities. In March 1967, Cresap, McCormick, and Paget submitted its "Master Plan for the Institute" to Director Butler and the board of trustees.

The purpose of the Cresap study was to lay out a ten-year plan for Dunwoody Institute. By way of background, the Cresap plan noted that the potential pool of students for vocational technical schools in Minnesota would be over 31,000 by 1970, by which time there would be twenty-seven area vocational technical institutes with enrollment capacity of 28,000. To meet the growing competition from these public schools, Dunwoody would have to enhance its existing program strengths and expand its public relations efforts to make more young people and their parents aware of what the Institute had to offer.

Specific recommendations in the Cresap plan included:

- The primary service area of Dunwoody should continue to be the five-county Twin Cities metropolitan area; Greater Minnesota should be a secondary market.
- Dunwoody's major objective should continue to be high-quality post-secondary training programs for skilled craftsmen, industrial service technicians, and industrial workers.
- Dunwoody should consider developing accredited programs in engineering technology as one way to differentiate itself from the area vocational technical institutes.
- Dunwoody should continue to provide Evening School programs to benefit employed workers.
- Dunwoody should continue to be the leader in vocational/technical education. It could do this by:
  - expanding its international programs
  - assuming a leadership role in educational consortiums
  - establishing a curriculum center at Dunwoody
  - expanding in-plant training for industry
  - offering courses for foremen and supervisors
  - developing teacher training programs
  - publishing Dunwoody Institute training materials
  - developing a research program in vocational/technical education
- Dunwoody should formalize its staff development program to ensure ongoing improvement of instruction.
- Dunwoody should consider eliminating its programs in Baking, Carpentry, Sheet Metal, and Painting & Decorating.
- Staff compensation should be improved so that Dunwoody could attract and hold the most qualified teachers.
- Dunwoody's administration should be strengthened by hiring a new president and reorganizing the management

structure to include four director positions, including a new director of development and alumni affairs.

Although the Cresap plan built on the information contained in the 1965 Butler Study, it went well beyond the recommendations made by Butler and his staff two years earlier. For example, the Butler Study had considered the possibility of developing accredited engineering technician programs but saw no reason to move in that direction. Nor had the Butler Study recommended the closing of any existing programs. And finally, Butler and his team had not proposed filling the position of Dunwoody president or creating three new director positions to rival Butler's one position. Clearly the Cresap plan envisioned more dramatic changes for Dunwoody than the in-house Butler Study had.

Upon receiving the Cresap plan, the board of trustees moved to act on the plan's recommendations by creating an Implementation Committee. Since most of the recommendations would have to be carried out by Dunwoody's administrative staff, the Implementation Committee made its priority evident at the board's annual meeting in October: the board should hire a full-time president as Dunwoody's chief executive officer. It would appear that the board suspected that a new president would implement the Cresap plan more aggressively than Director Butler would.

Once the decision was made to fill the vacancy that had existed for almost three years, the board moved quickly. On November 29 the board's Executive Committee interviewed Dr. John P. Walsh. Dr. Walsh had met Director Butler and Dunwoody staff during previous visits to Minnesota while working for the U.S. Office of Education and then the U.S. Department of Labor as assistant manpower administrator. Impressed by Dr. Walsh, the Executive Committee authorized Board Chairman Wishart to extend a job offer to him. On January 17, 1968, the full board elected Dr. Walsh as president of Dunwoody, with an annual salary of $27,000.

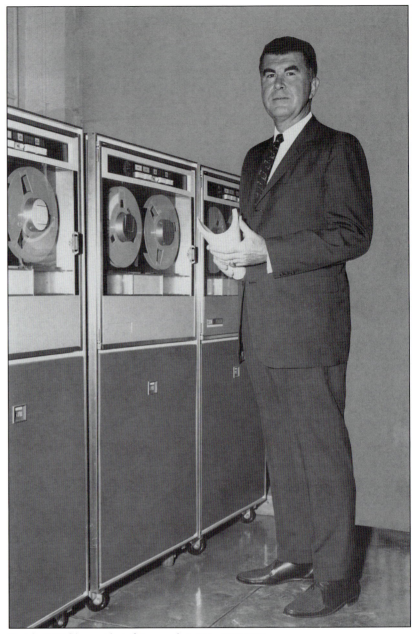

Dr. John P. Walsh, president of Dunwoody Institute, 1968-1978

Dr. Walsh was the first outsider chosen to lead Dunwoody since the appointment of Dr. Prosser in 1915. Although John Butler would remain as director for another six years* and

*When John Butler retired in 1974, the board of trustees honored him by naming him Director Emeritus and by presenting him with a Distinguished Career Service Award for his forty-three years of service to Dunwoody.

would serve President Walsh faithfully in that role—as he had President Kingman—a new environment was emerging.

As Walsh became settled in his role, Butler's influence and power began to decline. The Prosser/Butler era was ending.

CHAPTER V

Responding To Competition and Change, 1968-1989

The 1970s and 1980s brought several changes in leadership at Dunwoody. Former President Joseph Kingman retired as treasurer in 1970 and John Butler as director in 1974. Dr. John Walsh, elected as president in 1968, retired in 1978. He was replaced by Warren Phillips, who announced his retirement in 1989, the year of Dunwoody's 75th anniversary.

During these years, the competition and threat posed by the growth of Minnesota's public area vocational technical institutes (AVTIs) mounted, exacerbating the financial challenges facing Dunwoody Institute. Until the early '80s the strength of Dunwoody's international programs mitigated the school's financial problems to some extent. But ultimately, after thirty years, changing international conditions brought an end to this important source of external revenue, at a time when declining student enrollment was affecting tuition revenues.

The Butler and Cresap studies of the mid-1960s had addressed current and future challenges then facing the Institute. Similarly in the mid-70s and mid-80s, the Walsh and Phillips administrations developed major strategic plans for the board of trustees to point Dunwoody's way into the future.

The Walsh plan, presented to the board in April 1976, responded to the imminent construction of a new Minneapolis AVTI facility three blocks from Dunwoody on Hennepin Avenue. The Phillips "Futures" report, presented to the board in April 1985, responded to the computer and technology "revolution" that was dramatically accelerating the pace of change in American industry and the world of technical education. Keeping up with change was now becoming as big a challenge as keeping up with—let alone staying out in front of—all of the government-subsidized AVTIs.

How could Dunwoody, with its limited private resources, afford all of the new technologies necessary to ensure that its students were trained on the most current and relevant systems and equipment? The inevitable answer: fundraising. The immediate response to Walsh's 1976 plan was a capital fund drive, *A Vital Source*, which would raise $5 million in special funds for Dunwoody, and the response to Phillips' 1985 Futures report was a second capital campaign, the *75th Anniversary Campaign*, which would raise $4 million. By the end of the 1980s, fundraising from corporations, foundations, alumni, and other individuals had become integral to the Dunwoody culture. The celebration of Dunwoody's 75th anniversary in 1989 demonstrated an important way in which the Institute could and did separate itself from its public counterparts. History and tradition mattered to Dunwoody alumni and community business leaders. Aside from its technically oriented program offerings, Dunwoody was now functioning more like a private liberal arts college than a public AVTI.

President Walsh Takes Over

Dr. John Walsh attended his first board of trustees meeting as the new president of Dunwoody Institute on May 20, 1968. He told the trustees that an immediate priority was to

Opposite: HVAC instructor Merrill Engquist (center) assists students in sheet metal class. Jeff Ylinen, the student on the right, would later become an HVAC instructor, chairman of the HVAC Department, dean of learning, and provost of the college. Rod Albers, on the left, would later become part-owner of Northwest Sheet Metal Company.

review current Dunwoody operations and programs to determine the feasibility of the recommendations made the previous year by the Cresap study. Four months later, at the board's annual meeting on October 1, he was ready to share his personal observations.

Teacher compensation, communication between administration and staff, the management structure of the Institute, and program offerings were four Cresap issues about which President Walsh reported that October. Since faculty salaries were less than those of teachers in the public technical schools, the board had approved an average salary increase of 8.5 percent for the 1968-69 school year. Unfortunately Dunwoody salaries still lagged behind those in the AVTIs. Although Dunwoody faculty had defeated a second unionization vote in June, Dr. Walsh realized that improving communication with staff had to be a priority of his administration. Accordingly he established a President's Advisory Council, organized a Faculty Forum, developed a staff policy manual, and initiated in-service training in communications for department heads.

On the issues of management structure and programmatic change, Walsh's progress was more limited. The Cresap study had recommended not only the hiring of a president but also the expansion of the leadership team to include three additional director positions. And it had recommended the closing of Dunwoody's programs in Baking, Carpentry, Painting & Decorating, and Sheet Metal. After several months in office, President Walsh realized that Dunwoody could not afford to fund three new high-level administrative positions. His alternative was to reorganize the existing administrative structure. As for program closures, the president announced that Carpentry would be eliminated at the end of the 1968-69 school year and that the gym, which had been used as a carpentry shop for many years, would be restored to its original purpose as an auditorium/gymnasium. No mention was made of Baking, Painting & Decorating, or Sheet Metal.

During the next few years it became clear that the 1967 Cresap study was only partially implemented. As recommended, Dunwoody continued to provide high-quality training programs for Minnesota employers, both through Day School and Evening School, and it continued to operate a robust International Services Division. It phased out Painting & Decorating but did not close Sheet Metal or Baking (although in April 1969 President Walsh did propose the closing of Baking at the end of the 1969-70 school year). The Walsh administration introduced classes for foremen and supervisors during the 1970-71 school year, but it never developed a program in engineering technology. Dunwoody continued to increase compensation for its teachers, but staff salaries never caught up with those in the AVTIs. According to Warren Phillips, who became Walsh's assistant director of business affairs, one of Walsh's major contributions was to invite greater participation by faculty and support staff in the administration of Dunwoody Institute—a practice continued by Phillips when he became president.

For the first three years of the Walsh administration, student enrollment at Dunwoody remained strong. Cumulative enrollment in Day and Evening courses exceeded 4,000 students through the 1971-72 school year. The Day School totals of 1,731 students and 1.5 million hours of training during that year were the school's highest levels since 1951, and Evening School enrollment of 2,801 students and 220,365 hours of instruction in 1968-69 were the largest numbers since World War II. Five hundred ninety students graduated from Day School programs during the 1972-73 school year, and as usual, these graduates experienced outstanding employment opportunities despite the onset of an economic recession in the early 1970s.

Continuing education courses offered through Evening School continued to parallel the courses offered through Day School. For example, during the 1968-69 school year, Evening School instruction included Automobile Repair, Baking, Architectural Drafting, Building Construction,

Refrigeration instructor Harland Hayward (right) and student

Electrical Construction, HVAC (heating, ventilating, and air conditioning), Machine Shop, Mechanical Drafting, Printing, and Welding. Courses in these areas benefitted both labor organizations and businesses. Apprentice-related training was provided to Asbestos Workers Local 34, Electrical Workers Local 292, Pipefitters Workers Local 539, Plumbers Local 15, and Sheet Metal Workers Locals 34 and 547. Businesses that contracted for training with Dunwoody in that same year included Pillsbury Company, Pako Corporation, Honeywell, Minnesota Mining and Manufacturing (3M), Soo Line Railroad, Minneapolis Gas Company, and Northern States Power Company (NSP). One of the valuable services provided by Dunwoody board members was the negotiation of Dunwoody training contracts with their own companies. In 1968-69 trustees John Snyder (Pillsbury), Harry Dye (Pako), Paul Wishart (Honeywell), Cy Pesek (3M), Leonard Murray (Soo Line), Gerald Mullin (Minnegasco), and Allen King (NSP) all helped Dunwoody in this way.

> "Dunwoody gave me the work-related training I was looking for. Like my dad, I was hired by IBM before I graduated!" [Andrew, father Howard, and cousin Alex were all Dunwoody graduates.]
>
> —Andrew Heung Wong 2004

These kinds of continuing education courses and relationships continued throughout the 1970s. However, when the national and state economies were hit by recession, employers—both apprentice training committees and companies—cut back on extra training for their employees. This resulted in a decline in Dunwoody's fee income from Evening School and extension classes every year from 1969 to 1975.

Contract training was a different matter. One reason the board of trustees had hired Dr. Walsh was because of his national contacts through the U.S. Department of Labor and other government agencies. In 1972 the Walsh administration obtained a contract for $375,176 with the U.S.

Department of Health, Education, and Welfare to run the newly created Upper Midwest Area Manpower Institute for Development of Staff (AMIDS). AMIDS conducted staff training as well as development workshops and courses for ethnic minorities and the chronically unemployed. During the 1972-73 school year, Dunwoody converted the automobile showroom in the Warren Building into an AMIDS headquarters for fifteen staff, who delivered 480 training activities for 7,196 participants from eight states in the Upper Midwest. In early 1973 Dunwoody received an additional grant of $58,909 to assume responsibility for Northeast AMIDS, hiring another six employees for this training center.

During the two subsequent fiscal years, 1973-1975, Dunwoody further expanded its AMIDS activities with grants totaling $530,162. When the Education Department reorganized AMIDS in 1974, Dunwoody was forced to compete nationally with other schools and agencies for the opportunity to continue hosting AMIDS. When its proposal was ranked first out of thirty-five, Upper Midwest AMIDS was renamed AMIDS Center One. During that year, AMIDS Center One served 5,525 clients in eight states and two territories out of two offices (Minneapolis and Albany, New York), employing a staff of twenty. Dunwoody continued to run AMIDS Center One until July 1975.

AMIDS was an important source of supplementary income for Dunwoody. Another was the Institute's continuing international programs, which had begun in the 1950s. Between 1968 and 1975, Dunwoody's International Services Division operated projects in Chile, India, Jamaica, Saudi Arabia, Korea, Libya, Indonesia, Iran, and Ghana. The gross volume of international contracts during these years was $3.7 million, with administrative fees paid to Dunwoody totaling $670,743. In addition, 262 foreign students from more than fifteen countries enrolled in classes at Dunwoody Institute, paying $237,367 in tuition to the school, either individually or via international sponsors.

Notwithstanding the health of Day School and contract training, both domestic and international, the Walsh administration encountered many of the same financial challenges faced by its predecessors. First was the ever-rising cost of technical education. Between 1969 and 1975, Dunwoody's cost to educate one Day School student increased 69 percent, from $106.80 per four-week training unit to $180. Over the same years, the Institute's overall operating expenses increased 47 percent, from $1.7 million to $2.5 million.

The typical response to rising costs was to increase student fees. Between 1968 and 1975, student tuition for Minnesota residents* was raised from $48 per training unit to $82, an increase of 71 percent, and for non-residents from $68 to $108, an increase of 59 percent. (International students paid $160 in 1974-75.) In spite of these fee increases, the school still did not have enough revenue at the end of each year to finance all of its operating expenses. Whereas operating expenses had increased 47 percent since 1969, income had gone up only 40 percent.

To cover its operating shortfalls, Dunwoody had to look to annual appropriations from the William Dunwoody Endowment Fund, Kate Dunwoody Trust, and Dunwoody Development Fund. At the end of the 1968-69 fiscal year, appropriations from these three sources amounted to $486,075, leaving a small surplus of $33,870 on June 30, 1969. By 1974-75 the appropriation from investments and contributions had increased to $665,971; however, this 37 percent increase was now insufficient to avoid an operating deficit of $90,831 on June 30, 1975.

Although the value of Dunwoody's investments and the Development Fund had grown during the past six years, they had not grown enough to cover increased operating expenses, let alone provide extra money for significant

*In 1972 President Walsh changed the long-standing and unpopular policy of charging higher fees to U.S. veterans. From now on veterans would pay the same fees as Minnesota residents.

equipment acquisitions or campus improvements. During the 1968-69 fiscal year, 27 percent of the Institute's operating revenue had come from the Dunwoody Endowment and the Kate Dunwoody Trust, whereas in 1974-75 only 20 percent came from these two investment sources. Similarly the Development Fund had provided 6 percent of operating income in 1968-69, but by 1974-75, philanthropic contributions for operations had dropped to 4.5 percent.

To address the ongoing funding challenge, the board of trustees took three important steps in the early 1970s. First, it turned over the management of the Dunwoody Endowment Fund to Northwestern National Bank and First National Bank. Second, it withdrew $850,000 from the endowment fund to expedite some pressing capital improvement projects. And finally, since these capital expenditures created the need to replenish the endowment as well as underscored the importance of finding resources to fund other capital needs, the board began active planning to mount a major capital fund drive.

When Joseph Kingman retired as president in 1965, he had retained his position as treasurer of Dunwoody Institute, moving to a new office in downtown Minneapolis. He retired from that role in June 1970—after an amazing tenure of thirty-two years. In October 1969, with the treasurer's retirement pending, the board of trustees decided to assign the future management and investment of the endowment fund, then valued at over $7 million, to Minneapolis' two largest banks. Accordingly on January 1, 1970, the endowment was divided fifty-fifty between Northwestern National Bank and First National Bank. Now the banks would have the opportunity to improve Dunwoody's return on this critical investment. Even as Dunwoody was turning over the endowment fund

"I have always found the training I received at Dunwoody to be helpful throughout the last 60 years." [Lloyd came from a line of brothers, all of whom attended Dunwoody.]

—Lloyd Nyberg 1940

to the banks, it was moving forward with an ambitious plan to borrow funds from the endowment to implement capital improvements recommended by the board's Building Committee. Chaired by Clifford H. Anderson, president of Crown Iron Works Company, the Building Committee recommended six projects to the board in April 1970. During the 1970-71 fiscal year, the board authorized the expenditure of $300,000 to rehabilitate and expand the Machine and Mechanical Drafting Departments and to air-condition the east wing of the main building. In January 1972 the board authorized drawing $200,000 from the endowment to renovate the Baking Department.* Between 1973 and 1975

*Although both the Cresap study and President Walsh had recommended closing the Baking Department, the Building Committee targeted it for renovation in 1970. Apparently, influential Dunwoody partners like General Mills and Pillsbury encouraged the school not to close the program.

it spent another $350,000 to modernize the Architectural Drafting and Highway Departments and begin renovation of the Electrical/Electronics Department. The intent of the board of trustees and the Walsh administration was to use philanthropic fundraising to repay the $850,000 taken from the endowment.

Fundraising was not yet a major source of revenue for Dunwoody, but it was now recognized that it had to be a higher priority than it had been in the past. Growth of the Dunwoody Development Fund and acquisition of the Warren-Cadillac building had been signs of progress in the 1960s, along with the success of Robert Wood's trustee annual giving committee in obtaining corporate contributions for the school. Alumni volunteers on the board of managers of the Development Fund, led by board president

Architectural Drafting class: instructor Bernard Dols and students

and former assistant director of Evening School Floyd Schneeberg, demonstrated their commitment to fundraising when, in 1969-70, they created the Century Club for donors who contributed $100 or more annually to Dunwoody. The Century Club began with inaugural gifts from Schneeberg, Director John Butler, and Schneeberg's successor as board president, George Kelly. By 1974 it had nearly 100 members, and by 1982 it would have 286 members.

Although annual giving is an important foundation for any fundraising program, Dunwoody needed a major capital campaign to finance long overdue improvements to its physical plant. To determine the feasibility of such a campaign, the board's Executive Committee contracted with a professional fundraising firm, Marts & Lundy, Inc., to conduct a preliminary survey for the Institute. In January 1972, after the school had already moved forward with some capital improvements, Marts & Lundy presented its report to the board. Since the consultants concluded that Dunwoody could mount a successful campaign, the board authorized the Executive Committee and President Walsh to hire a development officer within the next six months. It also directed Marts & Lundy to develop Dunwoody's "case" for a capital campaign as well as provide consulting services to the new development officer, once hired.

Three months later Board Chairman Thomas Crosby reported on the status of campaign planning in "A Special Message for the Trustees of Dunwoody Industrial Institute." The son of founding trustee and long-time Building Committee Chairman Franklin Crosby, Tom Crosby believed strongly in the necessity of a major fund drive. For two years he provided the leadership for a potential campaign. In his "Special Message" he outlined the rationale for a $5 million campaign, and he issued a personal challenge to the board of trustees to assume responsibility for the campaign.

What is very curious is that no tangible progress was made to implement the recommendations of Marts & Lundy or

Machine Tool instructor Simon O'Loughlin (left) with student

Chairman Crosby for the next four years. In spite of much discussion at board meetings and one special session in 1973, no action was taken. It was not until President Walsh delivered an important strategic report to the board in April 1976 that Dunwoody finally took steps to launch the capital fund drive.

Thomas M. Crosby, chairman of Dunwoody's board of trustees, 1970-1973

by a land condemnation settlement with the Minnesota Highway Department caused by the expansion of U.S. Highway 12, and $247,975 by charitable contributions. A 1972 gift of $100,000 from the family of founding trustee Edward W. Decker to renovate the auditorium/gymnasium was foremost among these special contributions. Two years later the Decker Auditorium* was officially dedicated on Founder's Day during the celebration of Dunwoody's 60th anniversary. On the same occasion, Dunwoody presented a Charles A. Prosser Award to U.S. Senator Hubert H. Humphey and inaugurated a 50-Year Club for Dunwoody alumni who had graduated prior to December 14, 1924.

Dedication of the Decker Auditorium demonstrated the emergence of a fundraising strategy that would become widespread with time—the naming of school facilities in recognition of philanthropic contributions. This practice had, of course, begun with the naming of The William Hood Dunwoody Industrial Institute, and it had continued with the naming of the Warren Building for Henry Warren and his wife, Helen, in the 1960s. It was applied again in 1970 when the family and friends of alumnus and race car driver Donald Skogmo contributed money to renovate a training room in the Warren Building in memory of Skogmo, who had been killed in a racing accident, and in 1974 when the Crosby family donated funds to upgrade an executive conference room near the Decker Auditorium in memory of Franklin Crosby.

Other precedents for the future that occurred during the early Walsh years included the admission of the first woman student to Day School, the accreditation of Dunwoody Institute by an authorized educational organization, and changes in the size and leadership of the board of trustees.

Three possible explanations for the delay come to mind. One, in private conversations with trustees and other potential donors, Chairman Crosby and President Walsh may have discovered an unfavorable environment for launching a campaign. Two, advance-funding early projects by borrowing money from the endowment may have lessened the case for a larger campaign and sidetracked the board and the Walsh administration from the hard work of preparing for such a campaign. And three, Dunwoody had raised some special capital funds in the early '70s, which may have affected the timing of a larger campaign.

At the January board meeting in 1976, President Walsh reported on the status of twelve capital projects carried out at a cost of $1,246,112 since 1970, when he had replaced Joseph Kingman as Dunwoody treasurer. Of these projects, $850,000 had been funded by the endowment, $127,462

*In 1971 the board of trustees had voted to name the auditorium for Director John Butler, whose retirement was anticipated in the next few years. When the Decker family came forward one year later with its offer of a memorial gift, Board Chairman Crosby talked to Butler, who graciously agreed to let the school name a different area for him. Eventually the school's library was named as a memorial for Butler in 1989.

Auto Body shop in Warren Building, 1970s

As male veterans returned to the United States following the Second World War, Dunwoody's Rosie the Riveters—as well as women in wartime defense industries—returned to their homes or traditional female occupations. Dunwoody reverted to being an exclusively male-oriented institution. Not until the 1960s gave birth to the "Women's Liberation Movement" did Dunwoody face the prospect of again becoming co-educational. In 1971 Pam Spence, a student at St. Cloud State University with a lifelong interest in cars, heard about Dunwoody's Automotive Electric program and decided to

apply. Although Director John Butler suspected that Spence might be a feminist "test case," Spence's only goal was to become an auto mechanic. After her initial application was denied, President Walsh recommended to the board of trustees that Dunwoody change its males-only policy and permit the enrollment of girls and women in Day School. On July 20, 1971, the board approved this historic policy change.

Pam Spence enrolled at Dunwoody in January 1972. Soon

she was making the grade with her male counterparts in the Automotive Department. Of her performance, her instructors wrote: "sharp student," "good attitude," "works fast," "thorough," "reliable," "diligent," "confident." Spence graduated from Dunwoody in 1973 and went on to become the owner/operator of her own automotive shop in California.* By October 1972 seven women had enrolled in Dunwoody programs, and within six years, forty-eight women were attending Dunwoody.

*In 2006 Spence was recognized as a Dunwoody pioneer when she received the school's Alumni Achievement Award.

As significant as the decision to go coeducational was the decision to seek accreditation. By the early 1970s federal and state financial aid programs were becoming an important way for post-secondary students to finance their education. Although Dunwoody students had qualified for federal funds in the 1960s, such funds were now available only to students enrolled in schools accredited by officially sanctioned accrediting organizations. Four-year colleges and universities in Minnesota, like Carleton College and the University of Minnesota, were accredited by a regional organization, North Central Association of Colleges and Schools (NCA), whereas many vocational schools joined

Pam Spence (front row, fourth from right), with her 1973 graduating class

the National Association of Trade and Technical Schools (NATTS). Realizing that Dunwoody students would soon be denied the opportunity to receive federal or state grants or loans if Dunwoody were not accredited, the Walsh administration decided to seek NATTS accreditation.

When Dunwoody was officially accredited in October 1972, Dunwoody students become eligible for federal grants, loans, and "work study" via the U.S. Office of Education and through the State of Minnesota. With the cost of student fees rising every year—especially relative to those in the state's many AVTIs—governmental financial aid for students would now become an increasingly critical part of Dunwoody's financial picture. In the future, Dunwoody could not survive without the financial aid provided to its students.

The decisions to admit female students and seek NATTS accreditation were initiated by President Walsh and his administrative team, whereas changes on the board of trustees originated with the board itself. In 1965 the board had amended its bylaws to permit the expansion of the number of trustees from a maximum of fifteen to thirty. By October 1974 the board had grown to twenty-three members plus three honorary trustees (Dr. Laurence M. Gould, former president of Carleton College; Russell Bennett, longtime president and chairman of the board; and Joseph Kingman, past treasurer, director, and president of Dunwoody). In 1971, as another move to open up opportunities for service, the board established a mandatory retirement age of seventy for trustees.

Another change was one of practice rather than policy. Russell Bennett had been the leader of the board for nineteen years, first as president and then as chairman. Paul Wishart, who followed Bennett as chairman, held this office from 1961 to 1968. He was succeeded by Leonard Murray, president of Soo Line Railroad, who declined to serve more than two years as chairman. At the 1970 annual board

Architectural Drafting student Ann Bollmeier in 1976. Following her graduation, Ann started her own business, became the first woman president of the Dunwoody Alumni Association, and in 1993 received Dunwoody's Alumni Achievement Award.

meeting, Murray expressed his opinion that "a rotation of the chairmanship among members of the board would provide greater strength and understanding of Dunwoody and its needs." Although the two men who followed Murray—Thomas Crosby and John Snyder—served for three years each, the precedent of shorter tenures had been established. Following Snyder's retirement as board chairman in 1976, it became customary for the board chairman to be elected to two one-year terms of office, usually serving no more than two years in this leadership role.

The AVTI Challenge and Dunwoody's Response

Although the Cresap study of 1967 had identified the emerging competition from Minnesota's publicly supported vocational technical schools, it was not until the mid-1970s that the leaders of Dunwoody Institute woke up to the seriousness of the competitive challenge that Dr. Prosser and John Butler had helped to create for Dunwoody. At a board of trustees meeting in July 1972, Director Butler addressed the increasing competition. Four new AVTIs would open in the next year, and eleven of the state's thirty-three AVTIs had added new facilities in the past year. Moreover, since January, ten Dunwoody instructors had resigned to go to work for the AVTIs, five of them at the new Hennepin County Suburban Vocational School District 287, which had campuses in Brooklyn Park and Eden Prairie.

What really caught Dunwoody's attention was the announcement by the Minneapolis Board of Education that it intended to build a new facility for the Minneapolis Area Vocational Technical Institute (MAVTI) on Hennepin Avenue, only three blocks away from Dunwoody. With the capacity for 2,000 students, it would open in the fall of 1978. Since Dunwoody had experienced enrollment declines in 1974 and 1975, this announcement caused concern and soul-searching at Dunwoody.

On January 20, 1976, the board of trustees directed the Executive Committee and the Walsh administration to review the alternatives facing Dunwoody in view of the competitive threat, and to make their recommendations to the board at its April meeting. President Walsh and his leadership team* went to work immediately analyzing the challenges facing the school. The results of the in-house study—embodied in a "Special Message for the Trustees of Dunwoody Industrial Institute"—were first presented to the Executive Committee on April 14 and to the full board a week later.

The Walsh team identified the problems confronting

*From 1968 to 1974 Walsh's team had included Director John Butler and Assistant Directors Warren Phillips, John C. Hansen, and Robert Minarik. Following the retirement of Butler in 1974, Phillips had become director of Day School, Hansen director of Evening School, and Minarik director of International Services. In 1977 the three directors became vice presidents.

Dunwoody: (1) income from investments had remained relatively flat while school operating costs had gone up; (2) revenue from tuition increases, contract services, and contributions had only partially filled the investment gap; (3) AVTI competition for student enrollments had increased; and (4) plans to open a new Minneapolis AVTI had intensified the competitive threat. After analyzing the "competition factor" and the "finance factor," the Walsh report asserted that Dunwoody's financial situation, not public competition, was "the critical issue." Since the Institute had competed successfully against the AVTIs and MAVTI for many years, its real challenge was to increase operating revenues from the endowment, annual contributions, international and domestic contract services, and year-round scheduling of classes.

The Walsh report concluded by recommending four potential alternatives for Dunwoody's future, in descending order of priority. Ultimately President Walsh and his team recommended Alternative I and saw Alternative IV as "a last resort."

Alternative IV: sell Dunwoody's property and brand to a private company to operate as a proprietary school; maintain the endowment as an educational foundation under the control of the Dunwoody board of trustees.

Alternative III: convey Dunwoody's property and brand to the Minneapolis Board of Education or the State Community College Board to operate as part of MAVTI or some other AVTI; maintain the endowment as a foundation under the Dunwoody board.

Alternative II: seek formal affiliation with or assimilation into a public institution like the University of Minnesota, Metropolitan State University, or Metropolitan Community College. Under this model, Dunwoody could maintain its identity and gain public funding for operations and capital improvements.

Alternative I: take strong actions to increase income levels without raising student fees to "a self-defeating level." Essentially this alternative called for Dunwoody to work harder to generate more revenue from the endowment, the Dunwoody Development Fund, and contracts with foreign and domestic partners.

Even though the Walsh administration favored Alternative I, there was some sentiment on the board of trustees for a more radical alternative. Board Chairman John Snyder, for one, believed that the time may have come to close Dunwoody Institute and use the Dunwoody Endowment as a source of scholarship support for Minnesota students interested in attending other career-oriented technical schools. Clearly Dunwoody had reached a potential turning point in this, its sixty-second year of operation.

The stakes were high when the Executive Committee met on April 14 to consider the Walsh report. Attending the meeting was attorney David Bennett, who in 1968 had replaced his father, Russell Bennett, on the board and now held the office of board secretary. Upon studying the report, Bennett had concluded that Alternatives II, III, and IV would all encounter legal problems and that the courts might not approve such drastic actions. After considerable discussion, the Executive Committee, in the absence of Board Chairman Snyder, voted unanimously to recommend that the board of trustees approve Alternative I.

Chairman Snyder was absent again when the full board met the following week to consider the Walsh report and the recommendation of the Executive Committee. Here the outcome was the same. After more discussion, the board voted unanimously to keep Dunwoody open by adopting Walsh's Alternative I. More specifically, it directed the Executive Committee to set a fundraising goal for a capital campaign, develop a needs statement, and prepare an action plan. Fundraising would be Dunwoody's route out of the current competitive crisis.

Finally, after four years of delay, Dunwoody took action to move forward with a capital campaign. At the July board meet-

Instructor Joseph Hasbrouck (far right) with students in Electrical Construction shop

ing, the Executive Committee announced the members of a Fund Drive Steering Committee, which included Russell Bennett as honorary chairman and Stanley Nelson, a group vice president for Honeywell, who had replaced Paul Wishart on the Dunwoody board, as chairman. Subsequently Nelson's Steering Committee recommended that a campaign to raise $3-5 million should begin in 1977. On January 18, 1977, the board of trustees authorized the Executive Committee, Steering Committee, and President Walsh to launch a campaign to raise $5 million for plant improvements, additions to the endow-

Environmental Systems Design class: William Jordan, department chairman, with student. Jordan later became Dunwoody's director of facilities, implementing many improvements to the school's campus in the 2000s.

ment, scholarships, and assistance for minority students. One month later Dunwoody contracted with Zachary Associates in Winona, Minnesota, to provide consulting services for the campaign. At the July board meeting, Walter Collins, Zachary's "resident director" at Dunwoody, introduced the theme of the campaign, A *Vital Source*, and a new goal, $7.1 million. Collins, President Walsh, and the board began active fundraising in August, and during the next twelve months they raised over $3 million in gifts and pledges for A *Vital Source*—an encouraging beginning for the school's first organized, systematic fundraising campaign. The momentary talk of a possible school closing was now history. Once again Dunwoody would prove that it was "a vital source to Minnesota, the nation, and the world"—to quote from the campaign's case statement.

Continuing Financial Challenges

Less than one year into the *Vital Source Campaign*, President Walsh informed Dunwoody's board chairman, Robert Engels, president of NSP, that he intended to take early retirement at the age of sixty-three in October 1978. After Engels revealed this news to the board of trustees on July 18, 1978, the board immediately elected Dr. Walsh president emeritus and his executive vice president, Warren E. Phillips, as Dunwoody's next president, effective August 1. Walsh would continue as Dunwoody's treasurer until the board's annual meeting on October 3.

No one was more surprised by the speed of this leadership change than the new president. A longtime employee and administrator at Dunwoody, Phillips was well regarded by Dr. Walsh and by honorary trustee Russell Bennett. But he was taken aback when Chairman Engels called him, informed him of Walsh's pending retirement, and told him that he, Walsh, and Bennett wanted him to be president. Would he accept the nomination? Phillips said yes, and the executive search process was over. All that remained was the formal vote by the board.

With Walsh's retirement, President Phillips reorganized the leadership team at Dunwoody, promoting John Hansen to executive vice president, maintaining Robert Minarik as vice president of the International Division, and promoting Robert E. Poupore from head of the Automotive Department to director of educational programs, responsible for all of Dunwoody's training programs. Having worked closely with Dr. Walsh and, before him, Director John Butler, President Phillips was well positioned to keep Dunwoody moving along its current track without interruption, with one important exception: the *Vital Source Campaign*.

A *Vital Source* had begun on Dr. Walsh's watch, and he was instrumental in its early success. At the time of Walsh's retirement, Dunwoody had raised $3.3 million. As president emeritus, he continued to help with the campaign.

In January 1979 he reported to the board that Dunwoody had raised $4 million in gifts and pledges. But the campaign was apparently losing momentum, for the goal had been lowered from $7.1 million to $6.1 million. Only six months remained to reach the goal, Dr. Walsh reminded the board.

Between January and June 1979, Dunwoody raised only $200,000, leaving the school well short of its goal. Changing leadership in the middle of the *Vital Source Campaign* must have had an effect on its progress. Although Dr. Walsh remained a member of the board of trustees and President Phillips was a quick study, successful fundraising campaigns require focused energy, personal leadership, and consistent communication in the community. All of these were affected by the timing of Dr. Walsh's retirement.

Since the goal had not been achieved, *A Vital Source* was extended for two more years. In July 1980 President Phillips hired Dunwoody's first professional fundraiser, Development Director Fred Leighton, and in December, the board of trustees established a Development Committee. Nevertheless, gradually the board and the Phillips administration talked less about the *Vital Source Campaign* until finally, in mid-1981, it just faded away. There was no *Vital Source* victory celebration of any kind, and within three years Dunwoody was beginning to consider a new fund drive that would coincide with the school's 75th anniversary.

In the end, *A Vital Source* raised slightly more than $5 million, short of its more ambitious goals but still a worthy total for Dunwoody's first capital campaign. *A Vital Source* funded the final phase of renovation of the Electrical/Electronics Department, upgrades to the Printing and HVAC Departments, and construction of a new cafeteria, staff dining room (named for Russell Bennett), and new library (named for John Butler). Dunwoody also received a major grant from the McKnight Foundation to recruit low-income students of color and a gift from Mr. and Mrs. C. Charles Jackson to create a permanently endowed fund

to support the professional development of faculty and staff. *A Vital Source* was important in its own right as well as for ushering in the modern era of Dunwoody fundraising.

What *A Vital Source* did *not* do was to solve all the financial problems identified in the 1976 Walsh report. Alternative I had called for Dunwoody to increase operating revenues through annual giving, improved returns on investments, enhanced contract training overseas and at home, modest tuition increases, and improved institutional operating efficiencies. Few of these expectations were realized between 1976 and 1984.

President Walsh (far left) and Vice President Warren E. Phillips (behind podium) preside over student commencement in June 1978.

Despite the success of the capital campaign, annual contributions to the Dunwoody Development Fund did not increase significantly during these years. The Development Fund raised $300,759 during the 1976-77 fiscal year, $324,255 in 1978-79, $304,000 in 1980-81, and $334,739 in 1983-84. Although fundraising for *A Vital Source* no doubt hurt annual giving, a modest 11 percent increase over eight years did not fulfill the promise of Alternative I.

When Dunwoody turned over the Dunwoody Endowment to Northwestern National Bank and First National Bank, the expectation had been that the banks would produce better annual returns on the investments than the Institute had been able to generate on its own. This did not happen. At the end of the 1981-82 fiscal year, Dunwoody's financial audit showed a market value of $6.2 million for these investments, less than what Dunwoody had entrusted to the banks twelve years earlier. The board's Finance Committee became so dissatisfied with the banks' performance that it withdrew Dunwoody's funds in early 1982 and turned them over to Alliance Capital Management Corporation and Investment Advisers, Inc. By June 30, 1984, the total market value of these managed funds had increased to $8.3 million. It now appeared, finally, that Dunwoody would begin to receive increased operating support from the endowment, thanks to its new fund managers.

The situation was somewhat different with international training, from which Dunwoody continued to receive substantial revenue until the early 1980s. Between 1975 and 1981 the International Services Division ran projects in nine countries: Libya, Iran, Panama, Saudi Arabia, Indonesia (Irian Jaya), Liberia, Ghana, Korea, and Venezuela. These contracts produced $5.5 million in gross revenue and $1.4 million in administrative fees for the Institute. In addition, 297 sponsored students enrolled at the Minneapolis campus, paying almost $500,000 in tuition. This source of revenue seemed to be meeting the expectations of the Walsh report.

Then the bottom fell out. As several of Dunwoody's projects neared completion, political and economic conditions were changing overseas. Anti-Americanism was on the rise and many of the underdeveloped countries that had contracted with Dunwoody for technical training were now suffering from heavy debt levels. Between 1982 and 1984 Dunwoody's international projects literally dried up. The final project, a

maintenance training program in Venezuela, ended when Dunwoody's partner in Venezuela defaulted on $114,000 owed to Dunwoody. The International Division operated at a financial loss for the first time ever during the 1983-84 fiscal year. Dunwoody had no international projects the following year. Reluctantly but inevitably, President Phillips, who had begun his Dunwoody career overseas, was forced to close the International Division in late 1984.

Although domestic contract training had neither the ups nor downs of international training, it never produced the magnitude of business envisioned by Alternative I of the Walsh report. After the high levels of enrollment of the late 1960s, Evening School numbers declined in the 1970s. During the 1977-78 school year, Dunwoody provided 78,566 hours of

Lawn adjacent to east shop building prior to construction of new student cafeteria in late 1970s

training for 1,349 students. Apprentice-related training now accounted for approximately 50 percent of these hours. Despite annual fluctuations, enrollment in Evening School had not changed significantly by 1984-85: 1,872 students received 59,611 hours of training during the year. Evening School remained an important part of Dunwoody's program mix, but the net financial effect was no increase in revenues from contract training.

Since 1976 Dunwoody had not improved its financial position through annual giving, investment income, or contract training. Nor did it find a "silver bullet" through improved operating efficiencies or tuition increases for Day School students. Dunwoody had been a lean organization in 1976, and it remained lean in the mid-1980s. Its major operating

expense was staff compensation. Dunwoody had improved compensation and benefits for employees each year, yet these still lagged behind those in the public AVTIs. And year-round scheduling of Day School classes, especially during the slow summer months, remained a goal only, not a source of new revenue.

The Walsh report had cautioned against raising student tuition to "self-defeating" levels, and for the most part, both the Walsh and Phillips administrations had followed this advice. Nevertheless, by 1984, Dunwoody resident tuition of $200 per training period was twice that of the AVTIs. When the board of trustees had endorsed Alternative I of the Walsh report in April 1976, it also approved a tuition increase of 15 percent for the next school year. Thereafter

New student cafeteria under construction with funds raised through *A Vital Source Campaign*

Architectural Drafting class: instructor Gordon Beneke (left) with students. Eventually Beneke became department chairman.

the annual tuition increases had reverted to single-digit percentage increases. Although student tuition increased 100 percent between 1976 and 1984, the extra revenue did not prevent operating deficits in 1983, 1984, and 1985.

Contributing to the deficits were declines in student enrollment. From a high of 1,731 Day School students in 1971-72, enrollment had fallen to 1,441 during the 1978-79 school year, rebounded to 1,669 in 1981-82, and dropped to 1,305 in 1984-85. The deficits would have been worse if Dunwoody had not obtained NATTS accreditation in 1972 and reaccreditation in 1978 and 1985. A growing number of students now received federal and state financial aid to help pay for their Dunwoody education. For example, during the 1984-85 school year, Dunwoody students received 1,078 grants and loans totaling almost $1.6 million—a substantial, though indirect, source of revenue for the Institute.

Little had changed during the Phillips years. Finances had been President Walsh's critical issue at the time of his 1976 report to the board, and now they preoccupied his successor as well.

From "Futures" Study to 75th Anniversary

Another issue complicated and exacerbated Dunwoody's ongoing financial challenges: the accelerating pace of technological change. Evolving technology had long been a challenge for Dunwoody and the businesses it served, but the computer revolution of the 1980s made it more and more difficult to keep up with the changes. "Future shock"— a term and a concept popularized by futurist Alvin Toffler— hit Dunwoody hard during this decade.

One of the early signs of computers coming to Dunwoody was the installation of the hardware and software of an IBM System/34 in August 1981. Student Affairs and Development were the first departments to utilize the 34, followed by Evening School and Accounting. Then, responding to the emerging use of personal computers by individuals and employers, Dunwoody set up a personal computer laboratory and began offering Evening School classes in personal computers and their software. Computer-aided drafting and design (CADD) came next. With funding from Dunwoody alumnus Roy Olson, the school established a CADD lab with five work stations in 1985 and began offering continuing education in CADD technologies.

Since Dunwoody's board of trustees was made up of business leaders whose own industries were being impacted by new technologies, the trustees strongly encouraged Dunwoody staff to adapt quickly to the changing times. In 1983 the board created a "Futures Committee," chaired by Dr. Robert Adams, senior vice president of technology services at 3M, to lead a comprehensive process to study all of Dunwoody's technical programs and determine appropriate "futures" for these programs. This process, which took over two years, involved Dunwoody faculty and staff, board members, alumni on the board of managers of the Dunwoody Development Fund, and industry advisers in all of the Institute's program areas. On October 2, 1984, President Phillips and his leadership team presented the results of fifteen staff course evaluations to the Futures Committee, and on April 16, 1985, they submitted their final report, entitled "Marking the Future," to the board of trustees.

The Futures report opened with a reminder of the new challenge facing Dunwoody Institute:

> *Change is not new to the school. The difference is the rate of change. The slow, evolutionary patterns of past decades were much easier to deal with and assimilate into instructional programs. Not so today. Change is coming at an almost exponential rate. And the cost of change seems to multiply almost as rapidly.*

As it considered directions for an unpredictable future, President Phillips and his team reminded the board that "the ultimate goal is the continued positioning of Dunwoody on the lead edge of technical education."

In reviewing employment projections from the Minnesota Department of Economic Security, the Phillips team discovered that all of Dunwoody's course areas, except for Baking and Refrigeration, could anticipate continuing job openings during the next decade. However, since the population of college-age students was declining, the competition for this shrinking pool of potential applicants would intensify. Placement of Dunwoody graduates remained close to 100 percent at this time, but the competitive challenge from the AVTIs would continue.

One interesting conclusion from the employment analysis was that new technologies "will not initially employ large numbers of workers." Although Dunwoody would have to "keep pace with changing technology," the kinds of jobs filled by its graduates "will not change dramatically over the next 5-10 years." Therefore Dunwoody should continue to teach "the basics" and incorporate new technologies into existing curricula as appropriate.

To guide their deliberations over the previous two years, the

Automotive lab: instructor Glenn Rasmussen (center) with students

Phillips administration and the Futures Committee had refined a list of assumptions about the future. These are some of the assumptions cited in the Futures report:

- Dunwoody will continue to be a two-year, post-secondary technical school.
- Courses will evolve in step with the introduction of new technology into the jobs Dunwoody graduates fill.
- Dunwoody education will key on the higher level/higher paying technical jobs . . . .
- Dunwoody will seek to attract the more capable student.
- Dunwoody graduates will require better communication and computational skills.
- All students must master computer skills.
- Dunwoody will move to a quarter or semester system school year . . . .
- Dunwoody will adopt a single fee for each course regardless of student residence.
- Dunwoody will pursue cooperative programs with universities or colleges leading to the B.S. or advanced degrees.
- The school should seek authorization to grant the Associate of Science degree for selected courses.

Many of the assumptions were included in the formal recommendations made by the Futures report. These recommendations mapped out an ambitious program of change for Dunwoody:

- Curriculum Restructuring: adopt a quarterly or semester system and appropriate credit hour system to record student progress.
- Scheduling: consider an earlier starting time for the Dunwoody school day.
- General Studies: consider additional general education to improve the employability of future graduates.
- Current Course Enhancements: establish linkages with Metropolitan State University and other four-year colleges.
- Associate/Bachelor Degree Courses: apply to the State for authorization to offer Associate degrees.
- New Technologies: begin to offer training in computer-aided manufacturing (CAM), computer-integrated manufacturing (CIM), robotics and automated processes, fiber optics, and laser technology.
- Linkages with Industry: establish and convene technology action committees for all course areas.
- Service to Minorities and Non-Traditional Students: actively recruit students of color and consider new courses to attract more women to Dunwoody.
- Facilities: update Dunwoody's campus plan in preparation for a new capital campaign.
- Marketing: hire a public relations/marketing professional to lead the school's marketing efforts.
- Equipment Updating: prepare a detailed equipment needs list for inclusion in a capital campaign.

Unlike the 1976 Walsh report, which was basically a defensive plan to keep Dunwoody in business in face of the AVTI threat, the 1985 Futures report was a comprehensive blueprint for the future. The report ended with a detailed "Summary of Action Items and Recommendations," with estimated costs totaling from $5.9 million to $6.5 million.

Like the Walsh plan, it clearly pointed the way to a capital campaign. But it also called for other critical changes, some of which would occur during the next four years while others would take longer to implement.

In May 1986 President Phillips hired Dunwoody's first marketing director, Gayla Shoemake, and charged her with implementation of Dunwoody's first-ever marketing plan to build student enrollment. The next month, seven technology action committees (TACs), each chaired by a Dunwoody trustee and including members of the alumni board of managers, held their initial meetings to advise seven departments on future directions. Soon all departments would receive industry advice and input from their own TACs. In September 1988 Dunwoody moved from a four-week unit of instruction with different fees for Minnesota residents and non-residents to a quarter system with one uniform tuition charge for all students ($885 per quarter, or $2,655 for three quarters). In June 1989 the Minnesota Higher Education Coordinating Board granted Dunwoody the authority to offer the Associate of Applied Science (A.A.S) degree in seven programs: Auto Service, Engineering Drafting, Civil Technology, Computer and Digital Systems, Architectural Drafting, Printing, and Industrial Electronics. A.A.S. authorization was pending for seven other programs, including a new two-year Baking course.

In view of the many costs associated with the Futures report, a capital campaign was put on the fast track. In July 1985 the board of trustees had approved a recommendation from the Development Committee to retain a fundraising firm, Ernhart and Associates, to conduct a feasibility study for a $6 million campaign. At the same meeting, the Futures Committee organized Dunwoody's capital needs into four categories: $750,000 for program and staff development; $3,450,000 for equipment modernization; $1,500,000 for building and site improvements; and $300,000 for scholarships for minority and disadvantaged students.

C. Charles Jackson Jr., member of Dunwoody's board of trustees, 1982-1991; chairman of board's Development Committee and the *75th Anniversary Campaign*

With Dunwoody's 75th anniversary approaching in 1989, Dunwoody's second capital campaign would be called the *75th Anniversary Campaign*.

President Phillips and the board had prepared Dunwoody for a successful campaign. In September 1984 the president had hired the school's second development director, Dr. C. Ben Wright, who was working closely with the chairman of the Development Committee, C. Charles Jackson, to build a comprehensive fund development program. While recognizing the importance of the Century Club, Wright and Jackson also saw the need for gifts larger than $100. Therefore they created the William and Kate Dunwoody Club for contributions of $1,000 and more and began to solicit gifts at that level. They also understood, as former Board Chair Tom Crosby had in the early 1970s, that the board of trustees had to be leaders in any fundraising campaign.

With the moral support of Crosby, Jackson hosted solicitation meetings for all trustees in late 1984. The result was immediate and positive. Contributions from individual board members to the annual fund drive tripled, from $6,700 in 1983-84 to more than $20,000 in 1984-85.

President Phillips' knowledge of the difference between "fundraising" and "development" was evident by the mid-1980s. Fundraising is the short-term process or activity of asking for money today. Development is a long-term process of "cultivating" a person, foundation, or company for financial support at an appropriate time in the future. President Phillips understood the value of building relationships over time. This development mentality came easily to the friendly and sociable Phillips.

With "cultivation" in mind, President Phillips initiated several signature events and awards. In the '70s he had introduced an annual picnic for the Century Club and an annual luncheon for the 50-Year Club. In 1984 he inaugurated the Alumni Achievement Award for successful Dunwoody alumni and presented the award to twenty-two alumni at the Century Club dinner that summer. In 1985 he honored C. Charles Jackson for his active volunteerism with Dunwoody's first Institutional Advancement Award. In 1986 he encouraged alumni Floyd Schneeberg and Jack Woods, who spent their winters in Arizona, to organize the first Arizona alumni reunion. In 1987 and 1988 he presented the first Partnership Awards to Honeywell and 3M and the first Alumni Entrepreneur Awards to Joel Elftmann and Morrie Wagener, who subsequently became the first Dunwoody alumni elected to the board of trustees.*

Another example of President Phillips' development savvy was his low-key cultivation of what turned out to be the second largest gift in Dunwoody's history. Albert C. Kavli

*For complete lists of recipients of the Alumni Achievement Award, Partnership Award, and Alumni Entrepreneur Award, see the Appendix.

was a real estate investor with property holdings in Minnesota, Florida, and New York. Since he had no children, several Twin Cities nonprofit executives hoped to entice him to include their organizations in his estate plan. When President Phillips invited Kavli to lunch at Dunwoody, the cranky investor rudely rebuffed him: "You don't know me; I don't know you; I eat with people I know." Chastened, President Phillips waited patiently until, one day in 1981, Kavli called to request a tour of Dunwoody. Phillips agreed and Kavli ended up being quite impressed with the school and its practical hands-on education. Afterward he told the president that he wanted to "do something for the school." But he cautioned, "Don't bother me."

> "When I started at Dunwoody in 1939, the Depression was lingering on. I was told that my tuition was paid. General Mills had a machine shop, and I guess they helped some of us. I feel I'm capable of helping now. I want to do my part in relieving some of the financial stress students are facing."
>
> —Harold N. Anderson 1940

Four years later, Kavli called President Phillips again to invite him to his house on Lake of the Isles Boulevard. Terminally ill, Kavli had decided to inform the president of his plans. With Kavli's permission, Phillips brought Dr. Wright, his new development director, with him. Before showing the president and Wright his last will and testament, Kavli recalled that he had once attended a liberal arts college where he had been forced to study "useless" subjects like history and English. Phillips gave a stern look to his development director, who had a Ph.D. in history from the University of Wisconsin, as if to say, "Don't you dare open your mouth!" Unchallenged by the former history student, Kavli then revealed that he was leaving 70 percent of his estate to Dunwoody and 30 percent to the Salvation Army.

Kavli died on December 10, 1985, while Ernhart and Associates was deeply involved in the feasibility study for the *75th Anniversary Campaign*. The timing of Kavli's death was both positive and negative for Dunwoody. The good news was that Dunwoody would receive 70 percent of an estate estimated to be worth $15-20 million. The bad news was that a bequest of this size called into question the necessity of a $6 million capital campaign. Since The Minneapolis Foundation was named as one of the trustees of the Kavli estate, the philanthropic community soon knew of Dunwoody's good fortune.

When Ernhart and Associates reported to the Dunwoody board in April 1986, it acknowledged the impact of the Kavli bequest on the feasibility study. Potential donors understood that Dunwoody still had compelling needs that could not be deferred for ten or more years, the time it might take to sell Kavli's properties and distribute the assets to Dunwoody and the Salvation Army. But $6 million seemed to be more than Dunwoody needed now. Therefore Ernhart and Associates recommended that Dunwoody lower its goal to $4 million and look to early distributions from the Kavli estate to fund some of its projects. On April 29 the board of trustees accepted the Ernhart report and authorized the kickoff of the *75th Anniversary Campaign* on May 1.

Over the next three years, Dunwoody succeeded in raising $4,093,469 for the *75th Anniversary Campaign*, as well as $3.7 million in annual giving, gifts in kind, and bequests, for a total of $7.8 million in philanthropic gifts between 1986 and 1989. The bequests included $682,133 in early distributions from the Kavli estate. Ultimately, over the next ten years, Dunwoody would receive about $8 million from Albert Kavli's bequest, not the $10-$14 million projected at the time of his death in 1985. But it was still the largest gift Dunwoody received during its first century, apart from the original bequests of William and Kate Dunwoody, and a crowning achievement of President Phillips' tenure.

The *75th Anniversary Campaign* enriched Dunwoody through the funding of many of the projects recommended in the Futures report, including equipment purchases for Dunwoody's technical programs, curriculum enhancements, and building improvements. One improvement was the construction of a new west entrance, named the Jackson Entrance, in honor of trustee C. Charles Jackson, a generous donor and chairman of the campaign's executive council. Another project was the erection of a lowered ceiling above Timeclock Hall to link the mezzanine floors in the east and west shop wings, thereby creating access from the mezzanines to the elevator. The installation of a handicapped lift between the ground floor and the Decker Auditorium level also made the building more accessible to persons with physical disabilities.

Since the early 1970s, one of the goals at Dunwoody had been to enroll more women and students of color. Both the *Vital Source* and *75th Anniversary Campaigns* raised funds to provide scholarships and special tutoring for non-traditional students. Beginning with the admission of Pam Spence in 1972, Dunwoody had enrolled more women each year until there were eighty-four women attending classes during the 1988-89 school year—7.7 percent of the student body. During these years the board of trustees also opened its ranks to women. In 1982 Georgia Skogmo Bartlett, whose first husband, Donald Skogmo, had attended Dunwoody, became the first woman elected to the board, and in 1987 Alice Mortenson, a leader of M. A. Mortenson Company, joined her. Both would become active trustees, Bartlett for fifteen years and Mortenson for ten.

Recruitment of students of color proved more difficult. During the 1973-74 school year, only fourteen minority students had enrolled at Dunwoody. To determine how to attract more minority students, the board of trustees elected Oscar Howard—founder of "Meals on Wheels"—as its first African-American trustee in 1977. Then in 1979 President Phillips hired Dunwoody's first minority counselor, Walter Cox, and entrusted him with the task of recruiting and advising minority students. Within two years the number of minority students had increased to seventy-nine, but by 1987 the number had fallen back to forty-eight, less than

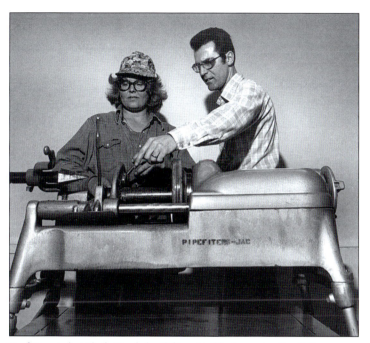

Pipefitting student Sheila Vanderlee (left) assisted by instructor Gerald Ponce, late 1970s-early 1980s

Georgia Bartlett, member of Dunwoody's board of trustees, 1982-1997. During Dunwoody's 75th anniversary celebration in 1989, Georgia showcased her classic Duesenberg (subsequently sold to comedian and television personality Jay Leno).

Counselors Ken Haagenson (standing) and Walter Cox (seated at right) advise two prospective students.

Marketing brochure for Youth Career Awareness Program (YCAP), inaugurated in 1988

4 percent of the student population. This minimal progress was particularly frustrating for President Phillips, whose administration had provided scholarships, pre-enrollment tutoring, and other support services for non-traditional students. The poor graduation rates for students of color were especially disappointing.

Although relatively inexpensive, one of the most important initiatives made possible by the *75th Anniversary Campaign* was the establishment in 1988 of the Youth Career Awareness Program, or YCAP. YCAP was the brainchild of President Phillips and Leon Rankin, a part-time minority counselor. A graduate of Dunwoody's Electrical program, Rankin had taught in Day School and Evening School. Having worked with students of color, Rankin believed that few of these students entered Dunwoody prepared to succeed. YCAP would improve student retention and graduation rates by introducing high school students to the academic requirements of a technical school like Dunwoody. The students would be exposed to the excellent jobs and careers open to Dunwoody graduates, and they would be encouraged to develop good math and communication skills so that they could be successful at Dunwoody. Recruited for YCAP following the ninth grade, YCAPers who remained in the program for the next three years would be eligible for a scholarship to Dunwoody.

Thanks to a start-up grant from the Pillsbury Company Foundation, twenty high school students enrolled in YCAP during the summer of 1988. Over the next 20 years more than 1,000 teenagers would participate in YCAP, and more than 90 percent of them would graduate from high school, with many going on to Dunwoody and other post-secondary institutions. YCAP would become a much heralded program in the Twin Cities, recognized for giving career opportunities to young people who might not have otherwise had them. A glowing success, YCAP was made possible by the *75th Anniversary Campaign.*

The completion of the capital campaign was only one highlight

Variety

Star Tribune   SATURDAY/SEPTEMBER 30/1989

DUNWOODY TURNS 75

Computers and women students evidence of change

By George Monaghan/Staff Writer

They still have a pencil sharpener on the wall in the computer drafting room in the Dunwoody Institute near downtown Minneapolis.

No one ever uses it.

No one even uses wood pencils. They don't have to. They not only don't use pencils and pencil sharpeners, they don't use erasers. Nor do they use T-squares or "French curves" or rulers. You will not find a compass or a caliper or even a slide rule here.

All the old basics of the draftsman's trade, from the "draftsman" down to his tools, are going the way of the pencil sharpener in the computer drafting room.

You can find them around, but you'll have to look. Beginning students who don't know computers still use basic drafting tools at Dunwoody. But where most people find them is in the hallway showcase near the drafting room. A sign behind the glass says: "Tools of years gone by."

Those tools were left in the dust in an electronic revolution that has reshaped the industrial trade school now celebrating its 75th year. It was founded by William Hood Dunwoody, who came to Minneapolis from Pennsylvania in 1871 and rose to prominence and wealth in the milling business.

The school has trained 250,000 students who went on to trades and business around the world. It has, according to its own publicity, become the largest of four private industrial and technical institutes in the nation.

"It's a leader," says Ben Ernst, president of Ranken Technical Institute in St. Louis, one of the other major institutions. "No question about it. They are extremely effective"

Staff Photos by Joey McLeister

Student Darcie Klick worked with instructor Al Jaedike in the computer-aided drafting class at Dunwoody Institute.

Minneapolis Star Tribune "Variety" headline, September 30, 1989

President Warren Phillips (left) and Board Chairman David Bennett (center) with Dunwoody graduate and State Representative Wayne Simoneau (right) celebrate the naming of Dunwoody Boulevard during the school's 75th anniversary in 1989.

of 1989, the 75th anniversary of Dunwoody Institute. The Phillips administration planned a number of activities to celebrate this milestone. Governor Rudy Perpich proclaimed the week of July 17 "Dunwoody Institute Week" in Minnesota. During that week Dunwoody held its thirteenth annual 50-Year Club luncheon, dedicated the library for the late Director John Butler, and hosted a gala party for 800 alumni and friends at Met Center in Bloomington, home of the Minnesota North Stars. The city of Minneapolis also re-named the segment of Wayzata Boulevard between Interstate Highway 394 and Hennepin Avenue "Dunwoody Boulevard." In November Dunwoody sponsored a day-long Technology Conference for educators and business leaders at the new Minneapolis Convention Center, with Edson Spencer, chairman and CEO of Honeywell, as the keynote speaker.

Another milestone was the change in Dunwoody leadership. President Phillips informed the board of trustees in January 1989 of his intention to retire in June 1990. The board soon formed a presidential search committee, chaired by trustee Fosten Boyle, Honeywell's vice president of human resources, to find a successor for Phillips. On September 1, 1989, Dr. M. James Bensen, formerly dean of the School of Industry and Technology at the University of Wisconsin-Stout, became president of Dunwoody. Phillips remained on the staff as vice chairman of the board until his formal retirement, assisting President Bensen with the NATTS reaccreditation process. Upon retirement, Phillips, who had served Dunwoody for thirty-six years, was named president emeritus, sharing that honorary title with his predecessor, Dr. Walsh.

"I learned from Dunwoody to work hard, not give up on a project, have a positive attitude and work together with your team. The instructors gave me the feeling that we were a part of their families and showed great interest in what we did and accomplished in their classes and labs."

—Morris Eisert 1962

CHAPTER VI

The Quality Journey, 1989-2002

For seventy-five years Dunwoody Institute had been known as a national leader in vocational technical education. In 1990 Dunwoody's educational leadership was publicly recognized when the National Center for Research in Vocational Education (NCRVE) at the University of California at Berkeley named Dunwoody as one of the top ten "institutions of excellence" in the United States. One of the indicators of excellence cited by the NCRVE study was an institution's awareness of "the importance of a quality climate—it shows everywhere."

Ever since the days of Dr. Prosser, Dunwoody had demanded quality curriculum, quality instruction, and quality performance by its students and its graduates. The Dunwoody Way was the definition of quality, as the term was understood in 1990 by Dunwoody faculty, staff, and other stakeholders, as well as by NCRVE. However, with the arrival in 1989 of a new president, Dr. M. James Bensen, the word "quality" began to take on a new, more precise meaning at Dunwoody, one that reflected changes taking place in American business and industry, and one that would become integrated into Dunwoody's culture over the next two decades.

Following World War II, American manufacturing had faced virtually no competition from the devastated economies of Europe and Japan. American industry had paid limited attention to the needs or demands of foreign or domestic customers for twenty-five years. By the early 1980s, however, the economic world had changed. The United States steel industry and automobile makers, two critical segments of the economy, were experiencing serious competition from Japan and western Europe. What became known as the "Quality Revolution" began in the United States in 1980 when NBC aired a television special titled "If Japan Can . . . Why Can't We?" which introduced American business leaders to the management philosophy and practices of W. Edwards Deming, who had introduced statistical quality control to Japanese manufacturers and workers during the 1950s. Deming, Joseph M. Duran, and Philip B. Crosby were the management "gurus" of a quality movement that had been adopted first in Japan and then embraced by Ford Motor Company and other automakers in the United States in the 1980s.

One definition of quality was "customer satisfaction and loyalty." A customer was anyone affected by a business' service, product, or process, and the measure of quality was the customer's satisfaction with or loyalty to that service, product, or process. By studying and measuring manufacturing processes, Deming and other quality practitioners believed that they could improve processes and thereby improve quality. "Continuous quality improvement" was a process for ensuring that services, products, and processes would always get better and never fall behind those of their competitors.

As an institution that had just been recognized as one of the ten best vocational schools in the United States, Dunwoody might have been vulnerable to complacency in the 1990s, content with doing business as it had during its first seventy-five years. However, President Bensen was a disciple of the quality revolution who introduced Dunwoody Institute to a new way of thinking about quality. When

Opposite: Civil Technology and Land Surveying students in the 1990s

Industry and Technology at the University of Wisconsin-Stout in Menomonie, as the best prospect "by far" to succeed him as Dunwoody Institute's next chief executive officer. A graduate himself of Stout, Phillips knew that Bensen was a dynamic leader who might be available. After meeting Bensen, Dunwoody Board Chairman David Bennett also became a booster. According to Fosten Boyle, chairman of the Search Committee, Bensen's experience at a four-year career-oriented school like Stout impressed the committee. He was the ideal candidate to lead Dunwoody's transition from two-year degree programs to four-year bachelor's degrees, as envisioned in the 1985 Futures study. Bensen was impressed with the business-oriented board of trustees and the relative lack of bureaucracy at Dunwoody. Dunwoody trustees were visionary and open to new ideas. Their influence was such that they "could open any door in town," he recalled. When offered the Dunwoody job, Bensen readily accepted.

The new president soon dazzled his Dunwoody constituents. Bensen was a compelling public speaker, exciting audiences with his passion for technology and exhilarating optimism about the future. He was a salesman for change, and he was as effective selling his message of change to individuals as he was to large groups with his popular "gee whiz" speech.

Bensen based his philosophy of organizational change on three concepts: mission, vision, and "mystique." Any organization had to live its mission, establish a vision of where it wanted to go, and build mystique about the organization to help it get where it wanted to go. As stated in a 1991 strategic plan developed by President Bensen and his staff, Dunwoody's mission was to "provide leading-edge technological education and service to learners preparing for and practicing in business and industry," and its vision was "to be recognized as a world-class institution providing leadership, development, and educational services in technology." Bensen tried to build the Dunwoody mystique by continuously publicizing everything the institution was doing to

Dr. M. James Bensen, president of Dunwoody Institute, 1989-1994

Bensen left Dunwoody in 1994, his successor as Dunwoody president, E. Frank Starke, brought with him the quality principles he had adopted at Alexandria Technical College. During his seven years at Dunwoody, 1995 to 2002, President Starke took quality to a deeper level of implementation. After Starke retired in 2002, Dunwoody continued on the quality journey, and by the end of the decade Dunwoody had made great progress in transforming itself into a quality-run organization that relied on data and measurement to ensure that it would always be an institution of excellence.

The Bensen "Mystique"

When the board of trustees formed a presidential search committee in 1989, retiring President Warren Phillips recommended Dr. M. James Bensen, dean of the School of

embrace and lead technological change. Later, as he reflected on his five years at Dunwoody, he cited as his major achievement "reigniting the energy of the community in support of our institution." Mystique was the perception that Dunwoody had already achieved "a new tomorrow" even as it was striving to get there. "We created a lot of positive energy about this institution and what it could do," Bensen recalled.

Introducing Dunwoody to quality contributed to the mystique, for there were few educational organizations in the early 1990s that had endorsed the principles of Deming, Duran, or Crosby. Jim Bensen had. While at Stout, he had read Philip Crosby's book *Quality Is Free* and attended an executive leadership seminar for corporate CEOs at Crosby's Quality College. After adopting quality at Stout's School of Industry and Technology, Bensen brought the Crosby principles to Dunwoody. To educate Dunwoody employees about quality and involve them in continuous quality improvement, he formed a "Quality Council" in 1990. One of its improvements was the adoption of a no-smoking policy in Dunwoody buildings. Quality training was soon offered to Dunwoody employees and students, and in the fall of 1993 Dunwoody created a "Center for Quality" to provide training in total quality management for businesses and other organizations.

Placing the customer at the center of any business was central to the quality movement. At Dunwoody the student now became the customer—an original idea in the world of education. Within the automobile industry, Cadillac had developed a poster called "What is a Customer?" which Dunwoody now adapted for education.

What Is a Student?

A student is the most important person in any school.
A student is not dependent on us.
We are dependent on the student.
A student is not an interruption of our work—a student
   is the purpose of it.
A student is an essential part of our job, not an outsider.

A student is not a problem.
A student is a human being with feelings and deserves
   to be treated with respect.
A student is a person who comes to us with needs and
   wants—it is our job to fill them.
A student deserves the most courteous attention we
   can give.
A student is the lifeblood of this and every school.
A student pays our salaries.
Without students, we would have to close our doors.

None of these seem like radical ideas today, but they were new to Dunwoody in the early 1990s. The culture of Charles Prosser and John Butler had believed in "Dunwoody's way or the highway." The school had had an "open door" policy, meaning that all students should have an opportunity to enter the front door to take advantage of the Dunwoody education but that they would be invited to exit the back door if they couldn't make the grade. One sign posted in the Accounting Office, where students paid their fees, read: "Poor planning on your part is not our problem." As the sign revealed, some attitude changes would be necessary in order for Dunwoody students to be treated like customers.

> "Dunwoody has given me values—the value of collaboration and confidence, the value of help and support, and the value of giving back."
>
> Harlan Hallquist 1960

To highlight the focus on students, President Bensen adopted a unique organizational chart for Dunwoody Institute. Instead of placing the board of trustees and president at the top of the organizational pyramid, this chart placed customers at the top and the board and the administrative team at the bottom.*

---

*The retirement of Robert Poupore as vice president and director of educational programs in December 1989 gave President Bensen the opportunity to reorganize the administrative team along more traditional "collegiate" lines. In the past almost all Dunwoody employees had been part of Poupore's administrative division, a continuation of the Prosser/Butler legacy when the director ran the school. In 1990 Bensen distributed employees more equally among three divisions and three vice presidents: administrative services, academic affairs, and institutional advancement.

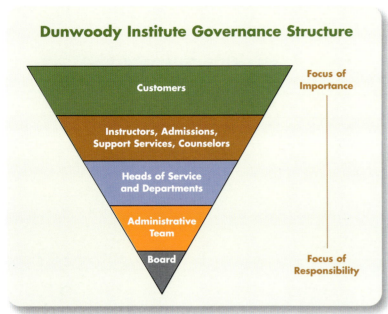

Dunwoody Institute Governance Structure

Customers

Instructors, Admissions, Support Services, Counselors

Heads of Service and Departments

Administrative Team

Board

Focus of Importance

Focus of Responsibility

President Bensen's "upside down" organizational pyramid. Bensen placed customers (i.e., students and employers) at the top of Dunwoody's pyramid.

Who were Dunwoody's customers? Its students and alumni, and businesses, industries, and organizations served by Dunwoody's training programs. This was a new way of looking at priorities within an organization.

Strategic planning—what Bensen called "planning from the future"—was another important element of quality. Although Dunwoody had done long-range planning in the 1960s, 1970s, and 1980s, it had not revisited these plans annually. Continuous quality improvement required planning, implementation, measurements of outcomes, and modifications along the way. Planning became part of such a continuous cycle under the Bensen administration. The president submitted the first five-year strategic plan to the board of trustees in April 1991. The board approved the plan in July and endorsed updated five-year plans in 1992, 1993, and 1994. Some of the objectives in these strategic plans included the implementation of total quality and customer service as modes of operation at Dunwoody, the design and implementation of new program initiatives, the study of an alternative model for delivering a Bachelor

of Science degree in industrial technology, and securing accreditation by the North Central Association of Colleges and Schools (NCA).

Although the core of Dunwoody's Day School programs remained essentially unchanged between 1989 and 1994, the Bensen administration did develop some new programs. It introduced a new A.A.S. degree program in Automated Manufacturing Systems/Packaging Technology in 1993, and in the fall of 1994 it enrolled its first students in HVAC Systems Servicing. In addition, in 1991 it added a second year to its Baking program, now offering an A.A.S. in Baking Production and Management. Adopting the revolutionary technology used by U.S. military forces in the Persian Gulf War in early 1991, Dunwoody's Civil Technology department offered one of Minnesota's first educational seminars in global positioning systems (GPS) in August of that year. GPS was not a new program per se, but it was an example of Dunwoody's long-standing practice of integrating new technologies into existing curricula.

Another program innovation was made possible by the philanthropy of former Dunwoody trustee Harold L. Holden. Founder of Holden Printing Company, Holden had great respect for Dunwoody's practical work-oriented education, yet he wanted Dunwoody students to understand and appreciate the challenges that managers faced in the running of competitive and profitable businesses. Therefore, between 1989 and 1994, he contributed $145,000 to create an endowed fund to support special classes in entrepreneurship and management. Initially these classes were offered to current students through the General Education department, and later courses were added for Dunwoody alumni and other employed workers through the Continuing Education department. The Holden Entrepreneurial Business/Leadership Center was eventually established through an estate gift of $250,000 and the remodeling and naming of a prominent multipurpose room in recognition of Mr. Holden's vision.

Above: Dunwoody's bakery sales counter
Right: Baking student prepares cookies for Valentine's Day.

The development of a four-year degree option for Dunwoody students and graduates was the most important program innovation called for in the strategic plans. Unfortunately accreditation by the National Association of Trade and Technical Schools (NATTS) was "an anchor dragging on us"—as President Bensen recalled, a barrier to offering a bachelor's degree. NATTS was an organization of one- and two-year vocational schools that did not provide the next level of higher education. Dunwoody would need to achieve accreditation by NCA, the regional accrediting body for

President Bensen (right) converses with Harold and Harriet Holden, 1991.

all of the major colleges and universities in the Upper Midwest, in order to offer a four-year degree that was authorized by the State of Minnesota. Therefore the development of a B.S. degree would have to take a back seat to the pursuit of NCA accreditation.

Even as Dunwoody sought and obtained reaccreditation by NATTS in 1990, it began the NCA process. At a board of trustees meeting on April 17, 1990, President Bensen reported on a visit he and former president Warren Phillips had made to Ranken Technical College in St. Louis. A private, endowed, non-profit school very similar to Dunwoody, Ranken had recently received NCA accreditation. Bensen and Phillips were convinced that Dunwoody should follow Ranken's lead, and they requested and received board approval to seek affiliation with NCA. Thus began a long NCA journey. In the fall of 1992 an NCA consultant visited the campus to advise the administration about accreditation. An eighteen-month self-study process followed. A formal "Self-Study" document was submitted to NCA in August 1993, and that fall an NCA evaluation team made its site visit to Dunwoody. The upshot of the evaluation

was a recommendation in December that Dunwoody be granted "initial candidacy" by NCA, with the proviso that the school address several areas of concern. After considering Dunwoody's "plan of action" to address the concerns, NCA officially granted candidacy status to Dunwoody on April 21, 1994.

As the accreditation process progressed, Dunwoody moved forward with a four-year degree program. Since it was not yet fully accredited, its first step was a collaboration with Saint Mary's College of Minnesota to offer a B.S. in Industrial Technology. In January 1994 the two institutions introduced their collaborative program. Thirty-eight semester credits of technical education plus two years of work experience were required for admission. Dunwoody provided or facilitated the technical education while Saint Mary's provided the upper-division courses and officially granted the degree. Students enrolled in classes at Dunwoody and Saint Mary's Minneapolis campus. Dunwoody expanded the collaborative model by introducing a B.S. degree with Bemidji State University and Metropolitan State University in 1995, and with the University of Wisconsin-Stout in 2001.

The Board Summit of 1993

Financial challenges had been a frequent issue during Dunwoody Institute's first seventy-five years of operation. Despite a substantial endowment, Dunwoody had often struggled to meet the need for annual operating revenue. In 1989, for example, the investment accounts of Alliance Capital Management and Investment Advisers had a total market value of $16.3 million, and the Kate Dunwoody Trust at First Bank had a value of $5.1 million. Income draws from these three accounts to support the 1988-89 operating budget amounted to $1.1 million. Nevertheless, at the conclusion of the fiscal year on June 30, 1989, Dunwoody still had an operating deficit of $546,238, which the board of trustees covered with an additional draw from endowed funds. This pattern of financing annual operating deficits by withdrawing extra funds from the endowment—

or using new funds coming to Dunwoody via periodic distributions from the Kavli estate—continued in the early 1990s. Finally, in the summer of 1993 when the annual endowment draw exceeded ten percent, the board's Finance and Executive Committees concluded that the time had come for the board to convene a high-level retreat to consider Dunwoody's long-range financial prospects.

Members of the board of trustees and President Bensen's leadership team met on November 18, 1993, at the corporate headquarters of Honeywell, Inc., hosted by past Board Chairman Fosten Boyle. The goal of the retreat, as stated in the agenda, was "to examine the long-range financial and resource needs of Dunwoody Institute and develop strategies that can be used to design a resource plan to meet these needs." Board Chairman Clifford I. Anderson, president and chairman of the board of Crown Holdings, Inc., opened the Honeywell meeting with a sobering presentation. Using data provided by Dennis Kenison, Dunwoody vice president of administrative services, Anderson graphically illustrated how the school would go out of business in the next ten years if it did not significantly reduce its annual endowment draw and increase other sources of revenue.

"That really seemed to be the bottom," trustee Charles Kiester recalled. "It was a dark, gloomy summit." Vice president of engineering at 3M, Kiester had joined the board three years earlier, and now he asked himself, "Holy cow, what did I get myself into?"

The retreat participants divided into four groups to discuss ways to make Dunwoody's programs more cost-effective and to reduce dependency on the endowment. "Just because we are a nonprofit organization," the chairman told his colleagues, "it doesn't mean that we can't operate some of our functions in a for-profit manner." The conclusions of the discussions were consolidated and refined in a "Business Enterprise Plan" presented at the next full board meeting on January 18, 1994. Some of the recommendations were:

Architectural Drafting and Estimating students. Jennifer Sutherland Larson (right) later became a member of the board of managers of the Dunwoody Alumni Association.

generate more revenue for school operations by charging tuition by credits and initiating laboratory fees;* identify high-cost programs and either discontinue them or price them at a higher level; redirect resources to programs that merit expansion; offer programs during the summer and on weekends; establish continuing education and corporate training as profit centers; and increase funds raised through the annual fund drive, estate gifts, and a new capital campaign.

Trustee Loren Taylor, president of NSP Electric, attended his first board meeting on January 18. He looked around the table and saw "a lot of frightened faces." Like Kiester, he wondered what he was getting into. Notwithstanding the

---

*One of the unanticipated consequences of introducing the A.A.S. degree in 1989 had been an increase in instructional expenses caused by a growing number of students enrolling in general education courses to earn A.A.S. degrees. The number of Dunwoody graduates receiving A.A.S. degrees had increased from 112 (or 38 percent of the graduates) in 1991 to 192 (62 percent) by 1994. Since A.A.S. candidates paid the same tuition as diploma students for more credits of instruction, Dunwoody received no compensating revenues for its increased costs. An immediate tangible outcome of the January 1994 board meeting was a decision to begin charging tuition by the credit hour. Beginning that fall, tuition became $55 per credit for lecture classes and $130 per credit for labs.

board's decision that day to integrate the Business Enterprise Plan into President Bensen's strategic plan, Taylor was skeptical. "It was not clear to me," he recalled, "how we were going to get where we needed to go." Another board member who had doubts about the immediate outcomes of the November "summit" was General Mills Vice President Donald Ryks, who had contributed to the development of the 1985 Futures study. In his opinion, the retreat had been "more of a session of concern than of leadership." He could remember "no strong decisions that led Dunwoody to any new dramatic outcome."

"I attribute my success as a designer to skills that I learned at Dunwoody. While going through the Drafting and Design program, we were taught how to work as a design team. There were many exercises where we had to work as a team to come up with ideas and analyze other ideas to come to a conclusion on a good final product design. I use the same technique today."

—Jeff Kraker 1993

David Crosby, the grandson of founding trustee Franklin Crosby and son of past Chairman Thomas Crosby, credited the summit with greater historic significance. Managing director of Piper Jaffray & Hopwood and vice chairman of the Dunwoody board, Crosby considered the 1993 retreat "seminal." More concerned about the Institute's endowment draw than perhaps any other trustee, he came to see years later that the retreat led to some critical long-term decisions for Dunwoody. Not all of these decisions were made in 1993 or 1994, but the summit paved the way for their future adoption.

There were several seminal outcomes. First, the board of trustees and administration realized that they must reduce the annual endowment draw to sustainable levels. Second, they recognized that a greater percentage of the real costs of educating students must be passed on to students through increased tuition. Third, they agreed that they must address the cost effectiveness of programs and make all programs more "profitable." Fourth, once programs no longer created annual operating deficits, the school could focus on enhanced marketing to increase student enrollments, which could then generate positive rather than negative cash flow. And finally, a decision would soon be made to launch another capital fundraising campaign.

An announcement in March 1994 caught the board of trustees, Dunwoody employees, and other stakeholders completely by surprise. Having been president for less than five years, Jim Bensen shocked everyone by announcing that he was a candidate for the presidency of Bemidji State University. Bensen described himself accurately as "a high-profile guy." He had delivered as many as one hundred public speeches annually since arriving at Dunwoody, and he recalled being nominated for twelve different positions during his last year at Dunwoody. He could not turn his back on Bemidji. He and his wife, Nancy, were alumni of the university, and this was one last opportunity to experience campus life at a university before retirement.

No one at Dunwoody doubted that Bensen would get the Bemidji job, and he did, departing for northern Minnesota in the summer of 1994. Board Chairman Anderson was "dismayed" by the Bensen departure, Chuck Kiester was filled with a "sense of gloom," and Foss Boyle, who had chaired the Search Committee that hired Bensen, wished Bensen could have stayed longer to continue working on the very serious problems facing Dunwoody.

Dunwoody board members credited President Bensen with enhancing the public profile and image of the Institute between 1989 and 1994, but there was a downside to his extensive public speaking and promotion of Dunwoody. The faculty felt neglected by his absences and came to lament the lack of academic leadership internally. The board chairman heard complaints about faculty unrest, and Vice Chairman Crosby believed that improving faculty morale should become a major priority for Dunwoody's next president.

Dr. Bensen's retrospective assessment of his own tenure may

be the most apt: "We set the table for another era." During Bensen's years at Dunwoody, the school initiated a quality movement, a customer service orientation, the pursuit of NCA accreditation, a B.S. degree, and a heightened focus on external relations. As Bensen saw it, Dunwoody's progress after his departure was "spectacular."

A New "Best-in-Class" Vision

For the second time in five years, Fosten Boyle—whose board term was almost over—was asked to chair a presidential search committee. The search would take several months. Upon the recommendation of outgoing President Bensen, the board's Executive Committee hired William Mamel as Dunwoody's interim president. He took the post in July 1994 and remained until the new president arrived seven months later. A former faculty member at the University of Wisconsin-Stout and past director of the south campus of Hennepin Technical College, Mamel had done training and consulting for Dunwoody during the previous year.

Mamel was not a passive caretaker. During his brief tenure he worked with the leadership team to build a stronger foundation for the next president. First, he made a change in leadership in the academic affairs division, a move welcomed by Dunwoody faculty and staff. Second, he consulted leaders in the Twin Cities baking industry to address curriculum and equipment deficiencies in the Baking department. The upshot of this program review was a decision in January 1995 to impose a one-year moratorium on the program, enrolling no new students in the fall and "teaching out" second-year students during the 1995-96 school year. Finally, Mamel developed a budget for the 1995-96 fiscal year that took into account the serious financial concerns of the 1993 board summit. The proposed budget included a tuition increase of 9 percent; it phased out diploma programs (for which Dunwoody could sell fewer credits than A.A.S. programs); and it froze wages for most Dunwoody employees and eliminated an employee bonus program. The budget did not address the persistent problem

of the endowment draw, but it did cut expenses and attempt to raise more revenue through student tuition.

Meanwhile the Search Committee found the perfect candidate to fill the void left by Dr. Bensen's resignation. In 1990 Alexandria Technical College had been the only school in Minnesota other than Dunwoody to be named one of the top ten institutions of excellence by the National Center for Research in Vocational Education. E. Frank Starke, Alexandria's president, had considerable experience dealing with financial challenges and academic issues of concern to faculty—two priorities of the Dunwoody board. Starke was committed to continuous quality improvement, had experience with NCA accreditation (Alexandria had been accredited in the 1980s), and was held in high esteem at his college and throughout his community. It took some months of wooing to persuade Starke to leave Alexandria, but ultimately he was attracted by the prospect of working with Dunwoody's outstanding group of trustees, by the appeal that life in the Twin Cities held for him and his wife, and by his conviction that Dunwoody was "the premier

E. Frank Starke, president of Dunwoody Institute, 1995-2002. President Starke initiated the practice of greeting students on the first day of classes each quarter.

school" in Minnesota. Starke accepted Dunwoody's job offer in November 1994, and he reported for duty as Dunwoody's president on February 13, 1995.

Like Jim Bensen, Frank Starke was a positive, high-energy leader. Whenever someone greeted him with the perfunctory question, "How are you?" he replied, "Great!" Other typical responses were "terrific," "wonderful," "outstanding." He was positive and upbeat himself, and he expected this kind of enthusiasm from Dunwoody faculty, staff, and students. "OK," "not bad," "can't complain," "good" were not acceptable responses, and before long he would infuse the Dunwoody community with this new expectation. Within a few months he would introduce a new slogan, "Definitely Dunwoody!" and begin wearing a "DD" lapel pin and distributing the pins widely to Dunwoody stakeholders.

President Starke attended his first board meeting on April 18. What he heard at that meeting might have dampened the enthusiasm of a less positive person. Donna Stephens, chairperson of the Finance Committee, as well as vice president and treasurer of Deluxe Corporation, informed those present that the endowment draw was nearly 12 percent. Her report showed that Dunwoody had made no progress in reducing the inflated draw on its endowed funds during the past year. Clearly one of the new president's immediate challenges would be to wrestle with this issue.

President Starke understood the challenges, and opportunities, in front of him. At the same board meeting he outlined his vision for the next five years, which he called "Dunwoody 2000." These were some of his forecasts, or goals, for Dunwoody at the turn of the century:

- Dunwoody's endowment and trust funds would total $30 million.

- The school's spending policy would reduce the endowment draw to 7.5 percent.
- Total Quality Management would be integrated into the strategic planning process.
- A customer service orientation would change the focus at Dunwoody from instruction to student *learning*.
- Dunwoody would implement "program health indicators" to ensure program quality.
- Fifty percent of program equipment would be donated, consigned, or funded by a capital campaign.
- Twenty-five percent of operating revenue would be generated by corporate training and continuing education.
- A campus remodeling plan would be in place.
- Dunwoody would be accredited by NCA.

Dunwoody would meet almost all of these expectations.

As president of Alexandria Technical College, Frank Starke had established continuous quality improvement as the college's business model. Since Alexandria was further along the quality journey than Dunwoody, the new president moved immediately to take his new school to the next level. Whereas President Bensen had been influenced by the quality perspective of Philip Crosby, President Starke was more in tune with W. Edwards Deming. Crosby and Deming were of like mind about many things, but they differed on the relative importance of *motivation* and *statistics*. Crosby believed in slogans, motivational speeches, and group meetings to win employee support for quality. Deming, on the other hand, ridiculed slogans and "rah-rah" motivational tools. He relied instead on the regular, systematic collection and analysis of statistical data. An organization could improve quality only by establishing benchmarks, measuring results, and improving business processes, he believed. President Starke did not eschew motivational slogans, speeches, or meetings, but he introduced Dunwoody to a new focus on data collection and process improvement.

President Starke (left) and David P. Crosby, chairman of Dunwoody's board of trustees, 1994-1996

To kick off his quality initiative, Starke convened all faculty and staff in a planning conference in the summer of 1995. This was the beginning of a strategic planning process that involved more employees than previously. At the staff conference, employees reaffirmed Dunwoody's 1991 mission statement but adopted a new vision statement, one that became President Starke's mantra: "To be recognized as a 'best-in-class' leader and innovator in learner-centered workforce development." American automakers and other manufacturers were striving to be best-in-class, and this now became Dunwoody's quality vision as well. The staff also identified four "core values" considered unique to Dunwoody:

- The ability to change
- A curriculum that ensures technical competence as well as life-long learning skills
- Work ethics and attitudes that support quality and maintain excellence
- Being a community of learners

These core values, the best-in-class vision, and new five-year goals and objectives were incorporated into a strategic plan for 1995-2000, published by President Starke later that year. Borrowing from his Alexandria experience, Starke used this and subsequent plans as his annual report to Dunwoody stakeholders.

The key to quality improvement was process improvement. Unfortunately processes did not change overnight. At the conclusion of the 1995 fiscal year, President Starke and the board learned, once again, that Dunwoody's operating expenses had exceeded revenues, notwithstanding the high endowment draw. Therefore, at its annual meeting in October, the board had to approve an additional draw of $157,707. When Dunwoody experienced another shortfall the following year, an embarrassed President Starke assured the new chairman of the Finance Committee, Loren Taylor, that he would not tolerate budget deficits in the future.

The hiring of a financial controller in 1997 was one step in fulfilling this pledge. The accounting department now began to monitor operating and equipment expenditures on a more regular basis rather than sporadically; it measured student credit counts closely to anticipate tuition revenue each quarter; and it conducted training in budgeting for all department managers.

Previously, Taylor recalled, "I was pulling my hair out," frustrated by budgets that were "meaningless." Now the board began to get numbers that were more timely and more reliable. Taylor gave President Starke high marks for demanding that Dunwoody operate "in a much more disciplined way." He praised the president for beginning to run Dunwoody "like a business." By improving internal financial controls and budgeting processes, the Starke administration was able to lower the budgeted endowment draw to 7.5 percent in 1998. By 2001 the draw was 6.8 percent—without the requirement of an extra draw at year's end. A rising stock market helped, too, having increased the value of Dunwoody's invested funds from $25 million in 1996 to $30 million in 2001.

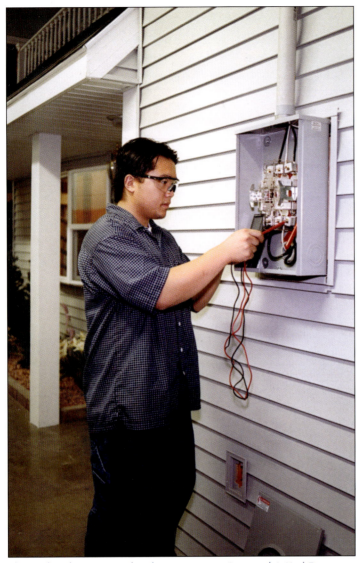

Electrical student acquires hands-on training in Dunwoody's Xcel Energy electrical wiring house.

Another target for process improvement was the systematic review of all of Dunwoody's technical programs. President Starke's concept of "program health indicators" would be refined as an ongoing quality improvement process within a few years. But he did not wait to address program shortcomings. In theory, faculty interaction with industry representatives on each program's technical action committee (TAC) was supposed to ensure that all programs were current and relevant to the needs of employers. President Starke discov-

ered that not all TACs met regularly. Some were filled with old-school thinkers who were either not aware of or not supportive of trends in their own industries. These TAC members were satisfied with the status quo. Starke did not consider himself an authority on technology, but years of experience in vocational/technical education had taught him to recognize a program in need of attention. Baking and Printing were two such programs.

The president's process for evaluating program health was to ask leaders in industry about the program, listen carefully to what they said, determine what resources would be necessary to upgrade the program, and then implement appropriate changes. In the case of Baking, interim president Mamel had begun the process for Starke. In effect, both the one-year diploma program and the A.A.S. program were closed during the 1995-96 school year. President Starke needed to decide whether to resurrect Baking in any form. He and his leadership team continued Mamel's process of consulting with leaders in the baking industry to determine their training needs. They learned that there was no longer a great need for one-year or two-year training programs for entry-level bakers but rather a desire for continuing education for persons already employed in the industry. Two organizations—the Bread Bakers Guild of America and the Retailers' Bakery Association—were very interested in becoming partners with Dunwoody in a new venture. By the summer of 1996, Dunwoody had developed a formal partnership with these organizations and received financial contributions from the baking industry to remodel its baking department into a new training facility.

The new National Baking Center opened at Dunwoody in the fall of 1996. It held its first bread baking seminar on November 17-21, and over the next two years it trained over 1,000 bakers and other interested students from more than thirty-four states and Canada. The Baking Center generated a lot of excitement about Dunwoody in the late 1990s. Board Chairman Robert W. Carlson Jr. saw the

Hands-on learning in Dunwoody's Manufacturing programs

Baking Center as a catalyst in Dunwoody's journey to become best-in-class. This feeling was reinforced when a U.S. baking team, trained at Dunwoody, took first place in the World Cup of Baking in France in February 1999. This was an example of one Dunwoody program that was dramatically changed by President Starke's quality improvement process.

Like Baking, Printing was one of Dunwoody's oldest programs, and it was also similar in that its curriculum and equipment had fallen behind industry standards. Since printing was one of Minnesota's largest industries,

Dunwoody Printing students

provided continuing education for employees in the trade. Dunwoody received contributions from the industry to renovate its Printing department, and PIM facilitated the donation of close to $3 million in equipment donations to the new Printing Center.

Turning problems into opportunities is a characteristic of any organization aspiring to be best-in-class. Much as President Starke had inherited the Baking and Printing challenges, he also had to address institutional concerns identified by NCA when it granted initial candidacy to Dunwoody in 1994. Although the NCA evaluation team had identified seven areas of concern, the major one was faculty credentials. NCA required that two-thirds of the faculty of an accredited school hold an academic degree *one level above* the degrees being awarded by that institution. Since Dunwoody awarded associate degrees, two-thirds of its faculty needed to have a bachelor's degree. This requirement posed a problem for Dunwoody, where most of the instructors had been hired without degrees directly from their trades or industries. Since the formative days of Dr. Prosser, a fundamental tenet of Dunwoody Institute had been the hiring of teachers directly out of industry. To achieve NCA accreditation, Dunwoody would now have to find a balance between hands-on experience in a trade and the necessity for these skilled practitioners to hold a bachelor's degree.

President Starke paid a personal visit to Kelvin Johnson, president of the Printing Industry of Minnesota (PIM), a trade association for the state's printing companies, to see whether PIM would be willing to help Dunwoody upgrade the program. Johnson was looking for a post-secondary technical school that could become a training site for PIM's member companies. The timing was right for a new partnership, and in 1998 Dunwoody and PIM established the Printing and Graphic Arts Advanced Technical Education Center at Dunwoody. Dunwoody provided instruction in an improved Day School program for entry-level students, while PIM

Dr. Bensen, Dunwoody's former president and current president of Bemidji State University, helped find a solution. In 1995 Dunwoody developed a collaborative program with Bemidji to provide a B.S. degree in Industrial Technology for Dunwoody faculty. Bemidji provided the technical courses for the faculty while Metropolitan State University provided the required liberal arts courses. That fall, thirty-four Dunwoody faculty enrolled in the Bemidji "cohort" program, and another ten enrolled in bachelor's courses at other institutions. Dunwoody's goal was for two-thirds of its full-time teachers to hold a four-year degree by the fall of 1998.

Minnesota Governor Arne Carlson opens Dunwoody's Printing and Graphic Arts Advanced Technical Education Center in 1998.

1998, NCA notified Dunwoody that the commission had granted full accreditation. Soon after receiving this good news, Dunwoody informed the Accrediting Commission of Career Schools and Colleges of Technology (ACCSCT), the new name for NATTS, that Dunwoody was dropping ACCSCT accreditation. After an eight-year journey, Dunwoody was now an NCA institution, two years ahead of Starke's vision for "Dunwoody 2000."

Living the Promise, Fulfilling the Dream

The necessity of a major fundraising campaign was one imperative emerging from the board summit of 1993. Even as Frank Starke was being interviewed for the Dunwoody job, he understood that a capital campaign was a board priority. Accordingly, during the first year of Starke's presidency, Dunwoody hired a fundraising consultant, completed a campaign feasibility study, and enlisted volunteer leadership for a five-year $15 million campaign, which began on July 1, 1996.

Upon the recommendation of its consultant Mark Davy, principal of Mark Davy and Associates, this comprehensive campaign would count all contributions received by Dunwoody between 1996 and 2001: annual fund gifts, equipment donations, estate gifts, and one-time capital and program gifts targeted exclusively for the campaign. If the *75th Anniversary Campaign* of the 1980s had been conducted as a comprehensive campaign, Dunwoody could have boasted of raising $8 million instead of $4 million. A $15 million campaign would elevate Dunwoody Institute in the ranks of Twin Cities philanthropic organizations and possibly motivate major corporations and foundations to increase the size of their contributions proportionately. To highlight the connections between Dunwoody's past, present, and future, Davy proposed *Living the Promise, Fulfilling the Dream* as the name for the campaign. William and Kate Dunwoody made a *promise* to the youth of Minnesota in 1914, a promise which Dunwoody Institute had been *living* ever since. The *dream* for gainful employment and a rewarding life for Dunwoody

To drive the accreditation effort, President Starke hired a new academic leader for Dunwoody in August 1995. Bonnie Hugeback, formerly president of Brown College, was appointed dean of learning, a title reflecting Starke's new focus on student learning rather than the act of teaching. Hugeback was a relentless worker who pushed the faculty and Dunwoody's NCA self-study team to address all of NCA's concerns, not only the issue of faculty credentials but also concerns about Dunwoody's library resources and the integration of general education into the school's technical curriculum. Dunwoody submitted its second "Self-Study" to NCA in March 1996, entertained a second site visit in May, submitted a third "Self-Study" in 1997, and received a third site visit in April 1998. Finally, in August

Dunwoody's technology exhibit at the Minnesota State Fair

students was one that each generation had an obligation to *fulfill*. Contributors to the campaign would be showing their support for a compelling promise and a lofty dream.

A dynamic group of board members led the campaign. Board Chairman David Crosby and Dunwoody alumnus Joel Elftmann, chairman and CEO of FSI International, became co-chairs. They were joined on the Campaign Steering Committee by Robert W. Carlson Jr., chairman of Quadion Corporation, who succeeded Crosby as board chairman; Richard "Pinky" McNamara, former University of Minnesota football star and CEO of Activar, Inc., a holding company for nearly twenty Minnesota companies; and Charles Kiester, senior vice president at 3M, who followed Carlson

as board chairman. The Steering Committee was supported by President Starke, Vice President of Institutional Advancement C. Ben Wright, campaign consultant Davy, and Campaign Director Steve Klingaman. Almost every month for five years, the group met to oversee the campaign, and much more. The committee—which included every board chairman and vice chairman who served during this time—functioned like a de facto executive committee of the board of trustees, dealing with issues not limited to fundraising.

The Steering Committee embodied the characteristics of a new kind of board that had evolved since the 1980s. Both David Crosby and Chuck Kiester noticed these changes in the board's personality. The board of his father had been "an old man's club of Minneapolis' downtown establishment," Crosby recalled. Entrepreneurs Joel Elftmann, Robert Carlson, Pinky McNamara, and others brought an impatience with the status quo to the board. They felt an urgency to make changes and make them quickly. 3M executive Kiester welcomed the move from a staid conservative board to "a totally engaged, action-oriented board." Indeed, as distressed as he had been by the financial summit of 1993 and the unexpected resignation of President Bensen in 1994, Kiester had confidence in the vitality and dedication of this new board of trustees to address and resolve any problems at Dunwoody. The can-do attitude led the Campaign Steering Committee, with the full support of the rest of the board, to support energetically President Starke's push to make Dunwoody best-in-class.

Trustee Bob Carlson epitomized this new energy more than anyone. President Starke thought of him as "the spirit of the board." Fellow trustee Cornell Moore, a member of the board since 1982, described Carlson as "a spark plug" who led by example. As chairman of the board's Development Committee, Carlson initiated a tradition of 100 percent participation by board members in all fundraising drives, a tradition adopted by the board of managers of the Dunwoody Alumni Association and continued year after year. As chairman of the Marketing Committee, he persuaded the administration to give students and guests preferred parking in the school's parking lot, install a "welcome" sign to greet visitors, and erect a large illuminated "Dunwoody" sign on the western façade of Dunwoody's main building. Once he became chairman of the board in October 1996, Carlson made a combined personal-company pledge of $500,000 in support of Living the Promise. He promoted camaraderie and teamwork among Dunwoody employees and trustees by hosting social events for these key stakeholders. President Starke was so grateful for Carlson's leadership and support that he awarded him Dunwoody's first and only Honorary Degree of Distinction in 1999.

As the board's primary champion of quality, Carlson continuously prodded and cajoled Dunwoody to do better. His drive paid high dividends for the Living the Promise Campaign. When Dunwoody reached the $10.8 million mark in the campaign in the first two years, he urged the board to increase the goal from $15 million to $20 million. When Dunwoody exceeded the new goal in 2000, he challenged the school to increase the goal again. Ultimately Dunwoody raised $25.1 million over five years, an unprecedented fundraising achievement for Dunwoody that propelled the school into the upper ranks of Minnesota's charitable organizations. Carlson was not singularly responsible for Dunwoody's success, but he was the most persistent spokesman for the principle that Dunwoody should always aim higher if it expected to be best-in-class.

In addition to Carlson, major contributors to Living the Promise included General Mills Foundation, Bush Foundation, 3M Foundation, and Honeywell, Inc. The list also included estate gifts from Twin Cities automotive dealer Rudy Luther and Dunwoody alumni Eugene Hunstad (Electrical, 1936), Roy Olson (Carpentry, 1926), and Richard Pinska (Pipefitting, 1929). One hundred percent of the board of trustees and

Living the Promise Campaign leaders celebrate the successful conclusion of the fund drive, May 2001. Left to right: Campaign Director Steve Klingaman; Campaign Steering Committee members Robert W. Carlson Jr. and Richard "Pinky" McNamara; consultant Mark Davy.

Robert Carlson (right) presents ceremonial *Living the Promise Campaign* contribution to Campaign Co-Chairman Joel Elftmann, May 2001.

east corner of Dunwoody's east shop wing was another major campus improvement. Completed in 2000, this new building was funded by the Minneapolis Plumbers Joint Journeyman and Apprentice Training Committee and Local 15 Union members. The building was owned by Dunwoody but leased long-term by the plumbers for their apprenticeship training program.

Much as the board of trustees displayed new energy in the 1990s, so too did Dunwoody alumni. To encourage greater participation in alumni activities, the board of managers of the Dunwoody Development Fund had temporarily adopted the name "Alumni and Friends of Dunwoody." In 1997 these alumni volunteers reorganized as a bona fide alumni association. Led by former board of managers President Gary Schulz (Electronics, 1965), the new "Dunwoody Alumni Association" was now open to any alumnus or alumna who made an annual contribution to Dunwoody Institute. The board of managers created standing committees to assist the Institute with fundraising, marketing, and education. In October 1998 it kicked off its support for the *Living the Promise Campaign*, announcing 100 percent participation three months later. Concurrently Dunwoody published the first-ever alumni directory, listing over 16,000 alumni.

alumni board of managers supported the campaign, as did 100 percent of Dunwoody faculty and staff, inspired by a dollar-for-dollar challenge grant from trustee Pinky McNamara.

Funds raised through the campaign supported over fifty projects. The new National Baking Center and Printing and Graphic Arts Center were the two most visible projects. Other changes were the development of new programs in Electrical Construction Design and Management, Computer Networking Systems, and Home Appliance Service Repair; the adoption of laptop computers in all areas of study; and the introduction of a new student support program called "Gateway," designed to improve student success and retention among non-traditional students. Other noteworthy campus improvements were the opening of the Holden Center, construction of an Xcel Energy wiring house in the Electrical department, renovation of the student cafeteria (subsequently named for its benefactor, Pinky McNamara), upgrade of the exterior façade of the Warren Building, and installation of a state-of-the-art packaging line for the Automated Manufacturing program.*

The Plumbing Technology Learning Center at the north-

The Steering Committee for *Living the Promise* often focused on more than fundraising. When problems arose that affected Dunwoody in other areas, members of the committee offered advice and counsel to President Starke. For example, in the late 1990s two major issues emerged that involved campaign success stories: the National Baking Center and the Printing and Graphic Arts Center. What had begun as innovative efforts to revitalize two struggling programs turned into conflicts between Dunwoody and the

*In 1997 the Machine Tool Technology, Engineering Design, and Automated Systems/Packaging programs were consolidated into one Manufacturing Learning Center, and the following year the center was named the Walsh Manufacturing Center in recognition of President Emeritus John Walsh and his wife, Marie, for their long service and philanthropy.

Above: Dunwoody's new Plumbing Technology Learning Center. *Right*: Plumbing apprentices receive hands-on training in the Plumbing Center.

respective trade associations that were ultimately resolved by ending both partnerships.

Problems with the Baking Center appeared first. After the center's first two years of operation, Dunwoody's leadership team and the board's Finance Committee became concerned about the center's declining enrollment and high expenses, especially the premium salaries being paid to the faculty. Neither the Bread Bakers Guild nor the Retailers' Bakery

Student in Automated Systems Packaging technology lab

Association were troubled about Dunwoody's financial losses. Instead they blamed Dunwoody for inadequate marketing and a lack of commitment to the industry. Following two years of negotiations, during which members of the Campaign Steering Committee attempted to repair a deteriorating relationship, the National Baking Center closed in the summer of 2001—thus ending one of Dunwoody's oldest programs.

The Printing Center encountered similar problems. Again a focused, even single-minded, industry trade association blamed Dunwoody when the partnership did not work out as expected. The enthusiastic launch of 1998 did not lead to significant growth in Dunwoody's Day School enrollment. And a previous source of revenue for Evening School had been lost when continuing education training was turned over to PIM. As the alliance with PIM became a financial drain on Dunwoody, relationships between the leadership of PIM and Dunwoody deteriorated. Again the Campaign Steering Committee tried to salvage the situation, but the result was the same. In the spring of 2002 Dunwoody notified PIM that it was terminating their alliance.

The Baking and Printing episodes taught David Crosby and other members of the Steering Committee the necessity for the board of trustees to pay closer attention to the financial health of its various programs. It also taught them that trade associations did not always know what was best when it came to training. Specialty baking for persons already employed in the trade had a finite market; it was not in Dunwoody's best interest to serve that limited need. PIM represented printing companies involved in offset printing, which was in decline; it was not in Dunwoody's interest to ignore future directions in printing, incurring financial losses in the process. Meeting the needs of business and industry was a more complicated challenge than most board members had realized. In the future they would pay more attention to the financial viability of Dunwoody's programs and marketplace demand for them.

A New Roadmap for the Future

Loren Taylor, chairman of the board's Finance Committee, and members of the Campaign Steering Committee were disappointed by the dealings with the two trade associations. If there had been a formal process for evaluating new program opportunities, the outcome might have been different. The promise of cash and equipment donations at the onset of the *Living the Promise Campaign* had been too enticing. Entrepreneurial initiatives were desirable, but they needed to be assessed in the context of a long-range plan. Although President Starke and his staff had developed five-year strategic plans, the board of trustees did not feel much ownership of them.

In 2000 Taylor introduced the board and President Starke to strategic planning consultant John Johnson and his company, Changemaking Systems. Over the next two years Johnson led the board, the Starke administration, Dunwoody alumni, and other stakeholders through a comprehensive visioning process. Trustees valued this process, seeing it as the first time since the 1993 summit that they were engaged in meaningful strategic planning. The strategic vision and plan that were approved by the board in January 2002 would become Dunwoody's roadmap for the next six years.

The context for the visioning was a five-year trend of enrollment growth, both in Day School and in Continuing Education, and outstanding graduate placement. In 2000, for example, Dunwoody had a placement rate of 95 percent and 9.9 employer requests for every Dunwoody graduate—the kind of record that inspired trustee Robert Carlson to promote "guaranteed jobs" at Dunwoody. At this time Dunwoody had fifteen associate degree programs and one diploma program. The largest programs were Electrical Construction and Maintenance (311 full-time students), Automotive Service Technology (151), Architectural Drafting and Estimating (146), Computer Networking (131), and HVAC Servicing Systems (72). With the addition of the new Electrical Design program with its forty-six students, the Electrical department faced an exciting opportunity to accommodate even more students if it could expand its classroom facilities, probably at the expense of a department that was not growing.

"Education in general has really helped to shape my life and career. We learned self-confidence and self-discipline as much as anything at Dunwoody. Instructors were always pushing us to learn new things, even if sometimes difficult, and once you learned them you left thinking, 'hey, if I can do this, I can do anything!'"

—Ray Newkirk 1965

The development of a formal system of program health indicators—one that went beyond President Starke's previous informal system—was the key to determining which programs could expand and which ones should shrink or be dropped. Gary Petersen, chairman of the Finance Committee at the time of the 1993 summit, was one of the trustees most engaged in John Johnson's visioning process. Petersen worked closely with Starke's vice president of academic affairs, Richard Pooley, who had replaced Dean of Learning Bonnie Hugeback as Dunwoody's chief academic officer. Together Petersen and Pooley developed a system and a process to evaluate the pluses and minuses of all of Dunwoody's technical programs. President Starke gave an interim report on their work at the board of trustees meeting in July 2001. All of Dunwoody's programs were now given one of these four "grades": strong and expandable; strong and maintainable; acceptable but needs attention; unacceptable and needs attention. Electrical Construction was strong and expandable; therefore, one of the ten visioning "design teams" was looking into how the program might grow. Since Civil Technology was unacceptable, it was being closed.* Since Electronics and Automotive Collision were acceptable but in need of attention, they were both undergoing redesign. This new quality process would be refined and heavily relied upon over the next few years.

Another design team had been addressing the issues of marketing and sales to determine how Dunwoody's full-time enrollment might grow from 1,300 students to 1,500 over the next three years. One strategy under consideration was changing the school's name to reflect the changing character of Dunwoody's curriculum and student body. Since more and more students who enrolled at Dunwoody had previously attended other colleges or had college degrees, and since a growing number of graduates were continuing their education after Dunwoody to earn bachelor's degrees, the institution was functioning more like a college than a traditional trade school. Working with the marketing design team, the board's Marketing Committee and marketing staff polled Dunwoody alumni to see how they felt about a possible name change. The consensus was that any name would be acceptable as long as the word "Dunwoody" was retained. Therefore, at the same board meeting where the program health indicators were unveiled, the Marketing Committee recommended that the school change its name from Dunwoody Industrial Institute to Dunwoody College of Technology. The board approved this name change but deferred its implementation until 2002, when the school would mount a full-blown branding campaign to introduce the world to Dunwoody College of Technology.

*Even though Civil Technology & Land Surveying could not be sustained as a full-time Day School program, it did survive as a viable three-quarter Land Surveying Educational Cooperative program.

The strategic plan adopted in January 2002 embodied both the optimistic can-do attitude of the 1990s and a conservative commitment to keep Dunwoody unchanged in its mission and organizational scope. The mission was "to provide leading-edge technological education and service to a diverse population of learners preparing for and practicing in business and industry." Dunwoody would remain primarily an associate degree technical college, providing hands-on, applied learning for a regional marketplace, and its principal customers would continue to be students and industry. The college's "driving force" would be *product leadership*. This meant that Dunwoody's product, i.e., technical education, must be best-in-class. "Our educational value must far exceed our tuition pricing," the plan stated.

The plan set four aggressive goals for the next five years:

1. Achieve best-in-class performance by improving quality evaluations each year and by meeting NCA's requirements for reaccreditation by 2005.
2. Expand academic programs to achieve student enrollment in degree programs of 1,500 by 2005-06 and 1,800 by 2007-08.
3. Expand custom training enrollment and revenues by 20 percent annually.
4. Thrive financially by reducing the annual endowment draw to 5 percent and raising at least $4 million annually in charitable contributions until the launching of the next capital campaign.

To achieve these goals, all of the design teams recommended their own strategies and action steps. Some of these included:

- Design a process for the development of new programs, as well as the evaluation of current programs
- Establish Learning and Student Services committees on the board of trustees
- Expand the Electrical Construction program and introduce a new program in "low voltage design"

- Hire a director of sales and marketing
- Address student concerns about technology, the parking lot, and campus life
- Increase diversity within the student body, on the faculty, and on the board of trustees
- Develop a space master plan to accommodate anticipated enrollment growth
- Continue to implement quality initiatives
- Create a financial forecasting model and five-year financial plan

For the strategic plan, the Finance design team prepared a detailed summary of Dunwoody's financial plan for fiscal year 2002 through fiscal year 2007, which included projections for earned revenues, enrollment growth, tuition pricing, operating margins, support area expenses, capital needs, and sources of funding.

Strategic and financial planning had reached a new level at Dunwoody—a long way from the dark days of the 1993 summit.

Dunwoody hosts the African-American UniverSoul Circus in June 2000.

CHAPTER VII

Highs and Lows In a Changing Economy, 2002-2012

As visioning gained momentum in 2001, Board Chairman Joel Elftmann and President Starke realized that leadership succession should be part of the process. Since President Starke might not be available to implement the entire new strategic plan over its five-year time frame (he would turn sixty-five in 2002), a decision was made to set in motion a search for his successor. To lead the search, Elftmann appointed Gary Petersen, who was more active in the strategic visioning than any other trustee, as chairman of the Presidential Search Committee. After conducting a national search, the committee recommended to the board in November 2001 that it elect Dr. C. Ben Wright, the school's vice president of institutional advancement, as Starke's successor. The board unanimously approved this recommendation, and on January 1, 2002, Wright became president-elect, assuming office as president on July 1.

Wright had served three presidents and one interim president during his seventeen years at Dunwoody. Although Wright was recognized primarily for his success as a fundraising executive, President Starke had given him an advantage in the presidential search by assigning him a principal role in staffing the board's visioning effort. According to Gary Petersen, the new strategic plan was a key factor in the search. The board had invested time and energy in developing the plan and did not want to retain a new president who would slow down or undo this progress.

Wright was "the right person at the right time," Petersen recalled. "He wowed the search committee." Emerging from his behind-the-scenes role as a vice president, Wright brought his passion for Dunwoody to the formal interview. After his presentation, Wright's appointment was a "slam dunk," Petersen said.

From Good to Great

The transition from President Starke to President Wright gave Board Chairman Joel Elftmann a great deal of pride and satisfaction. It was the best leadership transition he had ever witnessed. Having worked together for seven years, the president and president-elect respected each other and shared a commitment to Dunwoody and its new strategic plan. From the chairman's perspective, the transition was "so seamless and smooth that Dunwoody never missed a beat—it actually gained speed."

Dr. C. Ben Wright, president of Dunwoody College of Technology, 2002-2009

Opposite: Instructor Lee Frisvold with Automotive student

When Starke became president emeritus in July 2002, President Wright asked him to continue working part-time to help the college with fundraising and alumni relations. Starke accepted this invitation and served Dunwoody in this part-time role for the next five years. As he was turning over the presidency to Dr. Wright, he made a personal gift to him. The gift was a new book destined to rise on the best-seller charts: *Good to Great: Why Some Companies Make the Leap . . . and Others Don't* by Jim Collins, coauthor of *Built to Last*, a previous best seller. In his typical upbeat manner, Starke wrote on the inside of the front cover: "Ben, Take us *there*! My best, Frank Starke."

Where was the new president supposed to take Dunwoody? From good to great. This was an excellent directive for a college dedicated to continuous quality improvement. Since quality is a journey without an end, to become great was a high ambition and a destination to which Dunwoody could aspire. Looking for a theme and slogan to kick off his administration, Wright had found a perfect one in Collins' book *Good to Great*.

Wright attended his first board meeting as president on July 16, 2002. He introduced the board to the *Good to Great* theme, and he also presented a detailed progress report on the strategic plan. The president considered the strategic plan his personal job description, and he intended to hold himself and the board accountable for its implementation. This would not be a plan that gathered dust on a shelf. Rather it would be a plan that for the next seven years continued to engage the board of trustees, Wright's leadership team, and employees at all levels of the college. Never before in the history of the school was strategic planning so fully integrated into the day-to-day work of the institution.

Beginning with the broad framework provided by the strategic plan's five-year goals, Wright's leadership team developed a "strategic operating plan" for 2002-2003, which included specific measurable objectives for fourteen separate departments, with each member of the team accountable for at least one set of objectives. Eventually members of the leadership team involved all managers and department chairs in developing annual operating plans and in being responsible for their implementation. These managers, in turn, involved faculty and staff in the planning. All employees incorporated personal goals related to the strategic plan into their professional development plans and annual performance reviews.

President Wright kept the board of trustees active in the planning process by providing updates on the plan at every board meeting and by adhering to an annual strategic planning cycle calendar. From the board's standpoint, the most important phase of the cycle was its approval at January board meetings of Dunwoody's five-year goals and objectives. Usually the board simply reaffirmed the strategic goals, but occasionally it made important revisions to them. For example, in 2004 the board demonstrated its commitment to increasing diversity in the student body, on the faculty, and on the board by adopting a strategic goal for diversity: "to create and sustain a college environment that encourages and nurtures diversity."* Although the college was making incremental progress in attracting female students and students of color to Dunwoody, the board elevated this goal to an even higher priority in 2005 when it challenged the Wright administration to increase the percentage of students of color from 18 percent to 30 percent and female students from 8 percent to 20 percent over the next five years. These goals became part of the 2005-2006 strategic operating plan, and they had the effect of forcing the administration to become more aggressive in its pursuit of diversity initiatives.

*Even as the strategic plan added a diversity goal, it dropped the goal for Custom Training. Despite the high expectations of the Custom Training design team in 2001-2002, neither Custom Training nor Continuing Education generated the kind of growth or revenues envisioned in the original plan. Their deletion from the strategic goals was an acknowledgement that both the board and the administration had become less optimistic about their financial potential.

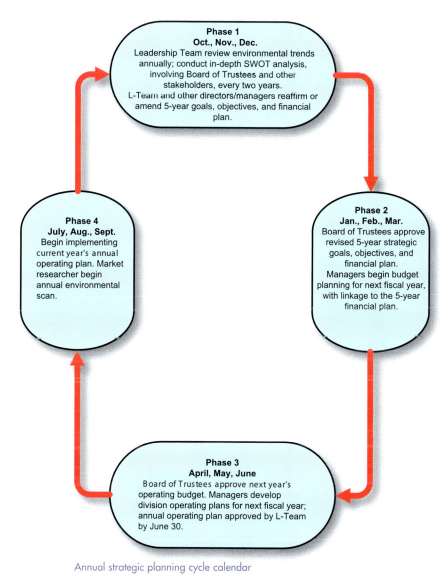

Phase 1
Oct., Nov., Dec.
Leadership Team review environmental trends annually; conduct in-depth SWOT analysis, involving Board of Trustees and other stakeholders, every two years.
L-Team and other directors/managers reaffirm or amend 5-year goals, objectives, and financial plan.

Phase 4
July, Aug., Sept.
Begin implementing current year's annual operating plan. Market researcher begin annual environmental scan.

Phase 2
Jan., Feb., Mar.
Board of Trustees approve revised 5-year strategic goals, objectives, and financial plan.
Managers begin budget planning for next fiscal year, with linkage to the 5-year financial plan.

Phase 3
April, May, June
Board of Trustees approve next year's operating budget. Managers develop division operating plans for next fiscal year; annual operating plan approved by L-Team by June 30.

Annual strategic planning cycle calendar

Since the strategic plan was a living document, it was modified in other ways as well. In 2006 the board of trustees and administration changed Dunwoody's core values and its driving force. In place of the four values adopted in 1995, they embraced these six values:

- We value practical, applied learning.
- We believe in instilling a strong work ethic.
- We are committed to providing our students with high-quality technical education that results in an immediate job and a fulfilling career.
- We are committed to continuous quality improvement.
- We value a diverse faculty, support staff, and student body and their unique contributions to an inclusive Dunwoody community.
- We value high performance within an environment of trust, respect, teamwork, and personal accountability.

And in place of product leadership as the driving force, they adopted "Graduates Who Are Worth More," a phrase originally suggested by Vice President Richard Pooley.

The new driving force emerged from extensive discussions within the leadership team about the "hedgehog concept," one of the characteristics of great organizations identified in Jim Collins' *Good to Great*. Collins had used the image of a simple yet determined animal, the hedgehog, to emphasize the importance of knowing what one can be great at and doggedly pursuing that goal with passion and consistency. According to Collins, a good-to-great organization had a clearly defined hedgehog concept that drove all of its planning and decision making. As the leadership team considered what made Dunwoody great and what should drive it, the answer became simple: the students who benefitted from a Dunwoody education. When they graduated, their value should be greater than it was before coming to Dunwoody—greater to themselves, to their employers, and to the community at large. The board of trustees readily agreed that Graduates Who Are Worth More had been Dunwoody's driving force for ninety-two years and should continue to be the driving force well into its second century.

Two years later, in January 2008, the board also made changes in Dunwoody's vision and mission statements. The change in vision was proposed by Andrea Newman, the first female chair of the board of trustees. She had no objection to the best-in-class vision adopted in 1995, but what really impressed her (and others) was the eloquent language of William Hood

Dunwoody graduates celebrate by tossing their caps in the air. Caps and gowns were adopted, upon student request, after Dunwoody became a college in 2002.

Dunwoody's last will and testament. In her opinion, the founder's vision to establish a school that would prepare young people "for the better performance of life's duties" and endure "for all time" was a timeless and inspirational vision. The rest of the board and the leadership team agreed. Therefore a new vision was adopted: "To provide *for all time* a place where people of diverse backgrounds receive learning opportunities that prepare them *for the better performance of life's duties*." At the same time, the strategic plan also borrowed some of the wording from the new core values to craft a new mission statement: "To provide career-focused, applied education leading to immediate jobs and successful careers in business and industry."

Continuous quality improvement was now integrated into Dunwoody's core values and the strategic plan. A focus on metrics and measurable outcomes had begun during the Starke years and was now even more prevalent. The annual operating plans tracked results in multiple areas, and Wright's leadership team established "leadership imperatives" to hold itself accountable for these results. "Key performance indicators," or KPIs, were developed as an essential ingredient of measurement and accountability. Displayed in a quality "dashboard," the KPIs were reviewed by the leadership team every week at its team meetings. In January 2005 and again in 2007, President Wright demonstrated the dashboard to the board of trustees at its quarterly meetings. The board was very impressed to see the KPIs for the operating budget, fundraising, enrollment, diversity, graduate placement, student retention, student satisfaction, and program health. It was clear that Dunwoody had become a quality-driven organization.

Embracing quality turned out to be a real asset for Dunwoody. When Dunwoody received initial NCA accreditation in 1998, it was informed that it would have to go through the reaccreditation process in 2003. However, before that five-year period elapsed, NCA developed a pilot program for colleges like Dunwoody that had adopted continuous quality improvement as their way of doing business. In 2001 NCA launched the Academic Quality Improvement Project (AQIP) as an alternative to its usual method of reaccreditation. AQIP combined NCA's traditional academic criteria with new educational criteria created by the Baldrige National Quality Program. The Malcolm Baldrige National Quality Award program had been established in the 1980s by the U.S. Department of Commerce and the National Institute of Standards and Technology to recognize and promote quality achievements in American business, and the program had recently been expanded to health care and education. NCA converted Baldrige's seven education criteria for performance excellence into nine AQIP criteria, and these were the criteria on which forty pilot schools would be evaluated.

The AQIP process gave Dunwoody the opportunity to use its quality journey as its path to reaccreditation. Quality and accreditation would now be linked at Dunwoody. The three leaders who drove these two processes were Director of Quality Mike White, Vice President Richard Pooley, and Pooley's successor as vice president of academic affairs, Dr. Richard Wagner. On May 8, 2001, Vice President Pooley submitted three "goals commitment declarations" to AQIP. These became what AQIP called Dunwoody's "vital few" goals. Dunwoody's ongoing progress in meeting these goals would now become the alternative to a 2003 self-study and NCA site visit.

Each of Dunwoody's "vital few" addressed one of AQIP's nine educational criteria. Assessment of Student Learning related to the criterion "Helping Students Learn"; Evaluation of Program Heath related to "Measuring Effectiveness"; and Alignment of Quality Initiatives related to "Planning Continuous Improvement." Since these "vital few" were existing priorities for Dunwoody, accreditation was now an integral part of the college's operations, not an inconvenient digression that occurred every five or six years. Dunwoody's quality team became so effective in meeting and exceeding AQIP's expectations that it was called upon to make quality presentations at NCA's annual meetings in Chicago in 2003, 2004, and 2005. By the time that an AQIP evaluation team made a site visit to Dunwoody's campus in April 2007, Dunwoody was regarded as one of the leaders in the AQIP program. Among the strengths noted by the evaluation team were the commitment and leadership of Dunwoody's board of trustees and the board of managers of the Dunwoody Alumni Association, strategic planning, graduate placement, the college's process for considering and developing new programs, and its diversity efforts. Thanks largely to the success

The acceptance of new students each quarter was one of several Key Performance Indicators measured by Dunwoody's quality "dashboard." This graph is an example of a KPI measurement tool.

Our perspective

Dunwoody

A promising new focus on quality

Minnesota has long been a national leader in quality practices in industry and in quality efforts in government and education. Now Minnesota's quality focus is getting an important boost at the Dunwoody Institute in Minneapolis. A $1 million grant from business leader Bob Carlson, his family, and his companies will make quality a significant vocational training focus at Dunwoody, already a highly regarded technical school. The result will be students better equipped to serve the needs of Minnesota employers—and employers better equipped to compete in the national and global economies.

The five-year grant will help train the institute's 1,100 regular two-year students, beginning in 2001. Teachers and staff will be trained, too. Training will be optional for several thousand part-time students in continuing education. Details of the training will be described Monday at a post-graduation meeting of Dunwoody teachers and staff.

Dunwoody will become a national leader in such vocational training, says Carlson, a Dunwoody trustee. Mostly, such training now takes place, if at all, after a student goes to work. Carlson's companies operate under the banner of Quadion and make such products as specialty rubber and plastic components for hydraulics, brakes, and valves.

Says Frank Starke, Dunwoody president: "We will give...students and their future employers another workforce advantage, an understanding that quality is the overarching strategy in all areas of business and manufacturing. This is more than a gift; it is a catalyst."

For example, students in auto repair will learn quality principles and techniques for making their work meet customer expectations, a basic quality goal. Dunwoody employees will learn how to improve telephone, information and tuition services. The school itself will participate in a national 40-school pilot process to make quality a key part of accreditation. Eventually, Starke hopes to apply for a prestigious national Baldrige quality award—an honor that has given Minnesota companies national leadership among states.

Other Minnesota institutions addressing quality issues include the Minnesota Council for Quality, a program launched by business and labor during the Perpich administration; the Juran Center, the nation's leading university research center for quality, located in the University of Minnesota's Carlson School of Management; and quality efforts by Minnesota state government and its employees. To that list, now add a valuable quality focus at the Dunwoody Institute—a tool for helping Minnesota industry, such as Quadion, remain competitive.

of Dunwoody's quality journey, in January 2008 NCA reaffirmed the college's accreditation through the 2014-15 school year.

The *Good to Great Campaign*

Following the successful conclusion of the *Living the Promise, Fulfilling the Dream Campaign* in 2001, Dunwoody moved immediately into the quiet phase of a new fundraising campaign. It was a major financial commitment by quality champion Robert W. Carlson Jr. that pushed the first campaign over its $25 million goal and launched the next campaign. Having already contributed $500,000 to the *Living the Promise Campaign*, former Board Chairman Carlson, his family, and his businesses made a pledge of $1 million to Dunwoody in 2000 in support of the school's quality initiatives. Thirty percent of this gift was credited to the *Living the Promise Campaign* and seventy percent to the as-yet-unnamed *Good to Great Campaign*. Dunwoody's investment in quality over the next eight years and its reaccreditation via AQIP owed a lot to the financial support and focus provided by the Carlson gift—the magnitude of which was recognized at the time by an editorial in the Minneapolis *StarTribune*.

Along with the Carlson gift, Dunwoody received several substantial estate gifts between 2000 and 2005 that gave the Wright administration and the board of trustees great confidence that fundraising would continue to lead Dunwoody from good to great. The $1.2 million bequest from alumnus Eugene Hunstad in 2000 was followed by bequests of $1 million from Vernon Thompson (Automotive, 1935) between 2001 and 2003, $1.9 million from Cecil Ness (Electrical, 1937) in 2002-2003, $1.1 million from Clarence Anderson (Electrical, 1939) between 2002 and 2011, $560,000 from Eunice Munck (a benefactor unknown to anyone at Dunwoody) between 2003 and 2005, and $831,553 from Edgar Grove (Baking, 1949) in 2004-2005. Receiving almost $7 million from six donors over such a brief period

of time convinced Dunwoody's leaders that it could count on a continuing stream of estate gifts from Dunwoody alumni for the foreseeable future. Contributing to this optimism was the growth of the Dunwoody Legacy Association, individuals who had included the college in their estate plans, from sixteen members in 1990 to eighty-two in 2002.

The influx of cash from bequests and the fulfillment of pledges through the *Living the Promise Campaign* created a unique opportunity for Dunwoody in 2002. Even before planning and organizing the next fund drive, the college had the resources to begin funding some of the capital improvement projects envisioned in the new strategic plan. President Wright's budget for the 2002-2003 fiscal year included $2.5 million for capital expenditures, which were fully funded. Another $3.4 million was also available for spending during the following year.

However, since this amount would not fund all of the projects in the strategic plan, the board of trustees authorized the administration in October 2002 to negotiate a line of credit with Wells Fargo Bank so that Dunwoody could fund all of the 2004 improvements in advance. To maintain the forward momentum of the strategic plan, the board was willing to borrow money in the short run, confident that the *Good to Great Campaign* and future estate gifts would enable the college to pay off the loan within five years.

> "The trade skills that I gained at Dunwoody were instantly valuable and continue to be valuable to me. What really benefits me now, though, is the discipline that I learned there. That discipline is what keeps us going through the tough times." [Chris was one of four members of the Zeman family who attended Dunwoody.]
>
> —Chris Zeman 1986

Over the next two years Dunwoody made significant changes on campus—a visible sign to many of the move from good to great. The exterior of the Warren Building was remodeled as were the Auto Collision and Auto Service labs

Opposite: Star Tribune editorial recognizes Dunwoody's commitment to continuous quality improvement, June 10, 2000.

Banners in the Warren Building recognize contributors to the renovation of Dunwoody's Automotive department.

inside the building. As the Collision program was redesigned and downsized, all of Dunwoody's HVAC programs were relocated to renovated space on the second floor of the Warren Building. The Machine Tool Technology program developed a partnership with Haas Automation in California, the largest machine tool manufacturer in the United States, and opened a new 1,900 square-foot Haas Technical Education Center, furnished with twelve state-of-the-art pieces of equipment. As part of the ongoing reinforcement of the foundation under the 1924 administration building, Dunwoody constructed attractive new offices for the Arts and Science faculty in new space under the administrative wing.

Most notable for students, alumni, employees, and many board members was the construction during the summer of 2003 of a paved parking lot and attendant landscaping. At a time when Dunwoody's vision was to be recognized as best in class, a gravel parking lot with large potholes, subject to flooding in heavy rains, had left visitors to the campus with a negative impression both upon arrival and departure. By the beginning of the 2003-2004 school year, Dunwoody was beginning to look like a best-in-class institution.

Dunwoody's merger with another college in 2003 was as dramatic as the paving of the parking lot. Never before had Dunwoody contemplated joining with another institution,

Machining equipment installed in the Haas Technical Education Center

yet in 2002 President Emeritus Frank Starke initiated informal, confidential conversations with NEI College of Technology about the possibility of merging with Dunwoody. NEI was a private, non-profit school that had been in operation since 1930. It offered competitive programs in electronics, computer networking, information management, and web design. NEI's enrollment was declining and its building in Columbia Heights, Minnesota, was a financial drain on its very limited resources. Starke knew NEI's Board Chairman Clinton Larson, who happened to be a 1950 graduate of Dunwoody's Electronics program. From Larson, Starke learned that NEI might be open to a merger with a viable partner. Starke introduced Larson and NEI's president

Parking lot under construction, summer 2003

Landscaping west of the Jackson Entrance was part of the improvement of the parking lot.

NEI graduate Jay Johnson (center) received Dunwoody's Alumni Entrepreneur Award in 2007. Standing next to Johnson are Raymond Newkirk (left) and Joel Elftmann (right), 1998 and 1987 recipients of the award, respectively.

to President Wright and his team, and in January 2003 the leaders of the two colleges signed a memorandum of understanding, which led to a formal merger on June 1, 2003.

According to the terms of the merger, Dunwoody acquired NEI's students, staff, and physical resources, including any funds remaining after the sale of the Columbia Heights property and the closing of the college. When NEI enrolled 250 full-time day students and 143 part-time evening students at Columbia Heights that fall, those students officially became Dunwoody students. As the transition proceeded, Dunwoody remodeled space in the west wing of its main building vacated by the HVAC programs as a new NEI Center. In January 2004 nearly 300 NEI students and many of their teachers and support staff moved to Dunwoody.

Good to Great Campaign Chairman Gary Petersen with Dunwoody students

Minneapolis Mayor R. T. Rybak helps Dunwoody publicly kick off the *Good to Great Campaign* in September 2006.

Alumnus Gib Severson (Automotive, 1974) and students dedicated the Alumni and Friends Walkway as part of the *Good to Great Campaign.*

NEI's programs in electronics, web design and other areas were soon merged with comparable Dunwoody programs.

The acquisition of another college, visible improvement of the parking lot and campus grounds, changes to the Warren Building, and the announcement of several million-dollar bequests combined to create a sense of intense progress at Dunwoody in 2003 and 2004. Highlighting Dunwoody's

progress, President Wright took members of the board of trustees on a tour of the campus in October 2003 to show them recently improved areas such as the NEI Center, Haas Center, and Warren Building. They also walked through areas still in desperate need of improvement, such as current Arts and Sciences classrooms, administrative offices, and Decker Auditorium. Wright also painted a vivid picture of the next phase of physical improvements that might include the construction of a new east entrance addition to the main building and, with the improvement of student retention and graduation rates in mind, the creation of a new tutoring center.

Meanwhile, fundraising consultant Mark Davy, who had guided Dunwoody successfully through the *Living the Promise Campaign*, was beginning his feasibility study for Dunwoody's next fund drive. In January 2004 he delivered his recommendations to President Wright and the board of trustees. After interviewing many donors and potential donors, and allowing for contributions received since 2001, Davy and Associates concluded that Dunwoody could raise $30 million in a second comprehensive campaign. Davy proposed that the campaign be called the *Good to Great*

Campaign in recognition of the college's adoption of the Jim Collins theme. These recommendations were readily accepted. During 2004 Dunwoody accelerated its fundraising under the leadership of trustee Gary Petersen, who agreed to serve as campaign chairman.

Although Dunwoody had already borrowed over $2 million from Wells Fargo to fund some of its capital improvements, in June 2004 the board's Finance Committee, chaired by David Crosby, held a special meeting to consider borrowing even more money to sustain the college's building momentum. Board Chairman Loren Taylor, past chairmen Joel Elftmann and Clifford Anderson, and Good to Great Campaign Chairman Gary Petersen also attended the meeting. President Wright reviewed the background of strategic visioning in 2001-2002; noted the capital projects that had been funded since 2002 through bequests, restricted gifts, and the Wells Fargo line of credit; and identified major capital improvements for the next five years that would cost approximately $8 million. The committee did not take action at this meeting, but it did direct the administration to work with Wells Fargo to develop a financing plan for some of the new improvements.

Outgoing Board Chairman Larry Taylor (left) hands the ceremonial gavel to incoming Chairman Bruce Engelsma, October 2004.

Several months later, on October 5, 2004, the Finance Committee recommended to the board of trustees that Dunwoody expand its lines of credit with Wells Fargo from $4 million to $8 million. The new line of credit would be used to fund construction of a student success center and the three-story addition to the east entrance of the main building, which together would cost $5.7 million. Of this total, $1.9 million would be funded by current estate gifts and the remainder through borrowing. The assumption was that gifts from the Good to Great Campaign would pay off Dunwoody's debt over the next five years, and in the interim Dunwoody could afford to make quarterly interest payments to Wells Fargo out of its operating budget if necessary. After reviewing a cash flow analysis for the next five years, the board unanimously approved the decision to move ahead with the proposed financing plan.

The decisions in 2002 and 2004 to borrow $8 million to advance-fund capital improvements prior to the Good to Great Campaign were critical ones. When the United States economy and Wells Fargo experienced a financial crisis in 2008 and 2009, Dunwoody would find itself in a precarious position relative to its lines of credit. The decisions to borrow money in 2002 and 2004 would then be second-guessed. However, in the context of 2002-2004, taking on some debt seemed reasonable. The Good to Great Campaign was just getting started, and the record of previous and current giving created the expectation that Dunwoody could receive sufficient contributions to retire its debt.

Board Chairman Taylor considered it imperative that Dunwoody maintain the momentum of the strategic plan. "Our facility was a dump," he recalled with characteristic candor. It was not student-friendly. As student tuition continued to rise, Taylor worried about the college's ability to attract students to the antiquated campus—an opinion shared by campaign consultant Davy and Dunwoody alumnus and past Board Chairman Elftmann. Even Finance

Joel Elftmann and family at the dedication of the Elftmann Student Success Center, June 2006

Committee Chairman Crosby, who disliked debt and worried that the *Good to Great Campaign* might not generate adequate cash flow to retire the debt, conceded later that the campus improvements financed by the lines of credit between 2002 and 2008 were long overdue.

With credit in hand, Dunwoody moved forward with the next wave of construction in 2005 and 2006. Board Chairman Bruce Engelsma, chairman and CEO of Kraus Anderson Companies, and William Jordan, the college's director of facilities, provided much of the planning and oversight of the Dunwoody building projects. Two inter-related projects were the construction of a student success center in the executive office area used historically by Dr. Prosser, John Butler, and other Dunwoody administrators, and the creation of new executive offices in the run-down space previously used for Arts and Sciences classes immediately above the former administrative offices. In June 2006 the Elftmann Student Success Center was dedicated in recognition of the leadership and philanthropy of Joel Elftmann and his family. Three months later, a 24,000 square-foot addition to the east entrance was named the Robert W. Carlson Commons in honor of former board chairman and benefactor, Robert W. Carlson Jr.

Top: Robert W. Carlson Jr. Commons under construction
Above: Grand opening of the Carlson Commons, September 2006

Along with the parking lot, the Carlson Commons was probably the most visible campus improvement of this era. It housed a student lounge, game room, offices for student activities, new restrooms, and spacious conference room overlooking downtown Minneapolis.

Other improvements and dedications followed. In December 2006 a new facility for students of color, the Wenda W. and Cornell L. Moore Multi-Cultural Center, was named for

175

longtime trustee Cornell Moore and his wife. In December 2007 the placement office was named the Anthony L. Ferrara Career Services Center in honor of the founder of Standard Heating and Air Conditioning Company, whose sons, Ted and Todd Ferrara (Refrigeration, 1977, and Sheet Metal, 1980), now ran the company and supported their alma mater generously. One month later John Adamich (Automotive, 1950) and his wife, Betty, were honored for their generosity and support of Dunwoody's Automotive program when a laboratory in the Warren Building was named the Adamich Automotive Lab. In June 2008 two benefactors from North Carolina, Ron and Katherine Harper, were recognized for their active role in resurrecting Dunwoody's Printing program when the renovated Printing laboratory was named the Harper Center of Graphics Technology.

Finally, in 2009, Dunwoody named two conference rooms to recognize families that had been very supportive of the institution during its long history. The Crosby Family Board and Conference Room, adjacent to the new executive offices and overlooking Dunwoody Boulevard and the Parade park south of the administration building, was named for members of the Crosby family who had loyally served Dunwoody since 1914. The Anderson Legacy Room, the new conference room in the Carlson Commons, was named in honor of Clifford I. Anderson, former Dunwoody board chairman, for his leadership and philanthropy.

Along with these named facilities, Dunwoody remodeled its business offices and the cafeteria. In the area outside the former administrative offices, it created a recognition hall for donors, alumni, and business partners. With contributions from Johnson Controls of Milwaukee, it converted one HVAC shop into a control lab for a new collaborative program, CAREERCONNECT. It built classrooms for a new Interior Design program and remodeled the National Baking Center and adjacent space for the introduction of new health sciences programs. And it built many new rest-

Wenda and Cornell Moore at the dedication of the Moore Multi-Cultural Center, December 2006

rooms to accommodate a growing student population and create a more inviting environment for women. All of these physical changes on campus reinforced the feeling among Dunwoody's key stakeholders and within the community that Dunwoody was truly moving from good to great.

The growth of student enrollment was an essential element of the strategic plan and the move from good to great. The assumption since 2002 had been that growth was imperative and would occur through enhanced marketing, the improvement of existing programs by the application of program health indicators, and the introduction of a systematic process for identifying and researching new program options. The strategic plan of 2002 had set a three-year goal of 1,500 full-time students, which was achieved in the fall of 2003 thanks to the merger with NEI, and a five-year goal of 1,800 students. When it became apparent that this larger number would not be realized, the board revised its goal in 2006 to one of "modest growth." Still, by the fall of 2008, Dunwoody had enrolled over 1,600 students in its twenty full-time programs—a 23 percent increase since 2002.

Most of the enrollment growth came in redesigned or new

programs. For example, after ending their partnership with the Printing Industry of Minnesota in 2002, Dunwoody's Printing faculty focused on the new program area of flexography (printing on flexible surfaces). The Printing program was rewarded for its expertise when Dunwoody was named "College of the Year" four times between 2002 and 2008 by the Flexographic Technical Association. Then, in 2005, Printing introduced a program in Graphic Design, which attracted new students to the department. Similarly the Automotive department made significant changes in its Automotive Service and Collision programs, much of it through new partnerships with Honda, Toyota, and Chrysler, leading to enrollment increases by the end of the decade.

Other new programs were Construction Project Supervision, Interior Design, and a "2+2" Bachelor of Science degree in Applied Management. The new B.S. degree was an alternative to the earlier B.S. degrees developed with Saint Mary's, Bemidji State, and the University of Wisconsin-Stout. This was Dunwoody's own degree program, designed for students or alumni who wanted a four-year degree. The "2+2" concept meant that a student with a two-year A.A.S. technical degree could add two years of upper level "applied management" to earn a four-year degree. Introduced in December 2006, the B.S. program enrolled close to one hundred students in the next few years.

Printing instructor Pete Rivard (left) and student

The board of trustees viewed diversity as one means for ensuring growth, a prerequisite of its strategic plan. As the population of white males in the pool of potential students in higher education declined, it seemed apparent that Dunwoody would have to attract more women and students of color to the college if it hoped to sustain, let alone increase, student enrollment. Making Dunwoody a more diverse institution had been a goal of the board and successive administrations since the 1970s. Now it became a case of enlightened self-interest. In 2005 the board of trustees charged the Wright administration with substantially increasing the number of students of color and women over the next five years. It clearly expected to see more aggressive action.

Aggressive action is what the board got. Dunwoody hired a diversity director, who worked with other Dunwoody staff to develop a five-year diversity plan. It expanded the successful Youth Career Awareness Program (YCAP) to prepare more youth of color for future enrollment at Dunwoody, and it expanded the Gateway program, now housed in the Elftmann Student Success Center, to improve student readiness and retention. In addition to the Moore Multi-Cultural Center,

YCAP community service activity: students painting a classroom at Minneapolis North High School

Dunwoody opened a Women's Resource Center. It introduced new programs that might attract female students: Interior Design, Graphic Design, Food Science, and the B.S. in Applied Management. By September 2008 students of color accounted for 23 percent of the student body—up from 17 percent in 2005, 13 percent in 2001, and 8 percent in 1998. Sixty-four YCAP students were now enrolled in Dunwoody's technical programs. Unfortunately, female enrollment remained flat at about 8 percent—far short of the board's goal of 20 percent. That failure accounted for efforts then underway to develop an entirely new platform of programs in health sciences to attract more women to Dunwoody beginning in 2009.

These diversity initiatives required great expenditures of effort and resources. No effort was more aggressive or more expensive than Dunwoody's sponsorship of a charter high school in north Minneapolis between 2006 and 2011. Named Dunwoody Academy in recognition of its close relationship to Dunwoody College of Technology, the high school was conceived and designed as a technical high school that would prepare youth of color for admission to Dunwoody College. The goal was to enroll 450 students at Dunwoody Academy and admit fifty of its graduates to Dunwoody College in

September 2011. Although the Academy created educational opportunities for some students of color, it never realized its enrollment or its academic goals. The college withdrew its sponsorship in 2011, at which time a smaller school continued to operate as MetroTech Career Academy.

Dunwoody's diversity initiatives, new programs, and campus improvements were all funded by the *Good to Great Campaign* and Dunwoody's lines of credit. When the board of trustees held a strategic planning retreat in November 2007, they acknowledged that both debt and fundraising were critical to finance important growth initiatives. Even though they would prefer to have no debt or minimal debt, the trustees continued to see it as a temporary way to forward-fund strategic initiatives like health sciences, e-learning, and electronic student services. They looked to the *Good to Great Campaign* to retire some of the college's debt. But they now realized that fundraising would have to continue beyond the end of the campaign and that expectations would be even higher over the next seven years. Instead of the current $4 million in annual philanthropic support, Dunwoody would have to increase this support to at least $7 million a year. As Dunwoody moved into the year 2008, both the board of trustees and the Wright administration remained optimistic about the future and committed to the implementation of a growth-oriented strategic plan.

The *Good to Great Campaign* was scheduled to end in 2007. Instead Dunwoody needed an extra two years to reach its goal of $30 million. At the time of the strategic planning retreat, it was apparent that fundraising had become more difficult than it had been during the *Living the Promise Campaign* of 1996-2001. Why? According to consultant Mark Davy, there were three reasons: the lack of sizeable estate gifts after the early 2000s; the relative decline in large gifts of equipment from corporate partners; and the difficulty of duplicating the strong volunteer leadership of the previous campaign. Campaign Chair Gary Petersen concurred with this assessment. Even though he had agreed, reluctantly, to lead the *Good to Great Campaign*, he understood that the board of trustees had been unable to recruit enough new volunteers to bring fresh energy and fundraising clout to the campaign. Dunwoody finally proclaimed victory in the campaign on April 1, 2009, when it reached the milestone of $31.3 million in gifts and pledges.

Leadership Transition

The years from 1995 to 2008 were a time of great progress for Dunwoody. Dunwoody Industrial Institute had become Dunwoody College of Technology, now offering four-year bachelor's degrees as well as two-year associate degrees. The college had introduced new programs and revitalized existing ones. It had made numerous, highly visible campus improvements. It had increased student enrollment and become a more inviting school for women and students of color. It had achieved NCA accreditation and recognition for its program of continuous quality improvement. It had raised over $56 million in two major fundraising campaigns. It appeared to be well on the path from good to great.

Anticipating his sixty-fifth birthday the next year, and confident of Dunwoody's prospects for the future, President Wright informed the board of trustees in April 2008 of his intention to retire at the end of the 2008-2009 school year. Announcing his plans this far in advance gave the board sufficient time to find his replacement and make possible the same smooth leadership transition that had occurred between himself and President Starke seven years earlier.

As it had done in the past, the board appointed a presidential search committee to find Dr. Wright's successor. Chaired by Bruce Engelsma, past board chairman, the search committee began its work in May 2008. After conducting a national search to identify the best-qualified candidate, it recommended one candidate to the board in November—Dr. Richard Wagner, Dunwoody's vice president of academic affairs. Without hesitation, the board elected Wagner as president-elect. He would assume office as president in July 2009.

Women's Resource Center

Pam Spence (right) tours the Automotive department with Chuck Bowen, department chairman, in 2006. She returned to campus to accept her Alumni Achievement Award.

Rich Wagner was well-suited to be president of Dunwoody. He had served for ten years in the U.S. Navy, where he developed his appreciation for hands-on learning as an electrical instructor and earned an M.B.A., which prepared him for a brief career in financial services and investment banking after he left the navy. In 1996 he joined the Dunwoody faculty as an electrical instructor. Within a few years he was

Interior Design instructor Colleen Schmaltz (standing on right) with students

promoted to chairman of the Electrical department and then to dean of learning. After earning his doctorate in education, he left Dunwoody temporarily to become vice president of academic affairs at Hennepin Technical College. When Dunwoody Vice President Richard Pooley informed President Wright of his intention to retire in 2005, Wright met personally with Dr. Wagner to invite him to return to Dunwoody to fill Pooley's position. Wagner welcomed the opportunity to resume his career at Dunwoody, and in April 2005 he became academic vice president.

As vice president, Wagner was a key member of President Wright's leadership team. He helped develop the new programs in Interior Design, Graphic Design, Construction Supervision, and the B.S. degree in Applied Management.

He oversaw Dunwoody's quality program and the accreditation process through the Academic Quality Improvement Project (AQIP). He coordinated the opening of the Elftmann Student Success Center and the Harper Center of Graphics Technology. And he led the design and development of new programs in health sciences.

After his appointment as president-elect in late 2008, Dr. Wagner worked closely with President Wright during a seven-month leadership transition. Unfortunately the transition was anything but smooth—not because of any differences between the president and president-elect but because of national economic events that created huge financial problems for Dunwoody in 2008 and 2009.

The Financial Crisis of 2008-2009

Problems began for the United States and world economies when a housing boom, which had peaked in 2007, collapsed in 2008. The collapse caused a drastic fall in the value of securities tied to real estate, widespread default on bank loans, the proliferation of home foreclosures, and the failure of large financial institutions. Suddenly the world was faced with the most severe economic recession since the Great Depression of the 1930s. In September 2008 the U.S. Treasury took control of mortgage lenders Fannie Mae and Freddie Mac; Lehman Brothers filed for bankruptcy; and several other financial giants were either sold at bargain prices or bailed out by the U.S. government. Unemployment rose to double-digit levels, and the stock market dropped from a Dow Jones peak of 14,000 points in October 2007 to a low of 6,600 in March 2009.

The effects of the "Great Recession" began to hit Dunwoody College of Technology in the fall of 2008. At the time of the annual meeting of the board of trustees on October 28, President Wright reported on a five-year high in student enrollment and a normal graduate placement rate of 88 percent for students who had graduated in June. His one concern was the impact of recent stock market losses on the college's endowed funds. These losses would reduce funds available for the operating budget, limit student scholarships, and harm employees' 403(b) plans. What he did not foresee was the pending conflict with Wells Fargo Bank over Dunwoody's lines of credit.

Ironically this conflict occurred with the bank that had merged ten years earlier with Norwest Corporation, successor to William Hood Dunwoody's very own Northwestern National Bank of Minneapolis. Wells Fargo was one of nine large financial institutions that had been compelled earlier in October to accept bailout money from the Troubled Asset Relief Program (TARP) to head off a national financial collapse. Along with other banks, Wells Fargo was now under intense pressure from the U.S. Treasury to improve the status

Gary Petersen (left) succeeds Andrea Newman as chairperson of Dunwoody's board of trustees, October 2008.

Dr. Richard W. Wagner (right) became president of Dunwoody College of Technology on July 1, 2009.

of its loan portfolios. Dunwoody's problem was that its debt with Wells Fargo had grown from $7.6 million in June 2006 to $8.2 million in June 2008 to almost $10 million by November 2008. Although the board had authorized the borrowing of $8 million for capital improvements in 2004, the availability of easy credit had enabled Dunwoody to take on extra short-term debt to fund cash flow during the summers of 2007 and 2008—loans that had not been repaid. Since Dunwoody used its endowed funds as collateral for its lines of credit, the sharp drop in the stock market put the college at risk of violating its debt covenants. Pressured by Wells Fargo to sell stocks to create more cash for collateral, Dunwoody had to liquidate endowment assets in a very poor market. Dunwoody was not alone. Other colleges and universities were also facing serious endowment and credit problems.

> "While being a Dunwoody graduate didn't guarantee a job offer, it is a name that is preferred and respected in the industry. I am grateful for the scholarships and experience I gained."
>
> —Rachel Jones 2008

Dunwoody was well served by the board's election in October 2008 of Gary Petersen as the new chairman of the board. Petersen had been Dunwoody treasurer in the 1990s, and he now found himself again immersed in Dunwoody's financial problems. The knowledgeable Petersen was available and willing to take on an active role in Dunwoody's financial affairs during this difficult period. Also chairman of the *Good to Great Campaign*, he understood better than anyone the importance of the capital investments that had spurred Dunwoody's growth after 2004 as well as the dilemma that these investments had created for the college by 2008. The challenge facing him, the administration, and the board was to negotiate a new line of credit with Wells Fargo or another bank and sort through financial issues that compounded the credit problem.

The college's growing liability for its employee pension plan had emerged as an issue a few years earlier. Like many other organizations, for-profit and not-for-profit, Dunwoody had established a "defined benefit plan" which was becoming more and more expensive as retirees lived longer and longer. In 2006 Dunwoody's projected obligation to the plan had been $8.7 million; by 2008 this obligation had increased to $9.5 million. This obligation was a problem due to the simultaneous decline in the value of the assets available to meet the obligation: from $6.8 million in 2006 to $6.5 million in 2008. In just two years the projected shortfall in pension assets had grown to almost $3 million. With the stock market crash of 2008-2009, this shortfall would increase to $5.3 million by June 2009.

As an alternative to the traditional pension plan, the college had created a voluntary 403(b) employee savings plan, to which both Dunwoody and employees made annual contributions. Although the goal was to phase out the defined benefit plan, Dunwoody now had to set aside money in its annual operating budgets for both the 403(b) contribution and the ongoing pension obligation. The 2008-09 operating budget included $179,000 to fund the pension shortfall. The next year's budget, it now appeared, would have to provide as much as $500,000 for this purpose. In 2006-2007 Dunwoody had frozen benefits for all employees younger than 55, and now in 2009 it was forced to freeze benefits for all participants. Unlike the credit issue with Wells Fargo, the pension plan liability was not a new problem, but its cost and immediacy were exacerbated by the national financial crisis.

A third financial issue was the increasing cost of Dunwoody's investment in diversity. Two examples were Dunwoody Academy and the Youth Career Awareness Program (YCAP). As part of the college's commitment to its charter high school, it had loaned $450,000 to Dunwoody Academy. When the Academy could not repay the loan, it had to be funded through the college's operating budget. The enrollment of seventy YCAP students in full-time college programs during the fall of 2008 also had a big impact on the budget.

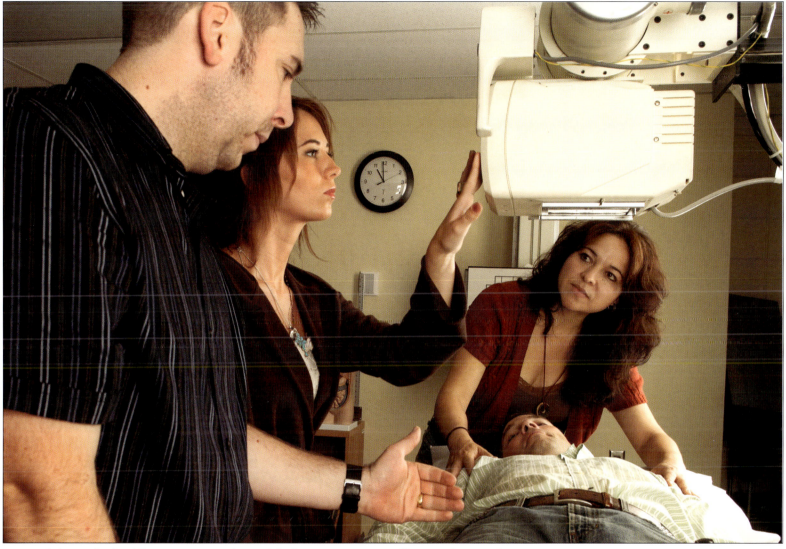

Radiologic Technology lab. Instructor Tom Brinkmann (left) demonstrates proper use of x-ray machine to students.

Although virtually all of these young people required scholarship assistance, these scholarships had not been funded through Dunwoody's annual fund drive or the *Good to Great Campaign*. Here was an example of poor timing—the college was hurt by its own success in attracting low-income students at a time when its resources were being hard hit on multiple fronts.

During the first six months of 2009, Dunwoody's converging financial troubles preoccupied Chairman Petersen, President Wright, President-Elect Wagner, and trustee Ted Ferrara, a member of the Finance Committee. Their immediate focus was two-fold: how to reduce operating expenses sufficiently to construct a viable budget for the 2009-10 fiscal year, which would commence on July 1; and how to secure a new line of credit to finance the college's cash flow needs during the approaching summer and beyond.

The budget cuts came first, and they were painful. Twenty-five employees, including eleven maintenance workers,

Dunwoody students play touch football at the Parade park across Dunwoody Boulevard from the college.

were laid off in May and June. Wages were frozen for other faculty and staff, and members of the president's leadership team took voluntary 10 percent reductions in their salaries. Pension plan benefits had been frozen, and Dunwoody made no matching contributions to employees' 403(b) plans in 2009-10. As a symbolic gesture, the college also cancelled the victory celebration for the *Good to Great Campaign*.

Another challenge was securing a new line of credit to ensure adequate cash flow during the summer. Collateral for a line of credit had become a serious problem, given the sharp drop in the value of the college's endowment from $26.3 million in June 2008 to $18.9 million in March 2009. Since Wells Fargo was unwilling to ease up on its collateral requirements, Dunwoody had to explore financing alternatives with other banks. Dunwoody alumnus and trustee Maurice Wagener, owner of multiple Morrie's automotive dealerships in the Twin Cities area, introduced the college's leaders to his bankers at Twin Cities Federal Bank. TCF was a local bank very interested in working with Dunwoody, an eminent educational institution. When Dunwoody's board of trustees held a special financing meeting on June 12, it authorized

Chairman Petersen and his ad hoc "financing advisory committee," which included trustees Wagener, Ferrara and others, to negotiate a new plan to finance the college's short-term and long-term debt. Such a plan was concluded with TCF on June 30, the very last day of Dunwoody's fiscal year. The new line of credit with TCF did not end Dunwoody's financial challenges, but it did end the financial crisis of 2008-2009. Dunwoody was now authorized to borrow up to $12.5 million from TCF. It immediately borrowed $11.5 million, using $10 million to retire its debt with Wells Fargo, and the balance of $1.5 million to fund Dunwoody operations during the summer of 2009. The intention was to pay back the summer loan during the school year, when tuition revenue would be available to fund school operations.

Adapting to New Realities, 2009-2012

On July 1, 2009, Dr. Richard Wagner became the seventh president* of Dunwoody College of Technology. He replaced Dr. Wright, who became president emeritus, sharing that honorary title with Warren Phillips and Frank Starke. In October Ted Ferrara, who had been deeply engaged with Chairman Petersen in the college's financial affairs in 2008 and 2009, became treasurer and chairman of the board's Finance Committee. A year later Morrie Wagener, who had also been active in the college's refinancing process, replaced Petersen as chairman of the Dunwoody board, a position he held for two years, and Charles Westling, CEO of Computype, replaced Ferrara as treasurer and Finance Committee chairman. In 2012 Ferrara became chairman of the board, serving in that role until Dunwoody's centennial in 2014. Wagener and Ferrara were both Dunwoody graduates. They followed Joel Elftmann as the second and third alumni to serve as board chairman.

*Numbering the Dunwoody presidents is somewhat problematic since Directors Charles Prosser and John Butler, who functioned like chief executive officers, never held that title. If they were included in the numbering, Dr. Wagner would be considered Dunwoody's ninth president. If Interim President William Mamel [1994-95] was included, Dr. Wagner would be the tenth president.

When Dr. Wagner took over as the chief executive, his immediate priority was the same as his predecessor's—finances—and this would remain his priority for the next three years. He needed to work within the limitations of austere operating budgets and to extend the line of credit with TCF, but his long-term goal was to develop a new financial model for Dunwoody that would retire the college's debt and rebuild its endowment.

Long-term improvements required many shorter-term actions. The new president instituted personnel and process changes. In his first two years Dr. Wagner hired a new chief financial officer and a new purchasing agent, who introduced new processes that saved Dunwoody money and improved financial reporting to the president and the board's Finance Committee. Board Chairman Morrie Wagener and former Chairperson Andrea Newman gave President Wagner credit for improving internal financial controls and developing more reliable cash flow projections. As financial reports became more reliable, the president and the board began to ask themselves a strategic question that had not been asked before the financial crisis: was continuing growth for Dunwoody necessary or desirable? Whereas the strategic plan of 2002 had envisioned enrollment growth to 1,800 students by 2007 (a goal that was subsequently modified), board members now pondered what optimum enrollment should be. They were open to the possibility that the college might stabilize at a smaller enrollment and set tuition pricing at a level sufficient to support a school of that size.

Since enrollment was the fundamental economic driver of Dunwoody, President Wagner created the new position of vice president of enrollment management. This executive

> "At Dunwoody you needed to learn how to learn, which made it easier in all areas of life. Dunwoody made it easy for me to compete [for a position with the Federal Aviation Administration]—you needed to be in the top 10 percent in order to even be considered."
>
> —Norman Welch 1972

In June 2011 Dunwoody moved its student commencement ceremony from the Decker Auditorium on campus to the historic Orpheum Theater in downtown Minneapolis.

was responsible for marketing, admissions, and student financial aid. Organizing enrollment as a comprehensive school-wide activity, the vice president integrated financial aid into the recruitment and admissions process, helping students not only select appropriate technical programs but also develop personal plans to finance their education. Concerns about student tuition and financial aid became especially acute during the 2011-2012 school year, when Dunwoody enrollment dropped to 1,100 students—a continuing effect of the severe downturn in the construction industry and the Dunwoody programs, such as Electrical Construction and

Architectural Drafting and Design, that served that sector.

As a former instructor, department chair, dean, and academic vice president, Dr. Wagner focused on Dunwoody's academic mission as well as its finances. One consequence of the economic downturn was the scaling back on the health sciences programs that had been scheduled for rollout in 2009. Instead of four programs, Dunwoody concentrated on one, Radiologic Technology, developed in partnership with North Memorial Medical Center.

Another new program was a B.S. degree in Industrial Engineering, Dunwoody's third "2+2" bachelor's degree, along with Applied Management and Applied Management/Management Information Systems. Thirty manufacturing students were enrolled in this program by 2012. President Wagner's vision was that all of Dunwoody's two-year technical programs would eventually offer "2+2" degree completion options.

Despite widespread national publicity about the outsourcing of American manufacturing, Dunwoody's manufacturing programs now enrolled more students than any other program area. The demand for computer numeric control (CNC) operators encouraged Dunwoody to develop a new semester-long certificate program called "Right Skills Now."* This program enrolled seventeen aspiring CNC operators in the spring of 2012, with another twenty registered for fall. Employers were lined up, ready to hire graduates of the program, who would also be able to continue their education in Dunwoody A.A.S. and B.S. programs.

Fortunately the historic demand for Dunwoody graduates

*During the 2012-2013 school year, Dunwoody moved from an academic calendar organized by quarters to a semester system.

Erick Ajax [center], co-owner of E. J. Ajax Company, observes the work of two Dunwoody manufacturing students working as interns at Ajax's metal-stamping plant in Fridley, Minnesota.

had rebounded from a low of 60 percent in 2009 to a more normal 90 percent by 2011-2012. As Dunwoody's first century of operation neared its end, Dunwoody was still doing what it had been doing for one hundred years—training people of all ages for employment in a wide variety of technical occupations and careers, and then placing them in the jobs for which they were trained.

CHAPTER VIII

Dunwoody at 100

Dunwoody College of Technology marked its 100th anniversary on December 14, 2014—Founder's Day. William Hood Dunwoody, the founder and principal benefactor, died on February 8, 1914, and ten months later his widow, Kate L. Dunwoody, ceremoniously turned on the power of the new William Hood Dunwoody Industrial Institute. Since then Dunwoody Institute, now Dunwoody College, has educated tens of thousands of students—locally, regionally, nationally, and around the world—and become the preferred training resource for countless businesses, industries, and other employers of technical personnel. During its first century of operation, Dunwoody distinguished itself by producing best-in-class technicians and preparing them for "the better performance of life's duties." William and Kate Dunwoody would be proud of the extent to which their school has fulfilled their promise and their dream.

More than anyone, Dr. Charles Prosser brought the Dunwoodys' promise and dream to life, for which he deserves to be considered the college's third major founder, alongside the Dunwoodys. As Dr. Prosser's "laboratory school," Dunwoody Institute became a national leader in vocational education, developing not only the curriculum and pedagogical practices that would be widely emulated, but also providing a training service to the nation during two world wars. After the Second World War, Prosser's loyal disciple, Director John Butler, expanded Dunwoody's leadership role by supporting the development of a system of public vocational education throughout the state of Minnesota and establishing international training programs that would endure into the 1980s.

Prosser, Butler, and their many academic colleagues were responsible for creating the Dunwoody Difference during the institution's first fifty years. The hands-on applied curriculum, emphasis on discipline and a strong work ethic, close ties to business and industry, replication of the workplace environment, perpetuation of a core body of technical programs taught in Day School and Evening School, and development and customizing of specialized programs for business, labor, and government—these were all elements of the Dunwoody Difference. The school's educational leaders and teachers passed these traditions on to their successors during the second fifty years of Dunwoody's history. When asked to identify major achievements of Dunwoody over its last few decades, President Wagner and trustees Andrea Newman, Bruce Engelsma, and Ted Ferrara all pointed to the Dunwoody Difference as a distinguishing feature of the college's legacy.

Another aspect of the legacy was Dunwoody's great capacity for change. The expansion of technologies and programs taught at Dunwoody was an essential development during its first century. When the school offered its first classes in December 1914 and January 1915, it provided seven areas of study in Day School. Five of these were still part of the curriculum one hundred years later: Machine Shop, Printing, Drafting, Automotive Repair, and Electrical Construction. Now there were seven A.A.S. programs, including Machine Tool Technology, offered in the department of Robotics and Manufacturing Technology. Printing was now part of a Design and Graphics department, which had three programs. Drafting was taught not only in Manufacturing but also in

Opposite: Instructor Frank Claude (right) demonstrates robotics equipment to students in the Robotics and Manufacturing Technology program.

Instructor Shawn Oetjen (left) with Printing students

the department of Construction Science and Building Technology, with three degree programs and three certificate programs. The Automotive department had grown to seven degree programs and three certificate programs. Electrical remained a stand-alone department with two programs, and it had spawned a Computer Technology department with three programs. Finally there were three degree programs and one certificate program in the HVAC department and four B.S. degree programs, including Interior Design. This was a comprehensive curriculum for a relatively small technical college.

As they reflected on Dunwoody's recent history, trustees Joel Elftmann, Robert Carlson, and Gary Petersen all commended the college for its ability to adapt to changing conditions and new challenges. In the days of Prosser and Butler, Dunwoody did not face much competition. However, by the 1970s, Dunwoody's leadership was being challenged by many of the public vocational technical colleges.

To meet the competitive challenge, Dunwoody became serious about strategic long-range planning and adopted the philosophy and operational practices of continuous quality improvement. Since its aging campus was a competitive liability—all of the public technical colleges had modern facilities—Dunwoody invested heavily in campus improvements from the 1970s to the early 2000s. It also invested significant resources in diversity initiatives, recognizing that the demographics of student populations were changing in the twenty-first century. Dunwoody's ability to attract more students of color than other private colleges and public technical colleges (with the exception of Minneapolis Community and Technical College and St. Paul College) was tangible evidence of the return on this investment.

An ongoing theme of Dunwoody's history has been the financial challenges faced by Dunwoody Institute and Dunwoody College as a private, not-for-profit institution. "Without money there is no mission," Ted Ferrara observed. The board of trustees and its Finance Committee played a critical leadership role in the financial history of the school. The founding board managed the institution's finances from 1914 into the 1930s, after which Treasurer Joe Kingman assumed the day-to-day responsibility for Dunwoody's finances until his retirement in 1970. Thereafter the Dunwoody president worked closely with the Finance Committee to ensure the financial health of the school. As Dunwoody's first century came to a close, President Wagner and Board Chairman Ferrara both regarded debt retirement, rebuilding the endowment, and establishing appropriate tuition levels as the keys to future health and stability.

Beginning with the economic crisis of the Great Depression, Dunwoody periodically dealt with problems of declining enrollment, loss of value of endowment investments, and rising operating costs. Common responses to these challenges were to reduce operating expenses, raise tuition and fees charged to students, and modify investment strategies. By

Instructor Timothy Gnitka (left) with Architectural Drafting and Estimating students

the 1970s the board of trustees began looking to another revenue source—fundraising. From 1977 to 2009 Dunwoody conducted four major fundraising campaigns, raising over $65 million in contributions to supplement revenue provided through endowments and student fees. The emergence of philanthropic support was another major achievement of Dunwoody's recent past.

Graduates Who Are Worth More became the driving force of Dunwoody's strategic plan in 2006 as the college moved from good to great. The achievements of Dunwoody alumni during the college's first one hundred years were widely regarded as another manifestation of the Dunwoody Difference. The career accomplishments of alumni built Dunwoody's elite reputation. Former board chairmen Chuck Kiester and Bob Carlson strongly believed that Dunwoody's record of graduate placement—consistently over 90 percent—proved that employers valued Dunwoody graduates highly. Many alumni advanced to leadership positions within the organizations that employed them, or went on to own and operate their own businesses, and this set Dunwoody alumni apart. Morrie Wagener, himself a

Dunwoody graduate and past chairman of the board, was not alone when he singled out Dunwoody alumni as "the biggest success story and legacy" of Dunwoody College.

Dunwoody thrived and excelled for one hundred years but never rested on its laurels. William Hood Dunwoody envi-

M. A. Mortenson Company receives Dunwoody's 2008 Partnership Award. *Left to right*: M. A. Mortenson Jr.; former Dunwoody trustee Alice Mortenson; Dunwoody graduate and Mortenson Vice President Greg Clark; Dunwoody trustee and Mortenson Vice President Paul Cossette.

sioned a school that would endure "for all time." Continuous quality improvement and the drive from good to great ensured that Dunwoody College of Technology would enter its second century with a continuing commitment to be best in class and fulfill the promise and dream of its founders. Former Board Chairman Clifford I. Anderson believed that William Dunwoody's will was as relevant in 2014 as it had been in 1914 and that it would continue to be relevant for as long as the institution endured.

Dunwoody graduate and Board Chairman Ted Ferrara sees a very bright future for Dunwoody. For one hundred years Dunwoody has provided "practical, real-world education leading to jobs, better lives, and better communities," he said. "Now the rest of the world is catching up with what Dunwoody has always stood for." If anything, Ferrara believes, the need for Dunwoody College of Technology is even greater than it has been in the past. By remaining true to its historic mission and adapting to changing times, Dunwoody will continue to "give people an opportunity where maybe they wouldn't have had one."

Minnesota automotive dealer and Dunwoody graduate Morrie Wagener (left) congratulates fellow auto dealer and graduate John Adamich at the dedication of Dunwoody's Adamich Automotive Lab.

Dunwoody graduate and Board Chairman Ted Ferrara (left) with Clifford I. Anderson, former chairman and honorary trustee.

For the better performance of life's duties. William Dunwoody set a lofty standard. The school of his imagination was transformed from a dream to reality. Its alumni embody the ideal. Now it remains for those to come to sustain that ideal during Dunwoody's second century.

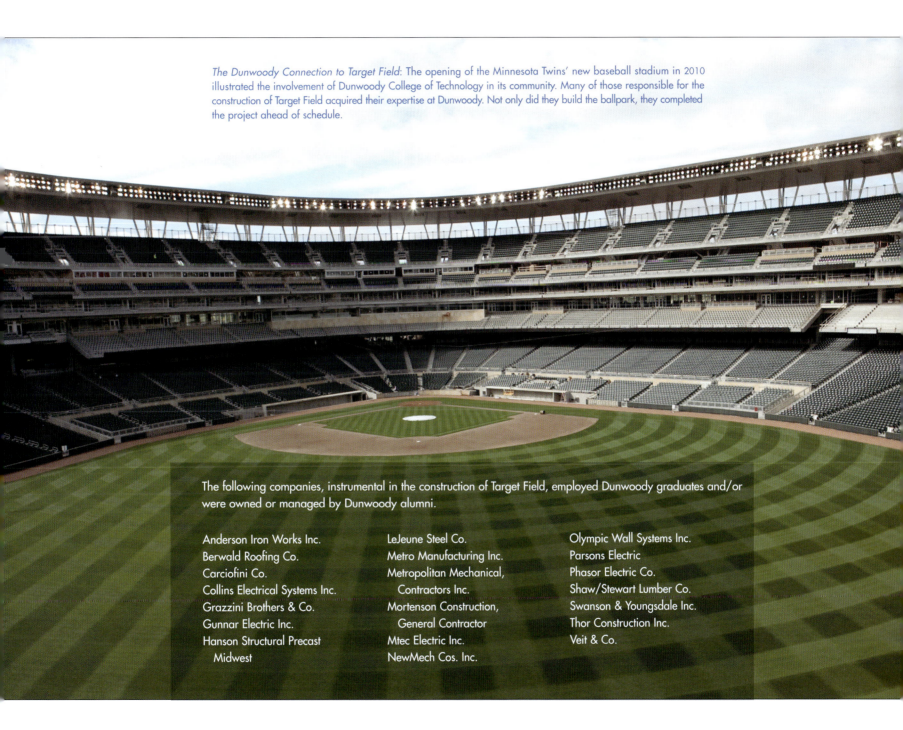

The Dunwoody Connection to Target Field: The opening of the Minnesota Twins' new baseball stadium in 2010 illustrated the involvement of Dunwoody College of Technology in its community. Many of those responsible for the construction of Target Field acquired their expertise at Dunwoody. Not only did they build the ballpark, they completed the project ahead of schedule.

The following companies, instrumental in the construction of Target Field, employed Dunwoody graduates and/or were owned or managed by Dunwoody alumni.

Anderson Iron Works Inc.
Berwald Roofing Co.
Carciofini Co.
Collins Electrical Systems Inc.
Grazzini Brothers & Co.
Gunnar Electric Inc.
Hanson Structural Precast
  Midwest

LeJeune Steel Co.
Metro Manufacturing Inc.
Metropolitan Mechanical,
  Contractors Inc.
Mortenson Construction,
  General Contractor
Mtec Electric Inc.
NewMech Cos. Inc.

Olympic Wall Systems Inc.
Parsons Electric
Phasor Electric Co.
Shaw/Stewart Lumber Co.
Swanson & Youngsdale Inc.
Thor Construction Inc.
Veit & Co.

APPENDICES

Members of Dunwoody Boards of Trustees

Leaders of Dunwoody Boards of Trustees

Presidents

William H. Bovey	1914-37
Russell H. Bennett	1937-48, 1953-57
Henry S. Crosby	1948-53

Chairpersons

Russell H. Bennett	1957-61
Paul B. Wishart	1961-68
Leonard H. Murray	1968-70
Thomas M. Crosby	1970-73
John P. Snyder Jr.	1973-76

Robert H. Engels	1976-78
Stanley J. Nelson	1978-81
Paul W. Kraemer	1981-83
Robert P. Fox	1983-85
Donald E. Ryks	1985-87
David T. Bennett	1987-90
Fosten A. Boyle	1990-92
Clifford I. Anderson	1992-94
David P. Crosby	1994-96
Robert W. Carlson Jr.	1996-98
Charles E. Kiester	1998-2000
Joel A. Elftmann	2000-02

Loren L. Taylor	2002-04
Bruce W. Engelsma	2004-06
Andrea L. Newman	2006-08
Gary N. Petersen	2008-10
Maurice J. Wagener	2010-12
Theodore A. Ferrara	2012-14

Treasurers

Joseph Chapman	1914-24
Cavour S. Langdon	1924-29
Henry S. Kingman	1929-38
Joseph Kingman Jr.	1938-70

Dr. John P. Walsh	1970-78
John S. Pillsbury Jr.	1978-83
Thomas M. Beckley	1983-87
Roger L. Headrick	1987-90
Robert A. Garvey	1990-92
Gary N. Petersen	1992-94
Donna G. Stephens	1994-96
Loren L. Taylor	1996-2002
David P. Crosby	2002-04
Jo Anne Anderson	2004-09
Theodore A. Ferrara	2009-10
Charles B. Westling	2010-

Principal Dunwoody Administrators

Harold Kavel, Principal	1914-15
Dr. Charles Prosser, Director	1915-45
Joseph Kingman Jr., Director	1945-57;
President	1957-65

John Butler, Director	1965-68
Dr. John Walsh, President	1968-78
Warren E. Phillips, President	1978-89
Dr. M. James Bensen, President	1989-94

Williiam Mamel, Interim President	1994-95
E. Frank Starke, President	1995-2002
Dr. C. Ben Wright, President	2002-09
Dr. Richard Wagner, President	2009-

Alumni Achievement Award Recipients

This award is presented in recognition of service to the college and exemplary contributions to one's profession and community.

1984
Edward F. Asproth
Russell H. Bennett
Ella M. Charley
Michael J. Childs Sr.
Kenneth A. Cronstrom
John R. Dolny
Charles E. Entenmann
Robert W. Entenmann
William J. Entenmann
Wayne Glanton
Allan O. Johnson
Odin S. Langen
Kenneth A. Malmstrom
Roy E. Olson
Richard A. Pinska
Arthur J. Popehn
Morgan H. Potter
Wilton W. Quist
Edward H. Ramsey

Gordon L. Schuster
Wayne A. Simoneau
William C. Wachtler
Maurice J. Wagener

1985
John Y. Elgin
Carl G. Magnuson
Walter F. Passe
Luther N. Radtke

1986
Floyd H. Schneeberg

1987
John C. Hansen
Cormac T. Woods
Jack F. Woods

1988
Francis Feyereisen

1989
Lester E. Goetzke
Victor E. Olson

1990
Douglas A. Hanson
Lee H. Jessen
Ernest J. Skramstad

1991
Rodney E. Erickson

1992
W. James Corbett
Duane G. Treiber

1993
Ann L. Bollmeier
Harold Juul

1994
Joseph A. Craig
Marc Falconer

1996
Robert E. Poupore
Gary W. Schulz

1997
Harvey D. Larson
Glenn T. Tilbury

1998
Gary Agrimson
Edward P. Hudoba
Dudley E. Woehning
Donald H. Zuercher

2000
John Holland

2001
Roy Otto
Roger H. Storms

2002
Michael Loegering

2003
David Schlueter

2004
Clinton O. Larson

2005
Theodore A. Ferrara

2006
Pam Spence

2007
Harlan Hallquist

2008
Steve Bryant

2010
John Adamich

2011
Larry Raasch

Alumni Entrepreneur Award Recipients

This award is presented in recognition of alumni who have started or significantly expanded their businesses and whose vision, initiative, and enterprise exemplify American entrepreneurship at its best.

1987	Joel A. Elftmann	1993	John A. Schumacher
1988	Maurice J. Wagener	1994	Edgar T. Grove
1989	Ralph B. Nordick		John M. Johnston
1990	Gerald L. Egan		James O. Stolee
1992	Frank E. Schochet	1995	Jon P. Kosmoski
	Vernon F. Thompson		Joseph C. Weis

1996	Howard L. Siewert	2002	Elgar C. Burgeson
1997	Donald D. Dolan	2003	Mike Hanson
1998	Raymond K. Newkirk	2004	Donald E. Snyder
1999	G. Howard Lund	2007	Jay Johnson
	Burton J. McGlynn	2008	Gil Arvig
2000	Charles Donatelle	2009	Morris Eisert
	Michael Donatelle	2010	Douglas L. Olson
2001	Keith P. Caswell Jr.	2011	Jack Mowry
	Peter J. Platzer		

Partnership Award Recipients

This award is presented in recognition of a company or organization that has made a significant contribution to further Dunwoody's mission.

1985	Pillsbury Company	1991	Beloit Corporation
1987	Honeywell	1992	Greater Metro Auto Dealers Association
1988	3M		
1989	Center Point Energy/ Minnegasco	1993	Minneapolis Pipefitters JAC
	General Mills	1994	North Central Electrical League

1996	The Minneapolis Foundation	2010	Graco and Graco Foundation
2003	Harper Foundation	2012	Pentair
2004	Peregrine Capital Management		
2005	Kraus-Anderson Companies		
2008	M.A. Mortenson		

BIBLIOGRAPHY

Papers and Records of Dunwoody Industrial Institute/Dunwoody College of Technology (Minneapolis, Minnesota)

"The Albert C. Kavli Bequest to Dunwoody Industrial Institute," pamphlet [1986].

Annual Reports, 1966-2012.

Annual Reports of the Director to the Board of Trustees, 1945-1968.

Annual Reports of the President to the Board of Trustees, 1957-2009.

Annual Reports of the Treasurer to the Board of Trustees, 1945-1970.

The Artisan, December 1915 - August 1924.

Audited Financial Statements, 1915-2011.

Bensen, Dr. M. James, and Administrative Team, "Bu$ine$$ Enterpri$e Plan," January 18, 1994.

———, "Plan of Action for Fulfillment of the Five Criteria for NCA Initial Accreditation as Recommended by the NCA Evaluation Team," January 24, 1994.

———, "Report of Action for Fulfillment of General Institutional Requirement #9," presented to NCA, March 20, 1994.

Board of Trustees meeting minutes, 1914-2012.

Butler, John A., et al., "A Study of the Objectives and Role of Dunwoody Industrial Institute," April 20, 1965.

"Charles Allen Prosser: A Testimonial in Recognition of His Service to Vocational Education," 1933.

The Compass, 2003-2012.

Cresap, McCormick, and Paget, "A Master Plan for the Institute," March 1967.

Crosby, Thomas M., "A Special Message for the Trustees of Dunwoody Industrial Institute," April 18, 1972.

Dunwoody Hi-Lites, 1992-1996.

Dunwoody Insta-Toot, 1990-1994.

The Dunwoody News, September 1922 - June 1987.

Dunwoody Newsletter, 1987-1990.

Dunwoody On-Line, 1991-2002.

Ernhart & Associates, Fund-Raising Feasibility Study, April 29, 1986.

"Good to Great," campaign scrapbook, 2009.

International Services Division brochure, c. 1980.

Leadership Team minutes, 2002-2009.

"Living the Promise . . . Fulfilling the Dream: The Campaign for Dunwoody," case statement, 1998.

Memorandum of Understanding between Dunwoody College of Technology and NEI College of Technology, January 9-10, 2003.

Minnesota Council for Quality, Baldrige Express Feedback Report, March 4, 1999.

North Central Association of Colleges and Schools, Commission of Institutions of Higher Education, Reports of Visits to Dunwoody Institute, October 18-20, 1993 and October 18-19, 1999.

Phillips, Warren E., and Administrative Group, "A Report to the Futures Committee and the Board of Trustees Summarizing the Impact of New Technologies on the Courses Taught at Dunwoody," October 2, 1984.

———, "Marking the Future," report to Board of Trustees, April 16, 1985.

Prosser, Charles A., "Conservation of Trade Skills for Continuous National Defense through Apprentice Training," December 16, 1940.

———, "The Disappearance of Trade and Industrial Skill and Knowledge," Summer, 1938.

———, "Dunwoody's Past, Present and Future," April 13, 1945.

———, "Then and Now: Twenty-Eight Years and the Smith-Hughes Act," August 22, 1945.

Prosser, Charles A., and James S. Lincoln, "The Employer, the Employee, and the Job," 1940.

Self-Study Reports to the North Central Association of Colleges and Schools, Commission on Institutions of Higher Education, 1993 and 1997.

Strategic Plans, 1995-2000.

Strategic Visioning Report, January 10, 2002.

Strategic Plan Progress Report, October, 2002.

Strategic Operating Plans, 2002-2011.

Summaries of Team Reports, Board of Trustees Retreat, November 18, 1993.

"A Vital Source," case statement brochure for 1977-1981 capital campaign.

Wagner, Dr. Richard, address to 50-Year Club luncheon, May 9, 2012.

Walsh, Dr. John P., and Administrative Group, "An Analysis of the Current Position of Dunwoody Industrial Institute and an Assessment of Alternatives for the Future," A Special Message for the Trustees of Dunwoody Industrial Institute, [April] 1976.

Wright, Dr. C. Ben, quarterly reports to Board of Trustees, 2002-2009.

Other Primary Sources

Anderson, Clifford I., interview with C. Ben Wright, September 2, 2009.

Bennett, Russell H., *Quest for Ore.* Minneapolis: T. S. Denison & Co., 1963.

Bensen, M. James, interview with C. Ben Wright, November 16, 2011.

Boyle, Fosten A., interview with C. Ben Wright, January 16, 2012.

Carlson, Robert W. Jr., interview with C. Ben Wright, October 27, 2009.

Crosby, David P., interview with C. Ben Wright, August 27, 2009.

Crosby, John, 1955 interview, Minnesota Historical Society, St. Paul, MN.

Davy, Mark, interview with C. Ben Wright, March 1, 2012.

Dunwoody, William H., Papers, Minnesota Historical Society, St. Paul, MN.

Elftmann, Joel A., interview with C. Ben Wright, August 19, 2009.

Engelsma, Bruce W., interview with C. Ben Wright, February 13, 2012.

Ferrara, Theodore A., interview with C. Ben Wright, May 7, 2012.

Kiester, Charles E., interview with C. Ben Wright, January 26, 2012.

Moore, Cornell, interview with C. Ben Wright, August 18, 2009.

Minnesota Department of Education, "A Study of the Need for Area Vocational-Technical School Expansion in Minnesota," June, 1964.

Newman, Andrea L., interview with C. Ben Wright, March 14, 2012.

Petersen, Gary N., interview with C. Ben Wright, February 24, 2012.

Phillips, Warren E., interviews with C. Ben Wright, July 29 and August 1, 2008; telephone conversations, April 26 and December 14, 2011.

Poupore, Robert E., interview with C. Ben Wright, October 15, 2009.

Prosser, Charles A., and Charles R. Allen, *Vocational Education in a Democracy*. New York and London: D. Appleton-Century Co., 1925.

Prosser, Charles A., and Thomas H. Quigley, *Vocational Education in a Democracy*. Rev. ed.; Chicago: American Technical Society, 1949.

Prosser, Charles A., with M. R. Bass, *Adult Education: The Evening Industrial School*. New York and London: The Century Co., 1930.

Prosser, Charles A., with M. R. Bass, *Evening Industrial Schools*. Rev. ed.; Chicago: American Technical Society, 1951.

Ryks, Donald E., telephone interview with C. Ben Wright, November 23, 2011.

Schneeberg, Floyd, interview with C. Ben Wright, November 6, 2008.

Starke, Frank, interview with C. Ben Wright, June 10, 2011; telephone conversation, March 30, 2012.

Taylor, Loren L., interview with C. Ben Wright, January 27, 2012.

Wagener, Maurice J., interview with C. Ben Wright, May 10, 2012.

Wagner, Richard J., interview with C. Ben Wright, May 3, 2012.

Secondary Sources

"2007-2012 Global Financial Crisis," *Wikipedia: The Free Encyclopedia*, en.wikipedia.org/wiki/2007-2012_global_financial_crisis.

Abbott Northwestern Hospital, "*Where Quality Is a Tradition: Abbott Northwestern Hospital, 1882-1982*." A history of the corporation and 1981 Annual Report.

———, "*Two Women, One Man, and Their Hospitals*." A profile of the founders of Abbott Northwestern Hospital and the Sister Kenny Institute, December, 1978.

Anderson, Andy, *Stagecoach; Book Two: Wells Fargo and the Rise of the American Financial Services Industry*. New York: Simon & Schuster Source, 2002.

Arnold, Kenneth L., and Michael Holler, *Quality Assurance: Methods and Technologies*. New York, etc.: Glencoe/McGraw Hill, 1995.

Baldrige National Quality Program, "Education Criteria for Performance Excellence," booklet printed by National Institute of Standards and Technology, U.S. Department of Commerce, 2001.

Blum, John M., et al., *The National Experience: A History of the United States*. 4th ed.; New York, etc.: Harcourt Brace Jovanovich, Inc., 1977.

Brown, Aneeta, *A Century of Educational Excellence: The First One Hundred Years of Ranken Technical College, 1907-2007*. St. Louis: Ranken Technical College, 2006.

Bushnell, John E., *The History of Westminster Presbyterian Church*. Minneapolis: The Lund Press, 1939.

Collins, Jim, *Good to Great: Why Some Companies Make the Leap . . . and Others Don't*. New York: HarperCollins Publishers, 2001.

Dobyns, Lloyd, "Ed Deming Wants Big Change, and He Wants It Fast," *Smithsonian*, August, 1990, pp. 74–82.

Edgar, William C., *The Medal of Gold: A Story of Industrial Achievement*. Minneapolis: The Bellman Co., 1925.

Edgar, William C., Loring M. Staples, and Henry Doerr, *Minneapolis Club: A Review of Its History, 1883-1990*. Minneapolis: The Minneapolis Club, 1990.

Evans, James R., *Quality and Performance Excellence: Management, Organization, and Strategy*. 5th ed.; Mason, OH: Thomson Southwestern, 2008.

Gray, James, *Business Without Boundary: The Story of General Mills*. Minneapolis: University of Minnesota Press, 1954.

Gryna, Frank M., Richard C. H. Chua, and Joseph A. Defeo, *Juran's Quality Planning and Analysis for Enterprise Quality*. 5th ed.; Boston, etc.: McGraw Hill Higher Education, 2007.

Hansen, Randall W., *The Servicemen's Readjustment Act of 1944 and its Beneficiaries*. Unpublished manuscript, 2003.

Hess, Jeffrey A., *Their Splendid Legacy: The First 100 Years of the Minneapolis Society of Fine Arts*. Minneapolis: The Minneapolis Society of Fine Arts, 1985.

Ivancic, S. K., *The Historical Development of Mission in Two Urban Colleges: St. Paul College and Dunwoody College of Technology*. E.D.D. thesis, University of Minnesota, 2004.

Kirkendall, Richard S., *The United States, 1929-1945: Years of Crisis and Change*. New York, etc.: McGraw-Hill Book Company, 1974.

Larson, Don W., *Land of the Giants: A History of Minnesota Business*. Minneapolis: Dorn Books, 1979.

Larson, Milton G., and Simon T. O'Loughlin, "A Follow-up Study of Selected Graduates of Dunwoody Industrial Institute." Master of Arts independent paper, Research Problems course, University of Minnesota, 1956.

Leuchtenburg, William E., et al., *The Unfinished Century: America since 1900.* Boston: Little, Brown and Company, 1973.

Millikan, William, *A Union Against Unions: The Minneapolis Citizens Alliance and Its Fight Against Organized Labor, 1903-1947.* St. Paul: Minnesota Historical Society Press, 2001.

Minnesota Vocational Association, pamphlet commemorating 20th anniversary of 1945 Minnesota Vocational Technical School Law, 1965.

Moss, George Donelson, *America in the Twentieth Century.* 4th ed.; Upper Saddle River, N.J.: Prentice Hall, 2000.

Reamer, Karen, telephone conversation with C. Ben Wright, September 29, 2010. [Reamer was executive director of the Woman's Christian Association of Minnepolis.]

Smith, Daniel M., *War and Depression: America, 1914 to 1939.* St. Louis: Forum Press, 1972.

Tatge, Doug, *Still Caring: The First Fifty Years of Alexandria Technical and Community College.* Fargo, ND : Forum Communications Printing, 2011.

Wachtler, Will C., *William Hood Dunwoody: A Portrait of Service, Benevolence.* Independent M.A. degree paper submitted to the University of Minnesota, 1963.

Weiner, Lynn, "Our Sister's Keepers: The Minneapolis Woman's Christian Association and Housing for Working Women," *Minnesota History*, Spring, 1979, pp. 189–200.

INDEX

Abbott, Amos Wilson, 22, 23
Abbott Hospital for Women and Children, 11, 22, *22*
Academic Quality Improvement Project (AQIP), 167, 169, 180. *See also* North Central Association of Colleges and Schools (NCA)
Accrediting Commission of Career Schools and Colleges of Technology (ACCSCT). *See* National Association of Trade and Technical Schools (NATTS)
Adamich Automotive Lab, 176
Adamich, Betty, 176
Adamich, John, *7*, 176, *192*
Adams, Robert M., 128
Ajax, Erick, *187*
Albers, Rod, *110*
Alexandria Technical College, 94, 147, 148
Allen, Charles R., 55
Alliance Capital Management Corporation and Investment Advisers, 126
Alumni Achievement Award, 131, *179*, 196
Alumni Entrepreneur Award, 12, 131, 197
Alumni 50-Year Club, 118, 131
"Alumni and Friends of Dunwoody," 156 *See also* Dunwoody Alumni Association
Alumni Fund, 30, 78, 102. *See also* Dunwoody Development Fund
American Institute of Baking (A.I.B.), 51
American Vocational Association (AVA), 79, 94–95
AMIDS Center One, 114. *See also* Upper Midwest Area Manpower Institute for Development of Staff
Anderson, Clarence, 169
Anderson, Clifford H., 85, 116
Anderson, Clifford I., 7, 145–146, 174, 176, 192, *192*
Anderson Legacy Room, 176
Anthony L. Ferrara Career Services Center, 176
Area vocational technical institutes (AVTIs), 83, 92–94, 111, 112, 121–123, 127, 130, 190
Area Vocational Technical School Law 121 (1945), 91–92
Argentina 96, 98
The Artisan, 34–35, *37*, 44, *49, 50, 58*
Asproth, Edward, 75
Associate of Applied Science (A.A.S.) degrees, 130, 142, 145
Atkinson, Frederick G., *18*, 30

Bachelor of Science degrees, 144, 152, 177, 187
Barnum, George, 23
Barnum Grain Company, 18

Bartlett, Georgia Skogmo, 133, *133*
Bass, M. Reed, *44, 52, 69*
Beal, Ivan, 90
Bell, James Ford, *18*, 30, *38*, 78, 84, 85
Bell, James Stroud, 14, 15, 17, *18*, 19, 30
Bemidji State University, 144, 146, 152, 177
Beneke, Gordon, *128*
Bennett, David, 123, *136*, 140
Bennett, Russell, 69–70, *70*, 78, 79, 83–85, *84*, 106, 121, 123–125
Bensen, M. James, *7*, 137, 139–147, *140, 144*, 152
"Big Four," 58. *See also* SKRA
Bolivia, *76*
Bollmeier, Ann, *121*
Bovey, Charles, *18*, 30, 84
Bovey, William H., *18, 30,* 30–31, 34, *38,* 39, 69
Bowen, Chuck, *179*
Boyle, Fosten, 137, 140, 145, 146, 147
Bread Bakers Guild of America, 150, 157–158
Brinkmann, Tom, *183*
Burma, *97,* 97–98
Bush Foundation, 155
Butler, John A., 84, 85, *85,* 92–93, 95, 97–98, *102,* 105–109, 111, 117, 118, 119, 122, 124, 185
Butler Library, 118, 137

C. C. Washburn Flouring Mills Company, 16
Cant, Taylor, Haverstock, Beardsley & Gray, 100–102
Capital campaigns. *See A Vital Source; 75th Anniversary Campaign; Living the Promise, Fulfilling the Dream Campaign;* and *Good to Great Campaign*
Carbonneau, J. J., *7*
CAREERCONNECT program, 176
Carlson, Arne, *153*
Carlson, Robert W., Jr., 7, 150–151, 154, 155, *155, 156,* 159, 168, 169, 190, 191. *See also* Robert W. Carlson Jr. Commons
Central Training Institute (Bombay, India), 98
Century Club. *See* Fundraising
Chapman, Joseph, 30, 31, *38,* 84
Chile, *96,* 99, 114
Chrysler, partnership with, 177
Clark, Greg, *192*
Claude, Frank, *188*
"College of the Year," 177. *See also* Flexographic Technical Association
Collins, Jim, 164, 165
Collins, Walter, 124

Cossette, Paul, *192*
Cox, Walter, 133, *134*
Craigo, Ralph T., *44,* 45, *52,* 60, 84
Cresap, McCormick, and Paget, 107. *See also* Strategic planning
Crocker, William G., *18,* 30
Crosby, David P., *7,* 8–9, 146, *149,* 154–155, 174–175
Crosby Family Board and Conference Room, 176
Crosby, Franklin M., 8, 30, 31, *38,* 39, 84, 117, 118
Crosby, George C., 85
Crosby, Henry S., 85, 99
Crosby, John, III, 8, 13, 14
Crosby, John, IV, 8, 14, 30, 31, 84, 99
Crosby, Philip B., 139, 141, 148
Crosby, Thomas, 8, 117–118, *118,* 121, 131, 146

Davy, Mark, 6, 153, 154, *155,* 173, 178
Decker Auditorium, 118, 133
Decker, Edward W., 30, 84–85, 118
Deming, W. Edwards, 139, 141, 148
Development. *See* Fundraising
Dinneen, Richard, 89
Disabled Veterans Rehabilitation Act, *77*
Diversity, as a goal and priority of William Dunwoody and Dunwoody College
    Students of color, 29, 123, 125, 133–134, 161, 164–165,167, 175, *176,* 177–178, 182–183, 190. *See also* Dunwoody Academy, Wenda and Cornell Moore Multi-Cultural Center, and Youth Career Awareness Program
    Women, 74–75, *74, 75,* 118–120, *120, 121,* 133, *133,* 164–165, 167, 176, 177, 178, *179. See also* Women's Resource Center
Dols, Bernard, *116*
Duluth Elevator Company, 18
Dunwoody Academy charter school, 178, 182
Dunwoody Alumni Association, 78, 156. *See also* "Alumni and Friends of Dunwoody"
Dunwoody Development Fund, 103, 115, 116–117. *See also* Alumni Fund
Dunwoody Difference, 11, 41, 55–59, 189, 191–192. *See also* Dunwoody Way
Dunwoody Endowment Fund, 29–30, 37–38, 62–66, 76–78, 80, 99–102, 104, 115–116, 118, 126, 144–146, 148, 149, 160, 182, 184, 185, 190
Dunwoody Grain Company, 18
Dunwoody Industrial Institute Alumni Fund. *See*

Alumni Fund

Dunwoody, James, 12, 13

Dunwoody, Kate, *10*, 11, 13, *21*, 21–22, 23, 25, 27, 30, 33, 36–37, 42, *53*, 55, 153, 189. *See also* Kate Dunwoody Trust and Kate Dunwoody Home/Hall

The Dunwoody News, 58, 59, 60, 73, 74, 75, 86, *91*, *100*

Dunwoody & Robertson, 13

Dunwoody Way, 55–60, 139. *See also* Dunwoody Difference

Dunwoody, William Hood, 4, *7*, 8, *10*, 11–25, *14*, *18*, *24*, 27, *28*, 29–30, 31, 34, 36, 39, 42, 45, *53*, 55, 74, 77, 100, 102, 153, 166, 189, 192. *See also* Dunwoody Endowment Fund

Duran, Joseph M., 139, 141

Elftmann, Joel, *7*, 9, 131, 154, 155, *156*, 163, *172*, 174, 175, *175*, 185, 190

Elftmann Student Success Center, *175*, 177

Emerson, L. A., *44*, 45

Engels, Robert, 124

Engelsma, Bruce, *7*, *174*, 175, 179, 189

Engquist, Merrill, *110*, 111

Ernhart and Associates, 130–131, 132

Federal Board for Vocational Education. *See* U.S. Federal Board for Vocational Education

Federal Cartridge Company, 74, 76

Ferrara, Ted, *6*, 9, 176, 183, 185, 189, 190, 192, *192*

Ferrara, Todd, 176

50-Year Club. *See* Alumni 50-Year Club

First Minneapolis Trust Company, 62, 63, 66–67. *See also* Minneapolis Trust Company

First National Bank, 115–116, 126

Flexographic Technical Association, 177

Ford Foundation, 83, 95–99, 102, 103

Founder's Day, 33, 74, 118, 189

Frisvold, Lee, *162*

Fundraising, 8, 30, 78, *86*, 102–104, 116–118, 125, 131, 191. *See also* Alumni Fund and Capital Campaigns

Galbraith, John Kenneth, *98*

General Mills, 11, 19, 72, 76, 104, 116. *See also* Washburn Crosby Company

General Mills Foundation, 155

Ghana, 96, 114, 126

G.I. Bill of Rights (1944), *77*, 85, 86–90

Gnitka, Timothy, *191*

Goetzke, Lester, *7*, *101*

Good to Great... (Collins), 164, 165

Good to Great Campaign, 169, 173–175, 178–179, 184

Gould, Laurence, 85, 121

Government Technical Institute (GTI) (Insein, Burma), 97

Graduates Who Are Worth More, 165, 191

Gray, James, 14

Great Crash of October 1929, 61

Great Depression, *60*, 61–67, 68

Great Northern Railway Company, 18

Grove, Edgar, 169

H. Darrow & Company, 13

H. E. and Helen R. Warren Building, 104

Haagenson, Ken, *134*

Haas Automation, 170

Haas Technical Education Center, 170, *171*

Hallquist, Harlan, *7*

Hansen, John C., *102*, 106, 107, 122, 124

Hansen, Randall W., 87–90

Harding, Warren, *47*

Harper Center of Graphics Technology, 176

Harper, Katherine, 176

Harper, Ron, 176

Hasbrouck, Joseph, *123*

Hawaiian Islands, 95

Hayward, Harland, *113*

Hedgehog concept, 165

Hess, Jeffrey, 21

Hewitt & Brown, 39, 40

Hewitt, Edwin H., 39–42

Hill, James J., 18–19

Holden Entrepreneurial Business/Leadership Center, 142

Holden, Harold L., 142, *144*

Holden, Harriet, *144*

Honda, partnership with, 177

Honeywell, Inc., 72, 76, 104, 106, 114, 131, 155

Hood, Hannah, 12

Hoover, Herbert, 61

Howard, Oscar, 133

Hugeback, Bonnie, 153, 159

Humphrey, Hubert H., 81, 118

Hunstad, Eugene, 155, 169

Hunt, Harold, 85

India, *97*, 97–98, 114

Indonesia, *94*, 95–97, *97*, 98, 114, 126

Institutional Advancement Award, 131

International Harvester Company, 76

International Services Division, 94–99, 102, 106, 107, 111, 112, 114, 122, 124, 126, 189

International Union of Flour and Cereal Mill

Employees, 17–18

Iran, 96, 114, 126

Jackson, C. Charles, Jr., *7*, 125, 131, *131*, 133

Jackson Entrance, 133, *172*

Jaedike, Al, *135*

Jamaica, 96, 99, 114

Jessen, Lee, *7*

Johnson, Allan, *95*

Johnson Controls, 176

Johnson, Jay, *172*

Johnson, John, 159

Johnson, Kelvin, 152

Jordan, William, *6*, *124*, 175

Kate Dunwoody Home/Hall, 22, *22*

Kate Dunwoody Trust, 37–38, 62, 63, 66–67, 76, 104, 115, 144

Kavel, Harry W., 32, *33*, 39, *44*, 45, *45*, 47, 49, 51–52

Kavli, Albert C., 131–132, 145

Kelly, George, 117

Kenison, Dennis, 145

Key performance indicators (KPIs), 166–167, *167. See also* Quality movement

Kiester, Charles, *7*, 145, 146, 154–155, 191

Kingman, Henry S., 64, 70, 78, 99

Kingman, Joseph R., Jr., 70, *78*, 81, 83–84, *84*, 85, 92, 94, 99, 100–101, *102*, 103–104, 106, 107, 109, 111, 115, 118, 121

Klick, Darcie, *135*

Klingaman, Steve, *7*, 154, *155*

Korea, Republic of, 95, *97*, 114, 126

Landon, Fred, 78

Langdon, Cavour, 85

Larson, Clinton, 171

Larson, Jennifer Sutherland, *145*

Larson, Milton, 90–91

Lebanon, 96, 99

Leighton, Fred, 125

Liberia, 96, 126

Libya, 96, 114, 126

Living the Promise, Fulfilling the Dream Campaign, 8–9, 153–154, 155–156, *155*, *156*, 159, 169, 173, 178

Lodhipur Institute (India), 97–98

Loegering, Mike, *7*

Lowry, Robert, 78

Lund, G. Howard, 12

Luther, Rudy, 155

M. A. Mortenson Company, 12, 133, *192*, *193*

MacArthur Concrete Pile Company, 40

Malcolm Baldrige National Quality Award, 167

Mamel, William, 147, 150, 185
Martin, Charles J., 14
Marts & Lundy, Inc., 117–118
McKnight Foundation, 125
McNamara, Richard "Pinky," 7, 154, 155, 155, 156
McQuay Company, 76
Metropolitan State University, 122, 130, 144, 152
MetroTech Career Academy, 178. See also Dunwoody Academy charter school
Minarik, Robert, 122, 124
Minneapolis Area Vocational Technical Institute (MAVTI), 92, 122, 190
Minneapolis Board of Education, 31, 122
Minneapolis Foundation, The 132
Minneapolis Institute of Arts, 11, 20, 20–21
Minneapolis Millers Association, 13
Minneapolis Plumbers Joint Journeyman and Apprentice Training Committee and Local 15 Union, 156
Minneapolis Society of Fine Arts, 20–21
Minneapolis Star Tribune, 135, 168, 169
Minneapolis Sunday Journal, 27, 28
Minneapolis Sunday Tribune, 70, 71
"Minneapolis Survey" (National Society for the Promotion of Industrial Education), 33–34
Minneapolis Trust Company, 37. See also First Minneapolis Trust Company
Minnesota Vocational Association (MVA), 92–93
Mission statement of Dunwoody Institute/Dunwoody College, 140, 149, 160, 165–166
Moore, Cornell, 175–176, 176
Moore, Wenda, 175–176, 176
Morrison, Clinton, 20
Mortenson, Alice, 133, 192
Mortenson, M. A., Jr., 192
Mortenson, M. A., Sr., 12
Moss, George, 61
Munck, Eunice, 169
Murray, Leonard, 121

National Association of Trade and Technical Schools (NATTS), 120–121, 128, 137, 143, 144, 153
National Baking Center, 150–151, 157–158, 176
National Center for Research in Vocational Education (NCRVE), 139, 147
National Society for the Promotion of Industrial Education, 33–34
NEI College of Technology, 170–173, 176
Nelson, Stanley, 123
Ness, Cecil, 169
Newkirk, Raymond, 9, 172
Newman, Andrea, 7, 165–166, 181, 185, 189
Newtown, Pennsylvania, 12, 13, 27, 29

North Central Association of Colleges and Schools (NCA), 142, 143–144, 152–153, 167, 169
North Memorial Medical Center, 186
Northern Pump Company, 72, 74, 76
Northwestern National Bank of Minneapolis, 19, 20, 115–116, 126, 181

Oetjen, Shawn, 190
Old Central High School, 31–32, 32, 37, 41
O'Loughlin, Simon, 90–91, 117
Olson, Roy, 128, 155

Panama, 96, 126
Partnership Award, 131, 192, 197
Patten, Catherine Lane. See Dunwoody, Kate
Pehling, Wilfred, 89
Pence, Gerald, 133
Perpich, Rudy, 137
Petersen, Gary, 6, 7, 159, 163, 173, 174, 178–179, 181, 182, 183, 185, 190
Philippine Islands, 95
Phillips, Warren E., 6, 7, 94, 96–97, 106, 107, 111, 112, 122, 124–125, 125, 126, 127, 128–134, 136, 137, 140, 144, 185
Pike & Cook, 40
Pillsbury Company Foundation, 134
Pillsbury, John S., Jr., 85
Pinska, Richard, 155
Plumbing Technology Learning Center, 156, 157
Pooley, Richard, 159, 165, 167, 180
Popehn, Art, 7
Poupore, Robert E., 124, 141
Presidential search committees, 137, 140, 146, 147, 163, 179
Printing and Graphic Arts Advanced Technical Education Center, 152
Printing Industry of Minnesota (PIM), 151, 158, 159, 177
Prosser, Charles A., 33–36, 34, 38–39, 40–41, 42, 43–47, 45, 48–50, 52, 55–60, 62, 67, 68, 69, 70, 76, 78, 78–81, 83, 84, 85, 86, 91–92, 95, 105, 106, 108, 109, 118, 141, 185, 189, 190

Quality Is Free (Crosby, Philip B.), 141
Quality movement, 8, 139–142, 147, 148–150, 155, 159–161, 163–169, 167, 168, 179, 180

Rangoon Technical High School (RTHS, Burma), 97
Ranken Technical College, 29, 69, 135, 144
Rankin, Leon, 134

Rao, K. Nagaraja, 96, 97, 102, 106, 107
Rasmussen, Glenn, 129
Renner, Raymond, 88
Retailers' Bakery Association, 150, 157–158
Right Skills Now program, 187
Rivard, Pete, 177
Robert W. Carlson Jr. Commons, 175, 175, 176
Robertson, Orrick, 13
Robinson, Steve, 7
Rogosheske, Walter, 91–92
"Rosie the Riveter," 74, 75, 119
Royal Milling Company, 19
Rybak, R. T., 173
Ryks, Donald, 7, 146

S. J. Groves & Sons, 40
Sahlin, Walter F., 84, 85, 106
Saint Mary's College of Minnesota, 144, 177
Saudi Arabia, 96, 114, 126
Schlueter, David, 7
Schmaltz, Colleen, 180
Schneeberg, Floyd H., 7, 86, 87, 106, 117, 131
Schulz, Gary, 7, 156
Servicemen's Readjustment Act (1944). See G.I. Bill of Rights
The Servicemen's Readjustment Act of 1944 and its Beneficiaries (Hansen), 87–90
75th Anniversary (1989), 125, 131, 133, 135, 136, 137
75th Anniversary Campaign, 111, 130–131, 132–133, 134
Severson, Gib, 173
Shoemake, Gayla, 130
Simoneau, Wayne, 136
Skogmo, Donald, 118, 133
SKRA, 58. See also "Big Four"
Smith-Hughes Vocational Education Act (1917), 44, 47, 49, 80–81, 92
Snyder, John, 114, 121, 123
Spence, Pam, 119–120, 120, 133, 179
Spencer, Edson, 137
St. Anthony & Dakota Elevator Company, 18, 19
Starke, E. Frank, 6, 7, 94, 140, 147–153, 147, 149, 154, 155, 156, 159, 163–164, 168, 171–172, 185
State Board for Vocational Education, 47
Stephens, Donna, 148
Stevens, Lloyd, 93
Stock market crash (1929), 61. See Great Crash
Storms, Roger, 7
Strategic planning
    Bensen and, 142, 145–146
    Board Summit (1993) 145–146
    Butler study (1965), 107, 111
    Cresap plan (1967), 107–108, 111, 112, 116, 121

"Futures" study (1985), 111, 128–130, 132, 140, 146
   Starke and, 149
   Strategic visioning (2000–2002), 159–161, 163
   Walsh plan (1976), 111, 122–123, 130
   Wright and, 163, 164–166, 176–178
Students of color. *See* Diversity
Sudan, *96*, 98
Sutherland, Jennifer. *See* Larson, Jennifer Sutherland

Target Field, *193*
Taylor, Loren (Larry), *7*, 145–146, 149, 159, *174*, *174*
Technical Teacher Training Institute (Bandung, Indonesia), 95
Technology action committees (TACs), 130, 150
Thompson, Vernon, 169
3M, 114, 131
3M Foundation, 155
Tiffany, Dunwoody & Company, 13
Time clocks, 41, 84, 106
Timeclock Hall, *58*, 133
Tollefson, Chester, 89
Total Quality Management. *See* Quality movement
Towner, Milton G., 95
Toyota, partnership with, 177
Twin Cities Federal (TCF) Bank, 184–185

United States government departments and programs
   G.I. Bill of Rights. *See* G.I. Bill of Rights
   Smith-Hughes Act. *See* Smith-Hughes Vocational Education Act
   Upper Midwest Area Manpower Institute for Development of Staff (AMIDS). *See* AMIDS
   U.S. Agency for International Development (USAID), 83, 98, 103
   U.S. Army Ordnance Department, 76
   U.S. Army Signal Corps, 45, *74*, 76
   U.S. Civil Service Commission, *73*
   U.S. Department of Health, Education, and Welfare, 114. *See also* Upper Midwest Area Manpower Institute
   U.S. Department of Labor, 114
   U.S. Federal Board for Vocational Education, 47, 49, 55
   U.S. Office of Education, *72*, 76, 121
   U.S. Veterans Administration, 76
   U.S. War Department, 47, *70*, *73*, 76
University of Wisconsin-Stout, 59, 79, 137, 140, 141, 144, 147, 177

Values of Dunwoody Institute/Dunwoody College, 149, 165, 166
Vanderlee, Sheila, *133*
Van Derlip, John R., 20
Venezuela, *96*, 126
Vision statement of Dunwoody Institute/ Dunwoody College, 29, 140, 147, 149, 165–166
A Vital Source campaign, 111, 123–126, *127*, 133
Vocational Education in a Democracy (Prosser and Allen), 55

Wagener, Maurice (Morrie), *7*, 9, 12, 131, 184–185, 191–192, *192*
Wagner, Richard J., 6, 11, *167*, 179–180, *181*, 183–187, 189–190
Walsh, John P., 85, 108–109, *108*, 111–112, 118–125, *125*, 128, 130, 156
Warren-Cadillac building, *103*, 103–104
Warren, Helen, 118
Warren, Henry E., 103–104, 118
Washburn, Cadwaller C., 13–14, 18

Washburn Crosby Company, 8, 13–18, *15, 18, 19*, 20, 21, 23, 25. *See also* General Mills
Washburn, John, 18
Washburn, William, 13
Webb, Robert W., 30, *38*, 78, 84
Wells-Dickey Company, *64*, 70
Wells Fargo Bank, 11, 169, 174, 181–182, 184–185
Wenda W. and Cornell L. Moore Multi-Cultural Center, 175–176, *177*
Westling, Charles, 185
White, Mike, 167
William H. Dunwoody Endowment Fund. *See* Dunwoody Endowment Fund
William and Kate Dunwoody Club, 131. *See also* Fundraising
Wirth, Theodore, 39
Wishart, Paul, 85, *105*, 106, 108, 114, 121
Wolf, LeRoy, 88
Women. *See* Diversity
Women's Christian Association (WCA), 21–22
Women's Resource Center, 178, *179*
Wood, Robert C., 85, 103, 104
Woods, Jack, 131
World War I, *26, 27*, 42–47, *44, 45, 46, 67, 74*
World War II, 70–78, *71, 72, 73, 74, 75*, 86–87
Wright, C. Ben, 6–7, 8, 131, 132, 154, *163, 163*–166, 169, 172, 173, 174, 177, 178, 179, 180, 181, 183, 185, *206*

Ylinen, Jeff, 6, *110*
Youth Career Awareness Program (YCAP), 134, *134, 177, 178*, 182–183

Zachary Associates, 124

Author
Dr. C. Ben Wright
President Emeritus
Dunwoody College of Technology

Ben is a native of Minneapolis. He received his bachelor's degree from the University of Wisconsin-Madison, master's degree in education from The Johns Hopkins University, and doctorate in history from the University of Wisconsin-Madison. After teaching American history at Chatham College in Pittsburgh, Pennsylvania, from 1972 to 1977, Dr. Wright returned to the Twin Cities and worked for the Minneapolis Park and Recreation Board and Voyageur Outward Bound for the next seven years. During his tenure with the Park Board, he wrote a history of the Minneapolis park and recreation system. As a member of the community faculty of Metropolitan State University from 1983 to 1999, he taught courses in the history of U. S. foreign relations.

In 1984 Dr. Wright joined the staff of Dunwoody Institute. He served Dunwoody for over twenty-five years—as vice president of development from 1984 to 1990, as vice president of institutional advancement from 1990 to 2001, and as president from 2002 to 2009, during which time the Institute became Dunwoody College of Technology. He retired as president in July 2009. Following his retirement he researched and wrote *For the Better Performance of Life's Duties*.

Ben lives in Minneapolis, only two miles from Dunwoody, with his wife, Donna. Ben and Donna have two daughters and three grandchildren, all residing in Minneapolis. Ben's son-in-law is a 2007 graduate of Dunwoody's Electrical Construction program.